The Graphic Arts

STUDIO MANUAL

Bert Braham

The Graphic Arts

STUDIO
MANUAL

Bert Braham

North Light

CONTENTS

First published in North America
by North Light, an imprint of
Writer's Digest Books,
9933 Alliance Road, Cincinnati,
Ohio 45242.

ISBN 0-89134-128-5

First Printing 1986.

**Designed and produced by
Robert Adkinson Limited,
London.**

Editorial Director Clare Howell
Art Director Christine Simmonds
Editors Diana L. Martin, Richard
Platt
Designer Bert Braham
Illustrator Rick Blakely

Phototypeset by Dorchester
Typesetting Group, Dorchester.
Illustrations originated by East
Anglian Engraving Limited,
Norwich, and Newsele S.R.L.,
Milan, Italy.
Printed and bound by SAGDOS,
Milan, Italy.

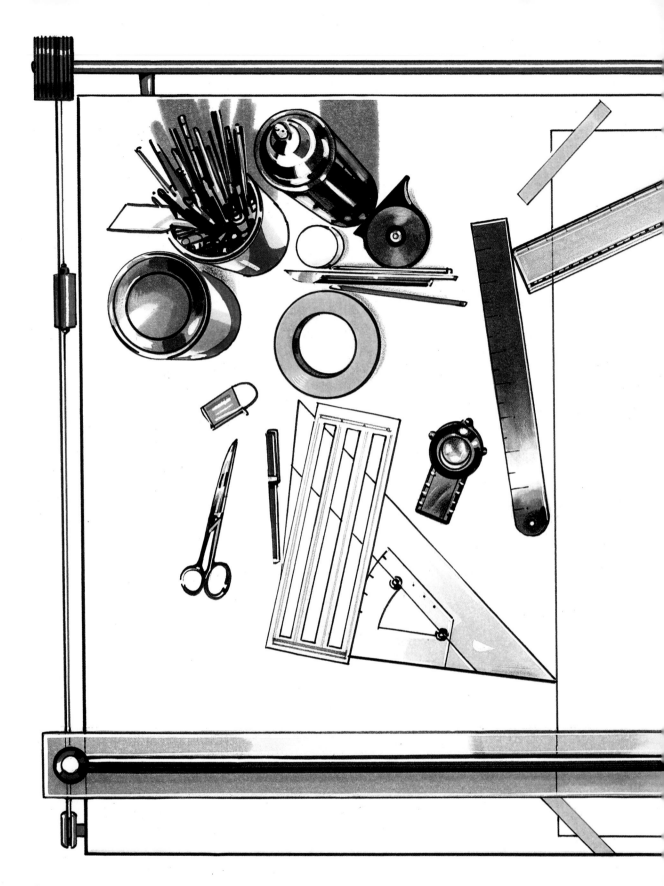

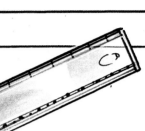

Introduction

The intention of this book is to illustrate and explain the practical ground rules of the graphics industry: the shortcuts, the tricks, and how to solve the multitude of problems that we face daily in the exciting world of graphics. This book is *not* about good or bad graphic design. It does not set out to judge the end product, because every piece of graphic work is unique, like the designer who commits it to paper. Set ten designers the task of producing a railway ticket, and you can guarantee that you will be presented with ten very different graphic approaches. Only one is chosen – does that make the other nine bad? Of course not, but in the world of commercial art, there can be only one winner, and somebody has to make the final choice.

The person who makes that decision is the client. The client judges the design not only on the basis of visual excellence, but also by commercial and economic standards: has the brief been followed? Is the work competent? How much will it cost to produce? Most important of all, what are the benefits for the client's company?

Good original ideas are often discarded because they cannot be adapted to meet the specifications of the client or employer. To be successful, it is not enough for a design to be innovative and original: the design must also satisfy certain practical requirements. A magazine with a cover that marks easily soon looks shabby, and gets left on the news-stand; unless a package carries a prominent brand-name, the customer won't be able to spot the product on the store shelf. The graphic designer therefore needs not only to create eye-catching ideas, but also to anticipate how those ideas will look when printed, and to do this on schedule, and within the budget.

The difference between success and failure in the business of graphic design is not primarily a question of talent. Some natural aptitude for visual things is essential, of course, but the hallmark of successful graphic designers is their ability to turn that creative talent into profit for themselves and their clients. In this book, I've tried to distill all the practical knowledge that I've learned in a long career as a designer. If you have the ideas and the visual ability, you'll find here the information you need to turn your skill into a salary.

The studio in your home

The first question facing the designer planning a business is 'where shall I work?'. Initially, most of us start out by working in our own homes, at least for a while. There are very good arguments for this: working in your home is usually convenient, and you save on studio overheads and travelling expenses. It is not a totally free office space, though: you still have to run heating and lighting, perhaps air conditioning in the summer. You'll use the telephone more and you may be surprised at the degree to which this affects the bill, especially if until now you've been working as an employee. The occasional private calls which used to be made at the expense of the studio now boost your own bill. Public utilities may also decide to charge you business rates, so that water, power and telephone bills rise, even if your consumption stays constant. There may be negative tax considerations: in some places tax is payable on the rise in value of commercial property, but not on the appreciation of residential accommodation. So when you come to sell your house,

the taxman is entitled to demand a share of the proceeds of the sale.

Tax laws can work for you, as well, though. A proportion of household expenses are tax deductible for the designer working in the home; power and telephone bills clearly fit into this category, and you may even be able to claim dog food!

It is wise to look into the other administrative or legal considerations before setting up a studio in a spare bedroom. Check the planning laws: your enterprise may be regarded by the authorities as unwanted commercial development in a residential area.

Making the break
The first year of work after the move into self-employment is a critical period. Make the transition smoother by looking objectively at your projected income and expenditure, and by making sure that you have a steady flow of work coming in. Ideally, try to negotiate a part-time contract to pay the rent while you build up work from other sources. If you are currently employed, and planning to start your own graphics business, your employer may be prepared to accept part-time working, particularly if this is coupled with on-the-job training for the designer who will take your place at the drawing board.

Many designers prefer to make a clean break with their employers, often because the former employer is seen as a competitor. If you are in this position, look for extra regular freelance work while you are still an employee. This will mean working 6 or 7 days a week, plus evenings and holidays prior to quitting full-time employment, but at least you can then rely on a steady trickle of income in the financially unstable early months.

Planning a home studio
If possible, set aside a room for exclusive use as a studio. Dual-function rooms invariably create problems of noise, dirt, and disruption. The disruption is two-way: your work may inconvenience other members of the household just as much as their activities disturb you. Choose a space that is out of the way of most other domestic activity; a well-used thoroughfare is not the best place for a drawing board.

Daylight is free, and easier on the eyes than electric light, so site your working area somewhere that gets a lot of light during the day. If you are right-handed, the window should be on your left, so that you are not working in your own shadow.

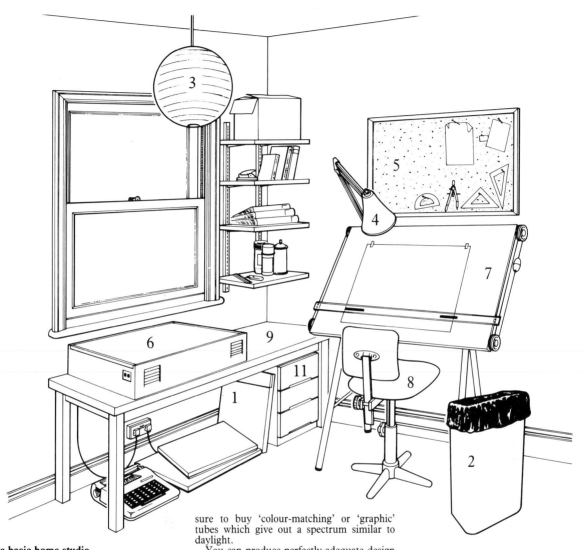

The basic home studio

Set aside an area for storage of paper and other materials (1). If the budget will not stretch to a plan or utility chest, try to obtain the large boxes or envelopes in which photographic film and paper is supplied. These are normally discarded by photo-labs. Get a large bin for waste paper (2). It's better to have this half empty than overflowing. Make sure there is some general overall light falling on the work area (3). An adjustable lamp should be your second purchase after the drawing board (4).

Put up a pinboard for job sheets, type charts and notes.

Hang small drawing instruments on nails or pegs (5).

A light-box or light-table (6) is essential for relaxed viewing of transparencies, and for tracing. It is not difficult to build one using fluorescent fittings and opal glass or acrylic sheet, but for critical evaluation of colour, be sure to buy 'colour-matching' or 'graphic' tubes which give out a spectrum similar to daylight.

You can produce perfectly adequate design work on the kitchen table, armed only with a T-square and a triange or set-square. However, a proper drawing board (7) with a parallel motion makes ruling up a great deal easier and quicker. Most boards can be propped up at a range of angles; those on stands are height-adjustable, too, so that you can work at them either standing or sitting.

Non-adjustable seating soon becomes very uncomfortable if you are seated all day, so it is worth spending money on a good drawing office chair (8). The angle of the chair back should be adjustable, as well as the height of the seat.

A flat area adjacent to the desk keeps transfer letters and other materials close at hand (9). Coffee cups and ashtrays must be separated from artwork and transparencies (10). Some basic office equipment (11) is essential for keeping job details in order.

Renting studio space

Renting premises is costly, but on balance the benefits almost always outweigh the financial outlay. These are just a few of the advantages.

Presentation Clients are not impressed by visiting your home. Separate premises inspire confidence, so that you are likely to be trusted with bigger jobs. Suppliers are more inclined to extend credit to a business that appears to be growing than to an individual running a budget operation in a residential area.

Inspiration If you are sharing with other creative people, you can learn from them and exchange ideas.

A business environment A self-contained studio solves the problem of family members disturbing you, and at the end of the day, you can lock the door and leave the work behind.

Location If you are working from home, there is no choice of location, but rented premises can be virtually anywhere you choose.

Working arrangements

The cheapest way to move your business out of the home is to rent 'desk space'. For a modest outlay, you move into a ready-made studio environment, with access to all the normal facilities such as a telephone, photocopier, secretarial help, and perhaps a PMT machine. The business arrangements that surround desk space vary considerably. You may just be left to get on with your own work, with perhaps a few jobs passed on by other designers who are overloaded. However, many companies renting out desk space do so in order to offer the client a broader range of services under one roof. In these circumstances, you are expected to work virtually full time for your 'landlord', but without the benefits enjoyed by employees, such as sick-pay and holidays.

Renting self-contained studio accommodation is more satisfactory provided you have the necessary capital, and a steady flow of work coming in. Costs can be cut by sharing with a colleague, but you should choose your companion with care. Either pick someone in a completely different line of business, such as a photographer or journalist, or else choose a graphic specialist whose work complements your own rather than competing with it. If your strengths are visualizing and illustration, pick a finished artist as a working companion.

When organizing shared use of a studio, make sure that the terms of the arrangement are absolutely clear. Try to strike a balance between petty rules and genuine respect for colleagues. Potential sources of friction are: smoking; noise; borrowing of equipment; untidiness; and shared responsibilities such as cleaning and locking up. Some of the worst problems can be avoided by careful studio planning, as explained on the opposite page.

Studio checklist

Rent is not the only overhead in a studio. When calculating costs, or apportioning them between several sharers, take into account the expenses listed below. Each partner should pay a portion based on floor area occupied, or on actual usage of the facility.

- Property taxes or rates.
- Power and water bills.
- Telephone bills – individual use can be monitored using a 'black box' so as to avoid arguments.
- Insurance.
- Cleaning.
- Secretarial help.
- Rental of office equipment such as photocopiers.
- Periodic redecoration and replacement of carpets.
- Shared supplies such as studio stationery, and PMT or photocopy paper.

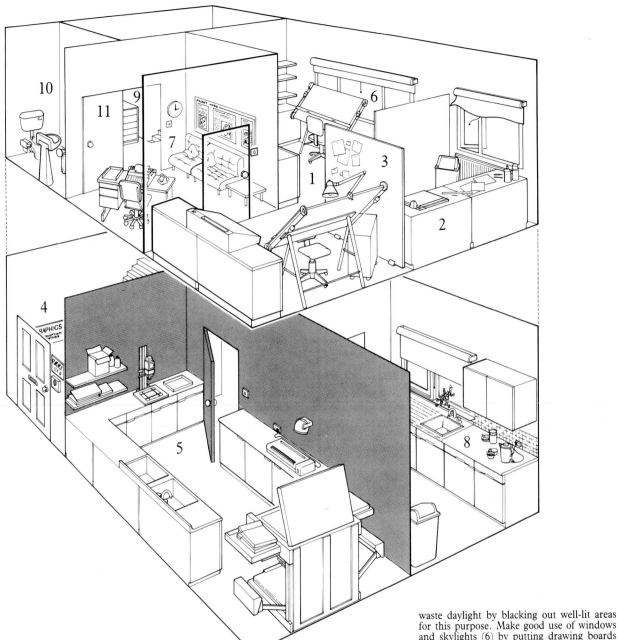

When looking for studio premises, try to visualize how the place will look once you've moved in. Old industrial buildings often seem cavernous and bleak (top), but very little building work is needed to turn them into bright and professional-looking working areas (bottom).

Design the main studio area (1) so that it is easy to keep clean: vinyl floors create less dust than carpets. Separate off an area for cutting, and another well-ventilated spot for using sprays (2). Movable dividers break up large spaces, and provide pinboards for island desks (3). If the premises are on several floors, make sure this is obvious to visitors, who might otherwise judge the studio to be a fraction of its true size (4). Set aside a quiet, smart area for presentations and meetings with clients. Put PMT darkrooms (5) in dingy, badly lit corners, well away from inflammable materials which could be ignited by the hot lights. Don't waste daylight by blacking out well-lit areas for this purpose. Make good use of windows and skylights (6) by putting drawing boards close to them. Screen off a reception area near the main entrance so that there is somewhere for clients to wait if you are not quite ready to meet them (7). This area could be used to display recent work. Kitchen areas (8) should not be clearly visible to visitors. Use awkward areas such as secure corridors (9) for artwork and material storage. Toilets are best sited on landings (10): cleaners then do not have to enter the studio itself when the building is unoccupied. Doors take up space. Remove them, or hang so that they are flush against a wall when open (11).

Anticipate expansion by renting more space than you need: the extra space can then be sublet on a short lease.

Financial considerations

Even if you have the capital to purchase major pieces of studio equipment outright, you may find that it is more sensible to buy such items on credit, or to lease them. The prevailing economic and taxation climate dictates the viability of each method of payment. For example, competition among photocopier manufacturers is intense, and one salesman may be prepared to offer a very advantageous credit deal or massive discount in order to close a sale. If you are unsure about which method of payment to choose, take professional advice from your accountant or bank manager.

Cash payment If you pay cash, you are likely to get the lowest possible price, so consider financing the purchase with a loan from another source. However, if you are buying complex equipment such as a photocopier or a microcomputer for cash, be sure to buy a maintenance contract at the time of purchase, or you could suffer from poor after-sales service. Beware of suppliers who insist on payment in currency and who do not issue receipts or invoices, or your purchase may be insufficiently documented for tax purposes and may even be illegal.

'Interest-free' credit Look carefully at these schemes. You will usually find that the same goods are available elsewhere for cash at a lower price, and most dealers offering interest-free credit often give substantial discount to cash buyers. True interest-free credit schemes do exist in highly competitive areas, though, and these may be very desirable options.

Repayment schemes or hire purchase Under these schemes, you make 12, 18 or 24 monthly payments until the item has been paid off. There are two disadvantages: Interest rates are very high, and the equipment remains the property of the finance house until the full balance has been paid off. Defaulting on one payment could lead to repossession. On the positive side, servicing is usually good and quick.

Talented designers don't always make good business people. If you find book-keeping baffling, you're probably better off employing an accountant to do the figures, thus freeing you to carry on with what you do best. Many financial companies run schemes specifically aimed at the small business.

Leasing If you are prepared to sign a long-term leasing contract, you will get good value for money, and the equipment will be maintained by the leasing company. Remember, though, that if your needs change and existing equipment is no longer adequate, you will still have to make the leasing payments to the end of the agreed contract.

Credit cards For long-term finance, credit cards are very expensive. However, if you time the purchase carefully, you can get up to seven week's free credit.

Credit accounts If you have a credit account with a supplier, try negotiating with the accounts department in order to spread payment on large items of equipment over several months.

Outside suppliers of goods and services

Even the most self-reliant designer cannot do everything, so outside suppliers inevitably have a role to play in the efficient running of a studio. Picking a supplier of goods or services is not always straightforward, especially in a city where there may be a choice of dozens of typesetters, photo-labs, graphic supply stores and courier companies. Don't base your decision entirely on cost, as there are other factors to consider, too: do these suppliers have good reputations in the business? Are they used to handling the kind of work you will be buying? Do they deliver? Can they meet deadlines? Do they stop work on the stroke of 5pm, or can they arrange late working for a rush job? All these factors will influence your choice.

'Put it in writing' is a business cliché, but failure to do so can cost you money. No matter how small the order, it always pays to keep a record of it. When ordering prints, write on the order all relevant details, including the size, the quantity, the agreed date and time of supply and – if it is a big order or a new supplier – the agreed price. Telephone orders should be recorded just as written orders are: when ordering headline setting by phone, write out what is required first, then read this over. When ordering messengers, write down the pick-up point and the destination, so that each trip can be checked against the courier account at the end of the month.

When commissioning outside work, the written order saves argument about fees later on. Your order should therefore not be ambiguous about the job: it should carry some indication of the fee if this is to be a flat payment, or the rate per hour plus allocated time for hourly workers. Clarify the cost of overheads, too: your order for commissioned photography, for example, should spell out whether film and processing is included.

Whenever work passes in or out of the studio, it should be documented. The value of graphic material lies in the time taken to produce it, and this may be considerable even for a small illustration. So whenever photographs, illustrations, or finished mechanical artwork change hands, write out a receipt or a delivery note detailing quantity, size, and brief description of each item.

Credit Running a credit account with a supplier has considerable advantages: it improves your cash-flow, because you have free use of goods and services for two or three months before payment falls due; it makes accounting simpler, because you receive monthly statements; and an account reduces the amount of petty cash floating round the studio. However, it is extremely easy to run up large outstanding balances, particularly if you allow junior members of staff to order goods on the account; always make sure that suppliers ask for a written order or at least an order number.

Almost all suppliers require two trade references and possibly also a bank reference. This presents few problems for the designer who already runs several established accounts, but how does the newcomer open a credit account? Most designers open their first accounts with local suppliers who know them well, and with whom they have been trading on a cash basis for some time. Once your face is known, and your word is trusted, the supplier will usually be happy to extend you credit purely on the basis of a recommendation from your bank.

When opening a credit account, you will have to negotiate terms of payment. Generally payment falls due 30 days after the end of the month in which the transaction took place, but some suppliers will agree to terms of 60 days.

Marking up If you buy in services on a job, you are responsible for payment of the supplier, and in recognition of this, and of the administrative work involved, it is customary to mark up the cost when invoicing the client. The mark-up should be agreed with the client at the start of the job. A typical advertising agency will mark-up by 15% of net cost, but smaller graphic studios sometimes mark up to a larger degree when buying print, typesetting, photography and other specialist skills. Materials such as PMT materials, paper, transfer lettering and art board are usually charged directly to the client at their original cost or occasionally with the addition of a small covering charge.

Locating & equipping the studio

Cost of floor space is inevitably a deciding factor in the choice of a studio location, but the proximity of suppliers can also influence the decision. You'll certainly need to be within easy reach of several of these suppliers or resources: a *typesetter* nearby is extremely useful, even if you send most of your setting out of town. In an emergency, the added cost of a local typesetter is more than outweighed by the time saved. The same applies to a *printer*: large print orders may well be placed with a plant many miles from the studio, but a printer round the corner is clearly more convenient for small jobs. A *photo-lab* is essential for colour and black-and-white prints from reflection and transmission originals. Unless you have a PMT camera in house, it is best to try and find a lab that offers the broadest possible range of services, including PMT prints and custom-made transfer sheets (rub-downs). A *graphic supply* store that delivers to the studio is an absolute necessity, and a *secretarial service* is very helpful particularly if it has word-processing facilities: floppy discs can be used for direct input for typesetting, as explained on page 37.

Graphic services tend to cluster together: a photolab lets out a spare room to a designer, who is eventually forced by expanding business to rent new premises just around the corner; he in turn lets out a floor of the new building to a typesetter. So in many major urban areas, it is possible to find studio space with all the services you'll ever need within a short walk of the studio door.

Studio equipment

It's best to take a very cool-headed approach when considering a major capital investment: use the guidelines on the previous page, and don't base buying decisions on over-optimistic assessments of future work. At the other extreme, don't hold back from buying a labour-saving piece of equipment if it will enable you to make more profitable use of your time.

A Grant enlarger or copy-scanner is a major investment, but as work expands, one of these units turns from a luxury to a necessity. Check the maximum enlargement and reduction ratios carefully before buying, as multiple re-tracing for major size changes in artwork is not only inaccurate, but may be as slow as just drawing a grid over the original, and copying the design freehand. Anticipate expansion by choosing a model that can be converted to a PMT camera.

A PMT camera is similar to a regular enlarger, but additionally has a pressure plate to hold negative paper against the glass top platen, and a timer to regulate exposure. A rapid-processing unit is also necessary when making PMT prints, and the combined cost of the two units can be crippling for a small studio. Before making such a large purchase, establish the current cost of sending PMT work out to a lab, and figure out what the saving would be if the same work was done in-house. Don't forget to cost in interest charges, the time taken to make the prints, and an element of material wastage.

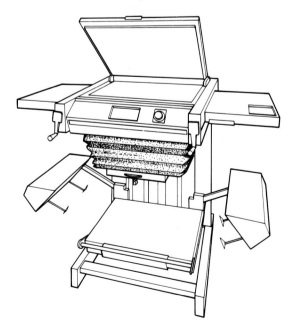

An in-house PMT machine seems at first glance to be an attractive and time-saving investment, but will it ever really pay for itself?

Photocopiers When choosing these, be absolutely sure of what your needs are, as each extra facility costs money. The most versatile kind has a zoom facility which allows you to key in the percentage enlargement or reduction required – this has obvious advantages to the visualizer. Do you really need an extra-large paper size? Will you be making multiple copies of a document? If so, choose a model with a collator and sheetfeeder. If you are unsure about your requirements, choose a basic machine that has these accessories available for fitting later on.

of a galley proof. For justifying text, and of re that is capable of justifying text, and of portion to their width. This text was produced using a rd personal computer, and a letter-quality printer with a ribbon.

For low-budget jobs, a microcomputer and a suitable printer can produce near-typeset quality text which can be pasted down in place of a galley proof. For best results, choose hardware and software that is capable of justifying text, and spacing letters in proportion to their width. This text was produced using a standard personal computer, and a letter-quality printer with a film ribbon.

For low-budget jobs, a microcomputer and a suitable printer can produce near-typeset quality text which can be pasted down in place of a galley proof. For best results, choose hardware and software that is capable of justifying text, and spacing letters in proportion to their width. This text was produced using a standard personal computer, and a letter-quality printer with a film ribbon.

For low-budget jobs, a microcomputer and a suitable printer can produce near-typeset quality text which can be pasted down in place of a galley proof. For best results, choose hardware and software that is capable of justifying text, and spacing letters in This text ation to their width. nd personal

Typewriters and computers Every design studio needs a typewriter for making out business-like invoices. Remember, though, that even the cheapest portable model can fulfil this basic need. Computers may superficially look like an attractive option, and certainly impress the client, but unless you have experience in their use, learning the necessary skills can be extremely time consuming. Word-processing (WP) is the simplest application to learn, and if you buy a lot of typesetting, you may find that purchase of a computer with WP software can save money and time on re-keyboarding. Accounts and financial planning (spreadsheet) programs are likely to save time and accountancy fees only in a medium-size or large studio: studios with three or less staff are better served by calculators and ledgers.

Studio furniture Save money by buying used equipment instead of new. A plan chest or utility chest is a particularly expensive purchase, though it is possible economize by buying the smallest model that can accommodate all sizes of paper and artwork in regular use. Extra-large special jobs can be kept in separate folders or folios.

Decoration/carpets This "hidden" cost quickly adds to the expense of a studio. Save money by decorating to a high standard only the areas seen by the client.

Small equipment and materials

Individually, small items of equipment and bread-and-butter graphic materials are inexpensive. But pull out a drawer in your desk, add up the cost of replacing every item, and you could be in for a shock. Total studio expenditure on these items over a period of time is considerable – and so is the scope for economy.

Adhesives The traditional studio adhesive, rubber cement, is still widely used. It has the benefit of being low-tack, so that small realignments are easy.

Spray-glues are excellent for many purposes, but the fine spray of adhesive tends to drift, so that studio surfaces become sticky and dirty. Fine adjustments of position on the artwork fixed with spray-glue are also more difficult.

Photo-mount, as the name suggests, is ideal for putting down photographic work.

Tapes One and two-sided tapes can be used for most common mounting tasks.

Double-sided adhesive pads are excellent for mounting, particularly in exhibition work.

Hot wax For finished artwork wax is probably the best adhesive. It is applied to individual graphic elements either using a hand-held roller, or with a desk-top machine. Both contain heated reservoirs of adhesive wax. Once waxed, the galleys or prints can be pressed into position, and repositioning is simple.

Transfer alphabets are no substitute for proper headline setting on large pieces of work, but do a business-like job on quick headings and simple one or two-line sentences. The principal advantage of transfer alphabets is choice: even a small graphic design supplier can offer a wider range of faces than a major city typesetter, albeit in a limited range of sizes.

Pads, like other graphic materials, come in various sizes and qualities. The differing show-through characteristics means that each type has separate and distinct uses.

Tracing pads have exceptional showthrough for easy tracing purposes.

Layout pads contain whiter, more substantial paper, ideal for layout and visual. The paper has a tracethrough quality, but fine copying requires the use of a light-box or window.

Drawing pads – good white cartridge paper, an ideal surface for markers and pastels.

Acetate pads have clear film sheets, often interleaved to prevent scratching. These are ideal when overlay material needs to be added to a base design.

Papers and films

Again, the cost of these paper products is considerable. Save by careful planning of a job, cutting shapes from the sheets in such a way as to leave the maximum possible useful area. Keep even small scraps of adhesive coloured film carefully – sometimes you'll need only a few square inches to complete a finished visual.

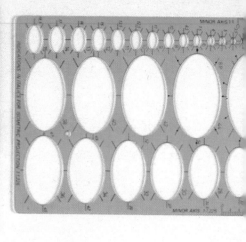

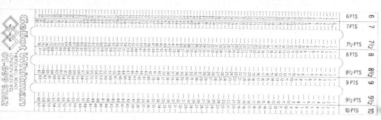

Rulers and straight-edges For measuring and ruling lines the most precise rules are transparent plastic. For cutting thin materials use a thin steel rule to guide the blade; for cutting thick cardboard, use a heavy non-slip aluminium straight-edge, which guards against injuries from the blade.

Curves, squares and angles Adjustable set squares (triangles) that can be set to intermediate angles are more versatile than traditional fixed 90° and 45° models, and make a cheap parallel-action drawing board almost the equal of an expensive ruling-up table.

Drawing accurate curves is very tricky: French curves help, but obtaining a clean joint as the direction changes requires practice. The 'snake' – a flexible rubber-coated guide – is adequate for roughs but not precise enough for curves on finished artwork. A template is the only practical way to draw accurate ellipses, and makes the task drawing small circles easier.

Cutting with the wrong sort of blade can cause serious injury or ruined work. Besides scissors, every studio should have several cutting knives in different sizes: scalpels or X-Acto knives are good for fine work, but for heavy work, knives with thicker blades are safer.

Markers Always try them before buying – some brands dry out if left in the sun or in a warm place.

Buy just a limited selection of black, red, blue and green markers, then purchase other shades only as the need arises. In a busy studio it does not take long to build up a substantial collection.

Pens Finished art keylining and precision ruling demands Indian ink pens – these come in widths ranging from about 0.1 to 2mm. Ink blocking occurs frequently unless the pens are kept scrupulously clean; when the nib is really blocked solid, take the pen apart and wash it with warm water, rather than trying fruitlessly to make ink flow by shaking the pen.

Pastels Combined with a marker, a pastel line smudged with the fingers produces excellent shadow effects.

Pencils An HB, a 2H and a 2B are enough for most purposes. However, no pencil collection is complete without a blue pencil for marking up grids. Though clearly visible on artwork, the blue line is not picked up by the process camera. Mechanical pencils (propelling pencils) don't need constant sharpening, and create much less mess than traditional wooden pencils.

Erasers Avoid the type of eraser that rubs more back on to the artwork than it takes off. For more accuracy in erasing, use a putty eraser moulded to a fine point, or cut a sharp edge on a standard composition eraser.

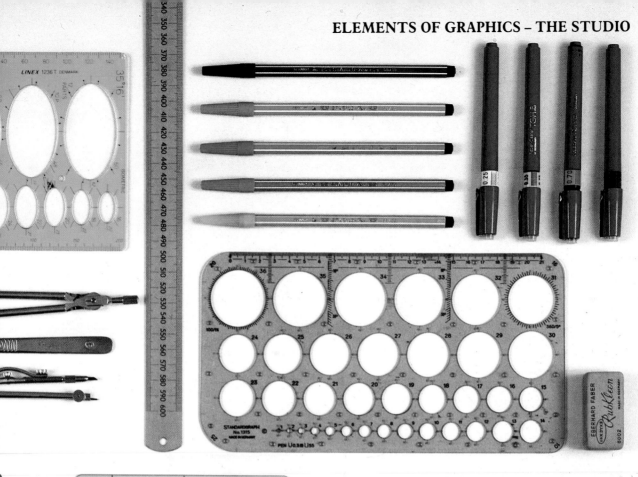

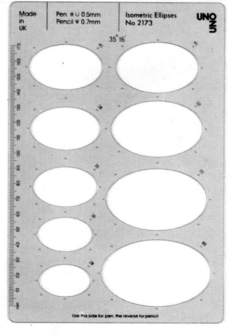

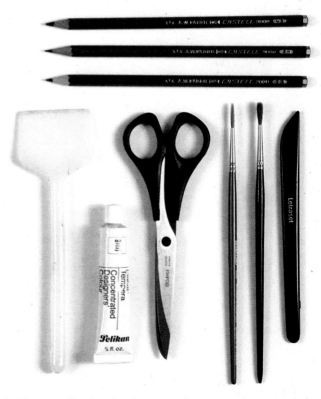

Taking a brief

The starting point for any design activity is the client briefing. This initial meeting provides you with your first opportunity to ask detailed questions, and to determine what is required. The shape of the briefing naturally varies: at one extreme, an advertising agency may supply you with a highly detailed, typed brief, outlining every aspect of the client's market performance, and including a precise outline of the target consumers for the campaign. At the other end of the scale, you may be talking directly to the management of a small business that has never before employed a designer; these people may well be wary of spending money on what they regard as cosmetics, and they may not be sure what service they want from you.

When dealing with an agency, your task is in some respects much easier, because there are more likely to be clear-cut guidelines, targets and objectives; answers to your questions are usually quick and concise, and much of the groundwork is already complete. When dealing directly with a client whose objectives are less well defined, the onus is on you to shape the commission and clarify your tasks as a designer.

Whatever the circumstances, though, it is wise to prepare yourself for a client briefing. If the client is a large, well-known corporation, ring their public relations department and ask for a copy of the annual report. This will detail the corporation's activities, including those of far-flung and less well-known subsidiaries. If you are dealing with a publisher, buy some of their books or magazines so that you can talk intelligently about the company's existing image. Enter a meeting with no prior knowledge, and your obvious ignorance could become an embarrassment.

Briefing checklist
No two client briefings are the same: each area of design has specific requirements, and some of these are outlined in the second half of the book. Every briefing has some common points, though, and if the client does not supply all of the information outlined below, you should ask questions until you have enough information to start work.

1 – Design objectives
First establish the broad nature of the design task. Exactly what are you required to do, and how will your design work coordinate with that of other people?
Existing products Find out whether you will be designing something totally new, such as a package for a new product, or whether your design is a facelift or relaunch of an existing product, such as a magazine.

Track record How is your client faring in the market? Are sales expanding or contracting?
Competition Are similar products already available? If so, what makes this one different? If it is a 'me-too' product designed to make inroads in the competition, how can your design make this product seem superior?
Target buyers Who are you aiming to sell to?
Stockists/outlets Where will this product be sold? In a store? Through a direct-mail offer? From a catalogue?

Identity To what extent is the design work to be integrated with an existing house style? In book publishing you may be required simply to feature the publisher's colophon (publishing house trademark) on the spine, elsewhere on the jacket, and on the title page. Packaging, though, often requires a look that is much more closely integrated with existing products.
Testing Has the product been market-researched? If not, is this research planned? If you are working on an advertising campaign, are there plans to test this locally or regionally before going ahead to a full launch?

2 – The raw materials
The next step is to determine whether or not all the basic materials are available so that you can commence

work on your design work.

Company identity Ask for a copy of the company's corporate manual, their logo or colophon, or for a range of existing printed material.

Stock photography If photographic material is to be supplied by picture libraries, is this already chosen? If not, who will do the picture research – you, the library, the client, or a professional picture researcher?

Commissioned photography Is there provision for special photography? Who is going to do it, and who

will oversee the shooting?

Text Is the copy/manuscript already complete? Will you be working closely with a copywriter?

3 – Production

At this early stage, it is possible that there are few fixed guidelines about the final form of your design. However, you should try to establish the broad production details, as these inevitably constrain your imagination and creativity.

Size and extent How big is the package? How long is the book? There may be constraints on size – leaflets, for example, may have to fit into an existing rack.

Foreign language If text is to be translated, you should avoid reversing headings out of pictures, as this will involve remaking colour film for foreign markets.

Form in which the artwork is required Are you to produce finished mechanical artwork, or just position guides from which a finished artist will work?

Special materials Is there scope for using special materials or finishes, such as metallics?

Print run This dictates the viability of certain print processes.

Use of colour How many colours are available? If the product is a book, does the imposition affect where full colour is available? For full-colour printing, is there provision for printing a fifth colour as a solid? Does the client have a house colour that must be exactly matched?

Special finishing work Die stamping, for example, is routine for packaging, but very unusual in book production.

Printer and colour origination house Have these suppliers been chosen yet?

Areas of responsibility Who buys print and other specialist services?

4 – Schedule, approval and delivery

Establish not only the dates by which the client requires the work, but also when you will receive the various elements that you need to complete the job. At what stage does the client want to see the design work before you proceed to the printed work? If you are organizing printing, where does the client want the finished work delivered to? How is it to be packaged and labelled?

5 – Budget

Clearly this is one of the most important areas. Find out not only the overall budget, but also how much money has been assigned to each of the areas of the project. Ask if there is any flexibility – perhaps a saving on commissioned photography could pay for a more elaborate printing process.

Be prepared for some questions yourself. If the commission is in a field of design that is totally new to you, think before the meeting about your ability to complete the job satisfactorily. You may be tactfully asked about this, so it is wise to prepare an answer which demonstrates that the task is well within your capabilities.

After a verbal briefing, always write to the client setting out what you think you have been asked to do, the time scale that you and the client have agreed, and the fee that you have jointly negotiated. This simple precaution avoids much misunderstanding at a later date.

Costing and controlling work

Naming a price for a job is never easy, particularly when there are many unknown factors. You may be asked to quote for a job, or the client may give you a budget within which to work. Either way, you'll have to work out how much time and money you can afford to spend on the work, and the checklist below should help you do this. This list assumes for simplicity that you are working alone. If you employ a studio junior or other staff the list would be more complex.

Your own time You first need to establish what is an appropriate hourly or daily rate. To do this, make a decision about the salary you plan to pay yourself, then divide by the number of working weeks in the year. Allowing for 3 weeks annual holiday produces a 49-week year, but public holidays account for at least another 5 working days annually, so a more sensible estimate is 48 working weeks a year.

Within the working week, not all time is productive. In a 5-day week, you probably spend at least a day doing administrative work which cannot be charged to any one client, leaving 4 productive days. So in a year, you will have 48 weeks × 4 productive days a week × 8 working hours per day = 1536 productive working hours a year. Divide 1536 into your notional pre-tax salary to produce an hourly rate.

Profit You may have included an element of profit in your fixed overheads. Otherwise, a reasonable margin is to divide the assets of the studio by 5 to obtain an approximate annual profit.

Variable overheads These are charged directly to the client, and appear on your invoice separately from the hourly rate. They include all goods and outside services which you buy specifically for the job; delivery of goods, and other expenses which you necessarily incur purely as result of the commission. Some of these overheads will be marked up as explained on page 13.

Contingency When supplying the client with an estimate, it is sensible to add 10% to the total to take account of unforeseen problems and costs, and idle time caused by delays outside your control.

Costing must be flexible
Estimates of cost must reflect the market rate. If you plan to pay yourself a high salary, you may find yourself with no clients. If another studio puts in a lower quote and gets business that you hoped for, ask yourself why. There can only be a few reasons why they are cheaper than you: their fixed overheads are lower; they pay themselves less; they make less profit; or they are able to buy goods and services for a lower price than you. New clients must be wooed, and this may mean cutting costs, and accepting a low return on the first few jobs. If work is flooding in, though, you can afford to be more selective, and perhaps raise your prices.

Always bear in mind that time spent in meetings with the client is not directly productive. If the client's premises are very distant, try to find further work in the same area, so that you can make two clients visits on a single trip. You may even decide that working for distant clients is simply not viable.

Fixed overheads
Obvious overheads include rent, heating and lighting for the studio, but there are other less tangible overheads that you have to pay, and which must also be charged to the client as part of your total hourly rate. These include basic studio materials such as rubber cement or tracing pads; membership of professional associations or trade unions; subscriptions to magazines; parking fines, and other incidental expenses. Estimate what these will come to over a year, and again divide by the number of productive working hours – 1536. Add the result to your hourly rate. Don't overlook any of the following costs.

- Rent.
- Power – gas, electricity, heating oil.
- Property taxes or rates.
- Telephone.
- Motoring expenses – or a proportion if there is an element of personal use.
- Travel between home and the studio.
- Stationery.
- Professional services – secretarial, legal, financial.
- Interest on loans and bank charges.
- Advertising and publicity.
- Depreciation of fixed assets – as a rough guide, write off 20% of capital value per year.
- Allowance for bad debts.
- Advertising and publicity.
- Insurance – for the studio, your life, sickness, motor, and public liability.
- Social Security or National Insurance payments.

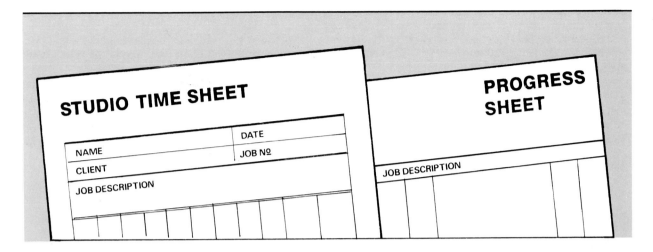

For a design studio to be financially viable, work must be carefully organized and documented. You'll need to keep accurate accounts of course, but in addition to these, it is essential that you are able to trace the progress of a piece of work through every stage of its creation, and to assign all costs to the relevant client.

Every studio does this in a different way. If you are just working on your own, you are unlikely to have more than 10 or 15 jobs in progress at any one moment, so keeping track of everything is easy. But in a large studio, it's not unusual to have 50 or 100 pieces of work going on at once. If you don't impose some sort of order on your way of working, jobs will soon get lost or forgotten, or clients will not be charged for the full cost of a job.

The simple solution

Any system you operate should be a compromise: too much paperwork, and you or your staff won't bother to fill in the elaborate forms; too little, and small items such as the cost of sheets of transfer lettering or motor-cycle messengers will slip through the net, and be paid for by the studio instead of the client. Many small studios keep the paperwork down to a single sheet per job, as shown here. This *job/time sheet* carries details of every aspect of the job, including: the time that each member of staff spent on the job; cost of materials and outside services; print and typesetting charges; and so on. The form is headed with the name of the client and a brief description, and with the *job number*. This is a unique number assigned to the job when it is commissioned, making the task of tracking work very much easier.

A variation on this simple system is to staple the job sheet to a large envelope, making a *job bag* into which

all but the largest finished mechanical artwork can be thrown. This has the advantage that all paperwork associated with the job is kept together. Cab dockets, receipts and delivery notes don't then go astray, and if a transparency falls off the layout to which it was taped, you don't lose a valuable picture.

Progress chasing

When there are dozens of pieces of work on the go, all with deadlines, keeping track of them can be chaotic. To progress them through to completion, keep a studio progress sheet as shown here. Coding the entries saves time:

I/H	*in house*
A/W	*artwork*
F/A	*finished artwork*
copy	*copywriting*
rec'd	*received*
awt	*awaiting*
L/O	*layout*
Vis	*visual*
Cl	*client*

In a busy studio with many simultaneous jobs, the task of progressing work can be eased by programming a computer to keep track of each stage.

Invoicing

Always itemize an invoice clearly. If necessary attach a separate sheet to show expenses. As with supplier credit accounts, always agree terms with the client, then stick to them: if a payment is not received on the agreed date, send a statement and phone to find out why you have not been paid. Always invoice promptly, but not before you receive monthly statements from your suppliers showing the costs that must be charged to the client.

Visualizing to presentation standard

All art directors, visualizers and studio layout personnel have their own techniques of putting ideas down on paper for the client's approval. These range from very rough quick sketches, through to elaborate presentations. The method chosen depends on numerous factors: the client's ability to understand and interpret what he or she is seeing; the graphic designer's knowledge of that understanding; the subtlety of the message which the client wishes to put across; the time available to commit the ideas to paper; and the talent or experience of the designer. There is little use in presenting very rough ideas without first considering whether the client will be able to make the necessary imaginative leap, and thus appreciate what the concept will look like in finished form. On the other hand, it is wasteful to produce very highly polished visuals when the client is quite capable of understanding something simpler.

After taking the brief from the client, don't try and solve the problem first time round. Instead make a series of 'doodles' on paper to represent different interpretations of the brief. Each can be represented as a simple line drawing, or perhaps as a headline that could later develop into a graphic approach. You can then discuss these ideas with the copywriter, or some other in-house person who understands what needs to be shown to the client. From a discussion around these rough visuals, and perhaps from just one idea, you can evolve a more definite direction.

The second stage need be no more than a further series of small, very rough sketches, but should now begin to take on more positive graphic outlines. This is the time to firm-up ideas, and, if there is copy involved, to draw in the headings to show how they will work. Finally bring the resulting rough ideas up to the size at which they will eventually appear.

Now your feel for visualizing really comes into play: If you have an ability to commit ideas to paper you should at this stage have created a piece of work that is good enough to show the client if budgets are small, or if time is short. Even at relatively early stages, graphic technique is very important: incorrectly-sized headings, bad spacing and poor use of coloured markers will be clearly evident.

Client presentations
The basic rough or layout is adequate when you are communicating graphic ideas to people who are familiar with the visual shorthand that designers use to express their ideas. Sometimes, though, you will be called upon to create highly finished presentations which simulate the final appearance of the printed job.

Book dummies are an example: the client requires a model that outwardly resembles the finished book. This is then presented to foreign publishers who are interested in buying rights to the book. Package designs are frequently tested on consumers in a similar way. The aim of a presentation is to simulate the printed image, and in fact many of the processes used are short-run printing methods. These techniques are costly, but they are economic when you must produce a run of several presentations – perhaps so that a simulated package design can be photographed on supermarket shelves. If you just need to make a single highly-finished presentation, you must seek ways to imitate the printed image at lower cost. Usually the colours on a presentaiton must be an accurate guide to the appearance of the printed work, so it is advisable to use materials from a colour system such as Pantone, which can be accurately matched by the printer.

SANS aeio capture the style of the TYPEFACE as closely as possible

Indicating headlines

First try to capture the approximate style of typeface that will eventually be used. This is largely a matter of practice; it is not necessary to trace out every letter for a visual, only to indicate the rough shape and style of the characters.

Ironically, too much care at this stage may slow things down later, because aiming for perfection early on sets standards which you must uphold for the remaining work. With practice, you'll develop a style that is a compromise between speed and quality.

Make each line of the letter with several strokes; you'll find that you can work very much more quickly this way than when trying to form perfect characters at a single pass. Don't choose a marker that has a tip as wide as the strokes of the letter – this does not provide sufficient control. Don't use a fine-point marker either, or you'll spend all your time filling in outlines.

Indicating body copy

Blocks of text should be drawn in neatly. This can be done in a variety of ways as shown below, giving an indication of bold or light type, of line length, and of whether text will be justified or ranged left or right (ragged right or left). This process may sound simple, but the way text and white space are indicated can make or break the look of a layout.

When indicating text with a pen or marker, try to capture the rhythm and character of the typeface you will be using. Naturally, you will not be able to do this as methodically as when lettering headings, but you can soon speed up your work if you practice lettering on tracing paper placed over set text.

Greek text – nonsense words – is useful if the client is not used to looking at layouts, and might be puzzled as to why "live" text did not appear. Save money by photocopying existing Greek body copy.

amititiao non modo fautrices filelssim sed al etiam
Lorem ipsum dolor si amet, consectetur adipiscing
incidunt ut labore et dolore magna aliquam erat
nostrud exercitation ullamcorper suscipit laboris nisi
duis autem vel eum irure dolor in reprehend

Using photographs

Colour prints are a valuable aid in presentation. Use them not only to simulate the appearance of a photograph in print, but also as the base material for a whole presentation, by applying lettering and coloured overlays directly to the picture surface as illustrated at right.

Print costs are high, especially when making prints from slides, but you can save money in a number of ways. One is to avoid using custom labs: instead use a 'mini-lab' that caters mainly for amateurs. Here you can make 36 postcard size prints for the same price as a single 8 × 10 in print from a custom lab. If you need several copies of a picture, simply use your camera to make several negatives, as this is cheaper than reprinting a single negative numerous times. For pictures larger than postcard size, have a whole roll of film printed to a bigger scale at the time of processing. This costs less than enlarging just 8 or 10 frames at a later date. Save money at custom labs by requesting 'enlarged contact prints'. The lab will place the whole roll of film in an 8 × 10 in format enlarger, and magnify each frame by a factor of 2 or 3. You receive a single print carrying an enlarged image of every negative on the roll.

Indicating pictures

If transparencies are to be used, indicate these on roughs by putting the picture on a Grant projector (Lucy camera) and carefully outlining the main content of the picture on tracing paper at the correct size. Then add the main colour content with markers so that the visual representation of the picture approximately resembles the original transparency.

Where the picture choice has not been finalized, you can indicate pictures by photo-copying a broadly suitable image to size, then colouring this with markers. However, for finished roughs, colour xerox prints provide a more accurate guide to the appearance of the finished job.

R-type prints are costly – reserve them for polished client presentations. Many finished layout studios offer a coloured marker interpretation that closely resembles the appearance of an R-type photographic print.

Putting lettering onto presentations

There are numerous ways to lay black text onto presentations – though coloured text is more difficult. The simplest method is to use a clear film overlay. First photographs and illustrations are sized as R-types and pasted in position. Then you paste up text and headlines on a separate board and make a clear

film copy of it using an ordinary photocopier, or a PMT machine for more solid blacks. The film copy acts as an overlay which both simulates the appearance of the text, and protects the pictures beneath. By loading the copier with coloured acetate, you can use this method to create black text on a coloured background, and if you have access to a colour photocopier (see page 83), you can produce coloured text on a clear acetate support very economically and quickly.

The disadvantage of this approach is apparent when the presentation is examined by a spotlight or in sunlight: where the overlay lifts, it creates a shadow, making the text difficult to read. Self-adhesive clear film overlays get round the problem, but are difficult to put down without creating air-bubbles.

Solvents For a few words in colour, you can use matt overlay, transfer letters and colour solvent spray. Rub down the letters in position on the adhesive colour overlay, then spray the work with solvent. After a few moments, you can wipe off the colour where it is not protected by the lettering. Finally, use an eraser or adhesive tape to lift off the transfer letters, revealing coloured letters on a transparent film support.

Multiple-picture presentations are very costly if each image is sized individually, so this dummy for a travel brochure was montaged together from several colour contact sheets as explained in the text

Rub downs Complex dummies with several colours of lettering are best prepared using rub-downs. These are effectively customized sheets of transfer lettering made from your artwork. You prepare finished mechanical artwork just as if you were sending it to the printer, and mark on an overlay the colours in which the various pieces of lettering are to print. A lab prepares one rub-down of the whole artwork in each of the specified colours. You then rub down the relevant areas from each transfer sheet onto the presentation. The colour is backed with an opaque white layer, so there is no show-through.

Hot-pressing For short runs of very highly finished presentations which must stand up to a great deal of handling, the hot-press method is ideal. From a line artwork, a metal plate is produced, and by a combination of heat and pressure, the plate is used to apply colour to a base material of your choice. The result can be indistinuishable from a piece of printed work, and metallic finishes are available, as well as many colours.

Colour overlays Overlays take the form of self-adhesive, flexible plastic film with a matt or semi-gloss surface that is ideal for visuals and mock-ups. The film is semi-transparent, so you can trace and cut shapes with great accuracy – perhaps to fill a black outline letter with colour. However, since the film is not opaque, you cannot use it to create areas of solid colour on a brightly-coloured background – the base colour shows through.

Colour papers Use these as base material for a presentation. They are available either on a matt, non-adhesive paper, or in a glossy finish on a self-adhesive base.

27

Artwork make-up

To produce printed work, a printer must have finished mechanical artwork – often known just as 'mechanicals' or 'finished boards'. Sometimes the printer's own artwork studio will produce these, starting from the designer's marked-up finished roughs. However, just as often, finished mechanical artwork will be made up by the designer.

Good artwork needs to be accurate. It also needs to be presented in a fashion which shows that care has been taken in its production. Mistakes made on visuals and roughs are easy to correct; errors at artwork are expensive to put right, and if they get into print, can be disastrous.

Preparation

Most artwork for printing is put down on stiff white board, or sometimes on thick smooth paper. The surface is important: it must take ink well, so that a ruling pen gives a true line width when keylining; and the board must respond well to adhesives, so that reproduction proofs (finished typesetting copies) and photographs can be stuck down securely, yet removed and repositioned without the surface breaking away. Lighter fuel often helps when lifting stuck-down setting and pictures.

Before starting on a piece of artwork, make sure that everything is clean – this includes the drawing board, the instruments and (especially) your hands. Cut the paper or board down to size (1), leaving it only slightly larger than the actual printing area. If the border is more than 2 in (5cm) wide, large artwork may not fit onto the printer's repro camera. Next, secure it to the working surface with masking tape (2), so that movement is impossible while work proceeds.

Ruling up

Carefully measure the extreme outside of the required working area – the untrimmed paper size – and mark with a fine pencil outline (3). The trimming edge (bleed) lies ⅛ in (3mm) within this outline. Often the edges of an illustration or photograph are purposely taken beyond this line, so that 'bleed-off' can occur when the paper is trimmed to size. If there are folds, mark these using a series of dashes or dots outside the printed area (4) of the page.

These marks must be accurate, as they act as a guide when trimming the work down to size. If there are overlays to indicate the position of a second colour or tone, these must be marked for position as well, so that they are kept in the correct orientation relative to the main artwork.

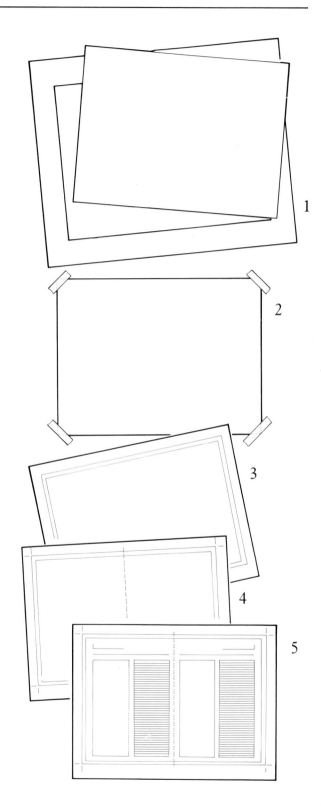

Positioning

The position of each visual element of the artwork is usually dictated by a grid (5) which defines where headlines, text setting or pictures should fall. It is therefore essential to mark accurately each position on the artwork before pasting anything down. Do this with a fine blue pencil so that the lines are not picked up when a negative is made from the artwork. Always measure down from the page top, and out from the gutter or from a single edge – measuring inwards from all four sides introduces errors. When laying typesetting (6), use a set-square and the parallel action on the drawing board to check for squareness of text and headings.

If you are pasting up many similar pieces of artwork such as book or magazine pages, you'll save time if you have blue grid sheets printed, so that you need then only rule up the page once. Get them printed on heavy tracing paper or thin cartridge, so that you can place the grid on a light box: you'll then see the blue lines projected through the repro proofs, making positioning much easier.

Before actually sticking everything down, make sure that all material is in hand, in the correct order. Read all captions to make sure that they correspond to the pictures beneath which they will appear.

Indicating picture positions

Only sized line illustrations are pasted down on the artwork in position. The position and scale of all other illustrations is indicated on the artwork, but the picture itself is supplied to the printer separately (7). Designers use many different methods to indicate picture positions, but the safest is to draw a keyline or corner marks on the artwork in ink to indicate the position of the picture precisely. Mark on the overlay 'keyline – does not print'. Then either make a tracing of the picture to size, and paste this onto the artwork, or else make a photocopy or PMT print of the picture and stick this within the keyline. This procedure acts as a check that the picture fits the space you have chosen; it helps the printer identify which picture goes where; and it ensures that all images appear the right way round and cropped correctly. A black rectangle which some designers use to indicate picture positions is much less helpful in this respect.

If you want a keyline printed around the picture – perhaps in a colour rather than black – rule the line on the artwork and indicate on the overlay that the line *does* print, and the colour in which it is to appear. Don't rule the line too thin, or accurate registration of picture and line becomes impossible: a practical minimum line width is $\frac{1}{25}$ in (1mm).

6

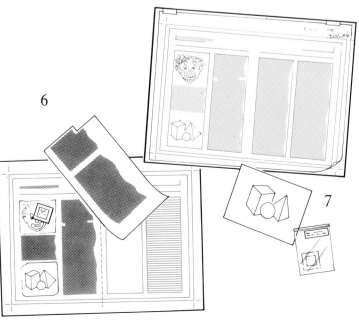

7

Overlays and cover sheets

If your artwork is to print in two or more colours, you do not necessarily need to supply two separate pieces of registered artwork. Provided the coloured areas do not touch, you can produce a single piece of artwork, and indicate the colour changes on an overlay attached to the board. This overlay also carries other directions for the printer, and should be semi-transparent so that the artwork beneath is visible: flimsy or typo detail paper is a good choice. Client's corrections to the artwork should go on a second overlay, so tape this over the first, and protect the whole artwork with a piece of good cover paper.

Using a finished artist

Not all designers are temperamentally suited to making up finished artwork in quantity: many of us simply do not have the patience and precision that this exacting work demands. Finished artists, though, specialize in pasting up finished mechanicals, and can work very quickly without sacrificing quality. It may therefore be easier and more economic for you to pass the final stage of the design process on to a finished artist – either at the printer or a third party.

If you opt to do this, you must take special care with the roughs that you supply to the finished artist. Your roughs will be used as a position guide, so that the exact location of every artwork element must be completely clear. If – as often happens – the typesetter is pasting up the artwork, you should supply two sets of corrected galley proofs. Paste one set in position on the finished roughs, indicating where lines have been cut or filled to make text fit the page. The second set carries the corrections in full.

Adding rules

Before ruling lines directly onto artwork with an Indian ink pen, make sure the ink is flowing freely by drawing a few trial lines. If you have difficulty getting lines of even thickness, it is best not to use a pen at all. Instead, get your typesetter to supply rules of the required width on photosetting paper. You can then paste these onto the artwork. Use tape rules and transfer lettering rules only for short lengths, as both types are apt to bow.

Spare setting

Don't discard spare setting – supply it with the artwork in case last-minute inspection reveals typographical errors. The spare setting may include the relevant word spelt correctly, thus avoiding resetting.

An eye for detail

Always aim for a straight, square edge when trimming waste white paper from setting or from prints that are pasted down on to the artwork. Although such edges will not reproduce, the overall appearance of the artwork is enhanced.

Single lines and characters stripped in at the last minute cast shadows that must be carefully painted out on the negative, and the additions can easily drop off the artwork. If you need to strip in small pieces of type, use double-sided tape, not wax or spray adhesive. Lay the item on the tape and cut around so that no tape is showing before carefully peeling off the backing and sticking down. Mark on the overlay the position of the line or character you have stuck down, so that the printer can then check that the strip-in has not dropped off.

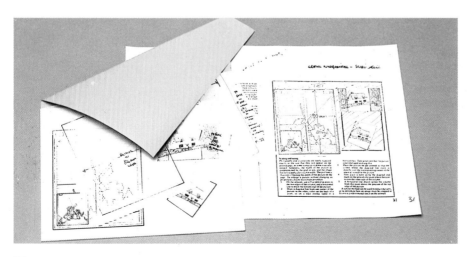

Overlays serve a dual function – they protect the artwork from dirt and damage, and they carry comments and instructions for the printer.

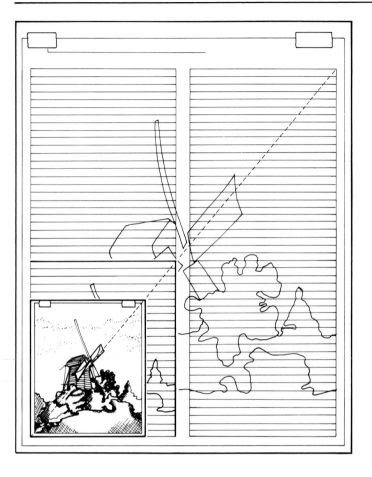

Scaling and sizing

Photographs and illustrations are rarely supplied exactly to the size that they will appear on the printed page, so some sizing up or down is usually needed. Generally, the width of the picture is predetermined by the grid in use, and the image has to fit a particular column width. The problem is thus one of finding the depth of the picture on the page. To enlarge a picture without changing its proportions, follow this simple procedure:

1   On the artwork, use a blue pencil to draw in the two edges of the column, and a horizontal line to mark the bottom edge of the picture.

2   Draw a diagonal line from one corner of the picture to the other, either on the back of a print, or on a trace overlay taped to a transparency. Take great care that the picture is not damaged in doing this.

3   Place the picture on the artwork so that the corner where the diagonal line starts is directly over the corresponding corner of the space allocated for the picture.

4   Now place a ruler along the diagonal and mark on the artwork the point where the ruler strikes the other side of the column.

5   A horizontal line drawn across the column from this point shows the position of the top edge of the picture.

A similar method can be used to reduce pictures, or to determine how an image must be cropped to fit into a predetermined space on the artwork.

Type and typography

On one level, typography is just the selection of a typeface to do a specific job, so that a piece of copy or a headline can be read with minimum effort. On closer examination, though, it is clear that there is more to typography than simple legibility: typography means literally designing with type. An area of body text can be seen not just as words on paper, but as a tone of grey, the shade of which varies according to the weight of the type; and the shrewd choice of typeface for a headline can actually enhance the meaning of each and every word.

Typography is an uneasy mix of mathematics and magic: on the one hand there are strict rules which you must rigidly apply to ensure that the copy fits exactly into a set dimension; on the other hand, good typography gives an individual and exciting character to every piece of graphic literature, and gives every word emphasis.

Tools of the trade
In America and Great Britain designers use points and picas when specifying type. There are approximately 72 points to the inch, and one pica measures 12 points. One pica is often referred to as an em, and though this is ambiguous, typesetters understand the reference.

You'll need two kinds of rule to mark up copy: the *pica or em rule* is used to measure line length, and carries a scale of points and picas. To measure the depth into which the copy fits you must use a *type gauge or depth scale* which indicates the depth of a number of lines set in each type size. For copyfitting or cast-off (the process of calculating how much space the manuscript will take up when set in type) you also need a *copyfitting table*. For the utmost accuracy, tables which give you dimensions of individual typefaces are available from typesetters, but for approximate copyfitting, universal tables based on the number of characters per pica are perfectly adequate.

Most typesetters supply a *type selection*, usually in the form of a wall chart showing all the faces available. On this the faces held by the typesetter are divided into families, with the sizes and styles of caps, lower case characters and numerals all indicated.

Typeface names vary from one typesetter to another, but more important than inconsistency in names is variation in character width and weight. The appearance of nominally identical pieces of text from two different typesetting systems is rarely exactly the same, so corrections and additions to a piece of copy should always be set on the machine that was used for the original.

Type style

The graphic concerns of today's typographer were far from the mind of the jobbing printer in past times; almost anything went. Sometimes so many styles of type and hand-drawn letter were used that only the size of the paper appeared to keep the designers from being completely swept away by their own enthusiasm as shown here. Today, though, such a random hodgepodge of styles is used only to recreate a flavour of the past, and type styles are now carefully selected because each has individual desirable qualities.

Classical typefaces (Old Style Roman) are based on early English, Italian and Dutch designs. The open, wide characters make reading easy, serifs are pointed, and there is little contrast between the thick and thin strokes. These very attractive typefaces are widely used today.

Transitional Under this family heading come type-faces such as Baskerville and Century, which are popular choices as text type for magazines and books. Again, the letters are smoothly cursive with a vertical emphasis, ending in serifs that are more horizontal than Old-Style letters.

Sans Serif The term is self-explanatory: the letters have no serifs. Helvetica, Univers, Futura and Gill Sans are all widely used examples. Compared to other styles, this type family has a greater degree of uniformity in its design, but care needs to be taken in the choice of weight to ensure legibility for text matter.

Modern Roman 'Modern' is a less appropriate name today than when these faces were first cast in the 18th century. The thick upright contrasts sharply with very fine cross-strokes and straight serifs. The faces are not widely used for text setting: Bodoni and Scotch Roman are perhaps the best known. The fine line does not easily reverse black to white, so this use should be avoided if possible.

Egyptian Slab Serif Rockwell is the best-known of this group of typestyles; the thickness of the serif matches that of the main letter, giving uniformity to family. Light and medium versions work extremely well as text faces.

Script Based on the hand letter or handwriting, this elaborate style of type is difficult to read if used extensively as text.

Decorative This blanket term covers a large number of typestyles. Only a few are held by typesetters, but many more styles are available as transfer letters. Though ideal for short, sharp headings or single words, decorative faces are not really suitable for text setting.

Classical

abcdeffgghijklmnop
ABCDEFGHIJKLM

Transitional

abcdefghijklmno
ABCDEFGHIJ

Sans Serif

abcdefghijklmnop
ABCDEFGHIJKL

Modern Roman

abcdefghijkl
ABCDEFGHIJ

Egyptian Slab Serif

abcdefghijklm
ABCDEFGHIJ

Script

abcdefghijklmnopqrs
ABCDEF

Decorative

abcdefghijklmn
ABCDEFGHIJK

The anatomy of a typeface

In normal type ranges, type sizes run from 6 to 72 points; to understand the other respects in which letter shapes vary, consider the widely-used Helvetica typeface. The first and most obvious variation on the basic letter shape is italic. Helvetica Italic has slanting letters, as opposed to the upright form of regular, or Roman Helvetica.

Varying the thickness of the lines produces different weights of type. Helvetica Medium is standard, but Light and Bold are both in common use, and there are also the extreme versions, Ultralight and Extrabold.

Squashing the letters vertically, makes an extended or expanded version on the theme. The reverse action makes Helvetica Condensed.

When selecting a face from the Helvetica or any other family remember that all variations from the basic medium roman or italic letter are designed to exaggerate the characteristics of the basic letterform. In this example, Helvetica Medium is the most legible face of all for body text, and the others are more specialized, and best reserved for headings and subheads.

ABCDEFGHI
JKLMNOPQR
STUVWXYZ&
abcdefghi
jklmnopqr
stuvwxyz
.,:;""-()/!?£
1234567890

Helvetica
Light

Helvetica
Light Italic

Helvetica
Medium

Helvetica
Medium Italic

Helvetica
Bold

Helvetica
Bold Italic

Helvetica
Light Condensed

Helvetica
Medium Condensed

Helvetica
Medium Condensed Italic

Helvetica
Bold Condensed

Helvetica
Bold Condensed Italic

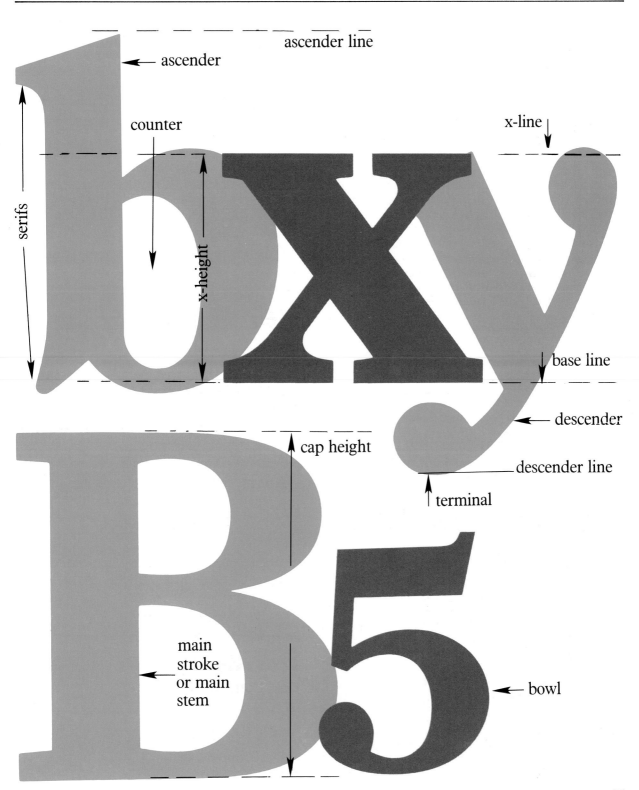

ascender line

ascender

counter

x-line

serifs

x-height

base line

descender

descender line

cap height

terminal

main
stroke
or main
stem

bowl

Typesetting methods

For centuries type was set by manually and laboriously selecting individual metal letters and placing them one by one into a 'composing stick' to make the required words. Today, this labour-intensive approach is used only for extremely high-quality fine-art books, and by job shop printers for very short pieces of setting such as posters or invitations.

Hot metal Setting for all other letterpress printing is carried out from a keyboard similar to that of a typewriter. The operator types in the text, and for each character in succession a matrix – a metal die from which a single character is cast – is selected from a set representing the whole alphabet. Once a whole line of matrices has been assembled, molten lead is poured into the matrix to form a metal cast of the type. Some varieties of hot metal machine have a keyboard which generates paper tape. This is then used to control a separate casting machine.

Photocomposition Many of today's printing methods do not require a raised metal letter to produce words on paper. All that is needed is a perfect copy of the text, precisely as it is to appear on the printed page. For some time, this was produced by setting type on a hot metal machine, making a proof copy, then pasting this into the appropriate space on the finished mechanical artwork – an elaborate and wasteful approach. Today most galley proofs are created photographically without recourse to metal letters. This method of typesetting is called photocomposition.

Just as on a hot metal machine, the starting point is a keyboard. The typesetter enters the text for setting at the keyboard, and checks accuracy on a visual display unit. In addition to the words of text, the operator also enters the designer's setting instructions from the marked-up manuscript. These are typed as 'control codes', and appear on screen as a string of apparently nonsense words such as $SZ18.

When all the text has been typed in and checked, it will be justified if the designer has specified this, and possibly hyphenated automatically, too. When setting justified text, hyphenation is essential to prevent ridiculously wide word spacing, and even on unjustified text, breaking words prevents the setting from looking too ragged.

Actual text setting is carried out in one of three ways. In the first, a beam of light shines through a photographic negative which carries an image of every letter of the font in use. A microprocessor flashes the light on and off, and a system of lenses projects the images of the letters, each in the correct position, onto a strip of light-sensitive paper. Processing of the paper reveals the set text in the form of galley proofs.

The control characters embedded in the text are not set. Instead they provide the typesetting machine with the instructions necessary for formatting the text. For example, the microprocessor might understand $SZ18 to mean 'set in 18 pt' and would therefore move a new lens into position to produce larger type for a subhead. A second control code would make the machine revert to 12 pt for body text.

'Second-generation' typesetting machines do away with the photographic negative of the font, and instead create the letter shapes on a high-definition cathode-ray tube. Using this system, typefaces can be stored as software – in digitized form on a floppy disc.

Finally, the most modern systems utilize a laser which scans across the paper, building up the letters as a series of dots or lines.

Electronic page make-up
Photocomposition systems are not limited to producing galley proofs. The console shown in the picture above can even position text on the page electronically, and put in rules, headlines and captions. This is variously known as electronic page make-up, video layout, or area composition. Once the process is complete the typesetting machine feeds out whole pages of finished mechanical artwork with every element except pictures in place.

Buying typesetting

Typesetting costs vary tremendously, so it obviously pays to shop around for a good price. Here are some steps you can take to get the lowest quote, and to save time and money on setting.

Use an out of town typesetter Do you really need the speed of a typesetter round the corner? If you are prepared to send off setting copy to a distant location, and wait a few days for its return, you could slash your setting bill by a third or a half.

Choose a common typeface If you pick a well-known typeface, you'll be able to choose from a much wider range of typesetters. Every new typeface costs money, and typesetters who hold a very large range are usually more expensive than those who keep just a few faces.

Reduce the number of galley proofs If you need to circulate galleys for approval, you can always make photocopies.

Cut down on corrections Under pressure, editorial staff often send out typescript for setting before all corrections have been made. Final changes are made at galley proof stage, adding to the cost of typesetting, and increasing the risk of errors.

Check setting on typescript If you are using photocomposition, your typesetter may be able to use a line printer to run out a proof of text that has been keyboarded. Though this typescript is not in the correct size or typeface, it does enable you to check for accuracy and typos. Only when your corrections have been taken in does the typesetter run out the galley proofs on expensive bromide paper.

Go straight to page If your pages are being made up electronically (see left), you may be able to save money and time by casting off the typescript accurately, and cutting out the galley proof stage altogether. The first time you see the set type it will have already been made up into pages. This approach suits only the most methodical of designers, though.

Give the typesetter plenty of time Rush jobs that require overtime, evening and weekend working are invariably more costly than setting done during normal business hours.

Keep it simple Fancy setting is expensive – printers describe it as penalty copy. Avoid running type around pictures and awkward shapes, and group together all setting of similar sizes and line lengths. Use a small number of typefaces, or a few variants on a single face, to eliminate constant font changes.

Send a clean, clear manuscript The operator keys more quickly and more accurately from a clean, carefully marked-up typescript than from a heavily-corrected one.

Key it yourself If typescript is produced on a word processor, you may be able to avoid re-keying altogether, as explained below. Even if this does not save money (it may not) it will almost certainly improve the accuracy of the setting.

Keystroke capture

A typesetter re-keyboarding typewritten text amounts to duplication of effort. If your typescript is produced on a word processor, you may already be storing on magnetic discs the keystrokes that the typesetter will repeat. Direct setting from word processor output is known as keystroke capture.

Unfortunately you are unlikely to be able to take a floppy disc out of your computer and slot it straight into the typesetting console. Even if the disc is the right diameter, the typesetting machine is unlikely to be able to read it directly. There are three ways around this problem.

Hard wiring If you can run a cable direct from your computer to the typesetting machine, you can send disc files directly from one machine to the other. This is only possible, of course, if the typesetter is in the same building, or if you have a portable computer.

Media conversion A more practical solution is to have your discs converted to the appropriate format. The typesetter may have a machine that does this, otherwise you should be able to find an outside agency to carry out the change.

Telecommunications If you attach a modem unit to your computer, you can send the data digitally down the telephone line. A similar unit at the typesetter's premises intercepts the copy, and stores it for later setting.

Text files or fully formatted?

The control codes used to change the appearance of the typeset text can be inserted either by the typesetter, or by the person who types the text onto the word processor. If you supply unformatted text files, the typesetter's keyboard operator will insert the control codes, and because of the time this takes, your financial saving is reduced. However, if you send fully formatted text to be set, there is always the risk that a coding error will produce body copy set in the wrong size. A good compromise is to agree with the typesetter a series of arbitrary code words which precede any change in style. For example, you would type CAPT before a caption, A-HEAD before a headline, and B-HEAD before a subhead. The typesetter then uses a 'search and replace' facility to turn your code-words into the appropriate control characters.

Headline setting

Photocomposition systems can produce headlines, though usually only up to 36 pt: this is the most economical way of putting headlines into copy. However, there is a size restriction, and most typesetting machines can set from only a limited number of fonts at a time, so choice of typeface is restricted, too.

Larger headings can be made by using a PMT machine to enlarge the output from photocomposition, but letters begin to break up if over-magnified. For larger headings, a special headline setting machine such as a Photo Typositor produces better results.

For short headings in a decorative face transfer letters are the most inexpensive and practical method. It is costly to buy all the different sizes of each particular typeface, and unnecessary, too. Instead, buy just a couple of sheets in the middle of the range,

and enlarge or reduce the heading on a photo-copier that has such facilities, or, for artwork, on a PMT machine. This is a particularly inexpensive way to produce a series of finished layouts when various sizes of 'adapt' need to be presented.

A collection of these sheets grows with time, and can soon get out of hand. To prevent alphabets from getting dirty and crumpled, buy cardboard storage boxes, and divide the large pile of sheets into families of typefaces: sans-serif, roman, italic, and so on, each with its individual box. When each box fills, further subdivide the sheets, perhaps by point size.

Old sheets of transfer lettering often seem reluctant to part with their characters, however hard you rub the backing sheet. To make the letters stick, spray a little adhesive onto the paper, let it dry, then try rubbing down the letter again, making sure that the rest of the sheet does not touch the tacky surface.

When applying transfer lettering, a wise precaution is to place the sheet of protective silicon paper over the section of artwork immediately below the line being lettered. This saves unwanted characters accidentally peeling off the lettering sheet through hand pressure. Another useful tip is to press letters onto the artwork with a blunt point – ideally a special burnisher designed for the purpose. Sharp points such as fine-tipped ball pens distort the plastic lettering sheet and break up the character.

The most common mistake when specifying headline setting is to choose a type that is oversized. White space around a headline adds impact and aids readability, particularly if an extrabold face is used. However, with one or two word headlines, and where size is available, it is possible to enlarge type over the normal 72 pt. Helvetica in particular gives good results, even when greatly enlarged.

To make inexpensive coloured headlines for roughs and dummies, simply duplicate regular setting on a colour photocopy machine.

Changing the scene
Changing the scene
Changing the scene

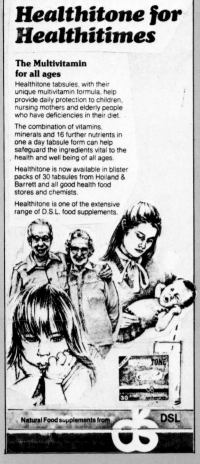

Clients often need several versions of the same advertisement, and when creating these adapts you can economize by ordering typesetting just once, and sizing the headlines and body copy to fit each different space.

Marking up copy

Before text and headlines go for setting, they must be marked with instructions so that the keyboard operator knows what typeface to set the material in, what line length, and all other relevant details. Occasionally this marking up will be done by a member of the editorial staff, but as often as not, the task falls to the designer. Full mark-up is not always necessary; the type style of a magazine, for example, is constant from issue to issue, and blocks of text would just be marked "style A", or with some similar pre-arranged code.

When text and headlines require a full mark-up, this must be done with utmost care. Errors in mark-up are costly to correct. Fortunately, there is a standard system of marks which all typesetters and studio staff understand and these marks are explained below. A few simple precautions are necessary, though, to avoid ambiguity and to make sure that copy does not get overlooked (see box).

The list of accepted proofreader's marks is very extensive, but many apply only to the correction of galleys and some just to hot metal setting. This abbreviated sample shows the marks that are appropriate to manuscripts: most text books on typography contain the full range.

Set in bold	∿∿∿
Set in italics	∠∠∟
Delete and close up	∂
Set in capitals	=
Insert	typed/
Take in new copy attached	⟨A⟩
Set in lower case	≢
Ignore marked correction	⊘
Change to full point	⊙
Indent	⌐1em
Reposition	⌐
Start new paragraph	⌐
Spell out	Spell out
Transpose	⊔⊓
Run on – no paragraph break	⌒

RAL / GRAPHIC ARTS STUDIO MANUAL disc C
Filename: ALACARTE.DOC   Folio:1/2

Magazine production: case history

A la carte is a glossy food, drink and entertainment magazine aimed primarily at A and B consumers, and is published monthly by ipc magazines. This story, about root vegetables, illustrates how the design and editorial staff turn a manuscript into printed magazine pages.

The author of the feature was Jane Grigson, Britain's leading food writer, and an an authority on vegetables and their preparation. THE feature was one of a series on unusual vegetables, and by convention the articles start with a strong, witty photograph that is specially commissioned--as is virtually all of the photography in the magazine;

The design staff were in the fortunate position of having few restrictions on their creativity. Colour printing is available on every page, and the house style is relatively flexible. The feature ran to 2 spreads in all, and none of the editorial pages faced matter advertising. The idea for the picture came from the photographer, Tim Hazael.

Some time before, he had brought in to the magazine a photograph of a fried egg and bacon on a shovel,

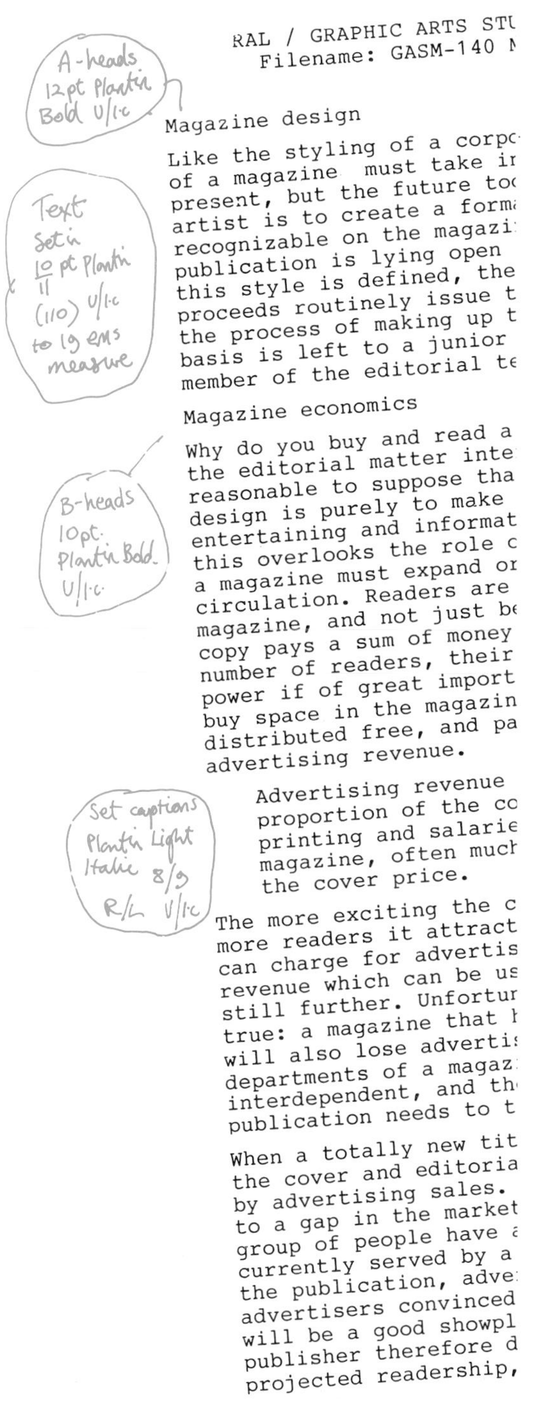

A-heads
12 pt Plantin
Bold U/l·c

Text
Set in
10 pt Plantin
11
(110) U/l·c
to 19 ems
measure

B-heads
10 pt.
Plantin Bold.
U/l·c·

Set captions
Plantin Light
Italic 8/9
R/L U/l·c

RAL / GRAPHIC ARTS STU
Filename: GASM-140 M

Magazine design

Like the styling of a corpc
of a magazine must take ir
present, but the future too
artist is to create a forma
recognizable on the magazi
publication is lying open
this style is defined, the
proceeds routinely issue t
the process of making up t
basis is left to a junior
member of the editorial te

Magazine economics

Why do you buy and read a
the editorial matter inte
reasonable to suppose tha
design is purely to make
entertaining and informat
this overlooks the role c
a magazine must expand or
circulation. Readers are
magazine, and not just be
copy pays a sum of money
number of readers, their
power if of great import
buy space in the magazin
distributed free, and pa
advertising revenue.

Advertising revenue
proportion of the cc
printing and salarie
magazine, often much
the cover price.

The more exciting the c
more readers it attract
can charge for advertis
revenue which can be us
still further. Unfortur
true: a magazine that h
will also lose advertis
departments of a magaz
interdependent, and th
publication needs to t

When a totally new tit
the cover and editoria
by advertising sales.
to a gap in the market
group of people have a
currently served by a
the publication, adve
advertisers convinced
will be a good showpl
publisher therefore d
projected readership,

- First and foremost, always send typewritten text, never longhand. Handwriting is often illegible, so typesetting takes longer, and errors are more likely.
- Typescripts should not be heavily corrected; if there are a lot of changes, particularly hand-written ones, have the manuscript re-typed. When adding more than a line or so of copy, type it on a separate sheet clearly marked "new copy"; attach this to the main manuscript and indicate how and where the new copy is to be taken in to the general text.
- All paper must be whole sheets: scraps and half-sheets are easily lost. When there are a large number of manuscript pages, number them and write "more follows" at the foot of each sheet except the last. On the last page write "ends".
- Don't allow the type specification to get con-fused with alterations to the actual text to be set. The universal rule is that instructions to the typesetter are always encircled – everything else will be set as it appears on the typescript. The only exceptions to this rule are the standard marks shown opposite. When writing type specifications, use a colour so that the typesetter can quickly tell the difference between instruc-tions and copy.
- Always photocopy a manuscript before sending for setting. This simple precaution not only avoids disaster in the event of a lost manuscript; it also enables the designer to look at an identical copy if the typesetter rings with queries.
- Supply the printer with a layout indicating the space that the copy must fill; then if there is far too much or too little text, the typesetter can tell by looking at the layout, and call for confirma-tion.

The typesetter is not a mind-reader, and will carry out instructions literally. Indicating clearly what is required is the only way to avoid mistakes.

Type specification

Before setting text or headlines, a typesetter must have other information to hand besides the typeface and variant chosen. The point size, the line length, the alignment, the leading or line spacing, and the letter spacing all need to be specified.

Point size

For most text purposes where there is a mass of reading, it is important to choose a type size that can be read without effort. 9pt, 10pt and 12pt are normal sizes for use when many pages of text are to be read.

When text is being reversed out, or printed on dark-toned coloured paper stock, it is better to use a larger or bolder face than when printing on white or pale paper. This is particularly important when reversing text out from a dark area of a colour illustration; medium type smaller than about 12pt becomes totally illegible with the slightest misregistration in the four-colour set.

Line length

Legibility depends not only on type size, but also on line length – long lines are very hard to read, especially when set in a small face. As a general rule of thumb 60 characters per line is the maximum that can be read easily. Avoid very narrow columns, too, as short line lengths invariably creates bad word breaks.

Line spacing Extra space or leading between lines makes for easier reading. Text without extra space between lines is said to be set solid, and extra space is specified by indicating in points how much space is needed, or by stating, for example, 12pt on a 13pt body (for 1pt leading). This is commonly abbreviated to '12 on 13' or just $^{12}/_{13}$.

4 POINT 1 point leaded

WHATEVER YOUR PRESENT METHOD OF COMPOSITION MAY BE, COMPUGRAPHIC CAN PUT GREATER SPEED, CAPAB
nd quality at your fingertips for the lowest possible cost. CG offers a wide variety of typesetting equipment, all incorporating the la
ctronic techniques for maximum reliability. In addition to a wide range of typefaces from the extensive basic typeface library, CG
peface development programme that is the most active in the industry. Typesetting today and in the future, requires equipment

5 POINT 1 point leaded

WHATEVER YOUR PRESENT METHOD OF COMPOSITION MAY BE, COMPUGRAPHIC CAN PUT G
er speed, capability and quality at your fingertips for the lowest possible cost. CG offers a wide variety c
setting equipment, all incorporating the latest electronic techniques for maximum reliability. In additio
wide range of typefaces from the extensive basic typeface library, CG has a typeface development pro
me that is the most active in the industry. Typesetting today and in the future, requires equipment that v

6 POINT 1 point leaded

WHATEVER YOUR PRESENT METHOD OF COMPOSITION MAY BE, COMPUGRA
can put greater speed, capability and quality at your fingertips at co
G offer a wide variety of typesetting equipment, all incorporating the latest electronic tec
ues for maximum reliability. In addition to a wide range of typefaces from the extensive l
typeface library, CG has a typeface development programme that is the most active in t

7 POINT 1 point leaded

WHATEVER YOUR PRESENT METHOD OF COMPOSITION MAY BE, C0
ugraphic can put greater speed, capability and quality at your fingertips for
owest possible cost. CG offers a wide variety of typesetting equipment, all i
porating the latest electronic techniques for maximum reliability. In additior

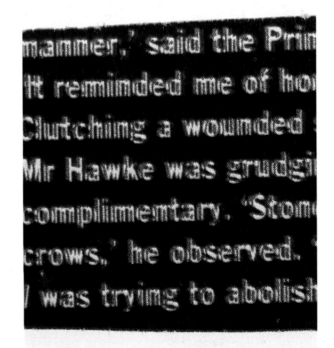

Alignment

Lines of text can be arranged in four ways, as shown here. Fully justified or ragged right text is easiest to read; use the other two alignments only when there is very good reason.

•

On one level, typography is just the selection of a typeface to do a specific job, so that a piece of copy or a headline can be read with minimum effort. On closer examination, though, it is clear that there is more to typography than simple legibility: typography means literally designing with type. An area of body text can be seen not just as

•

On one level, typography is just the selection of a typeface to do a specific job, so that a piece of copy or a headline can be read with minimum effort. On closer examination, though, it is clear that there is more to typography than simple legibility: typography means literally designing with type. An area of body text can be seen not

•

On one level, typography is just the selection of a typeface to do a specific job, so that a piece of copy or a headline can be read with minimum effort. On closer examination, though, it is clear that there is more to typography than simple legibility: typography means literally designing with type. An area of body text can be seen not

•

On one level, typography is just the selection of a typeface to do a specific job, so that a piece of copy or a headline can be read with minimum effort. On closer examination, though, it is clear that there is more to typography than simple legibility: typography means literally designing with type. An area of body text can be seen not

Gravure printing puts a dot pattern not only on pictures, but on text too (far left) making small type sizes difficult to read. Poor registration plays havoc with text reversed out of the four-colour set (near left), so again, keep type big and bold in this context.

Letter spacing Text set on a phototypesetting machine can have added or reduced space between letters – loose or tight setting. Altering letter spacing throughout rarely makes text more legible, but extra spacing between capital letters often gives improved appearance, particularly in headings. Certain combinations of letter look better with reduced letter spacing, and modern typesetting systems are capable of spotting these letter pairs, and moving them closer together, a process known as kerning.

POOR LETTER AND WORD SPACING MAKE FOR DIFFICULT READING

WRONG TYPE SELECTION MAKES FOR DIFFICULT READING

GOOD SPACING MAKES FOR EASY READING

try and avoid letter spacing lower case

try and avoid letter spacing lower case

Bold and Italic It is best to avoid large areas of italic and bold type in body copy, and reserve them purely for emphasizing single words or phrases. There are some specific uses for italics – for example, when there is a reference to the title of a book in body copy, the title is often set in italics to separate it from the rest of the text.

Subheads These are headings set within the body copy and in a different typeface or size, to break the text up. Bold and extrabold versions of the main text face make good subheads; they are normally set a size or two larger than the rest of the copy. When subheads require a more forceful impact, you may want to use sizes up to 18pt in a bolder face.

Casting off and checking galleys

Calculating the number of characters in a piece of text is a simple task, and can be done with nothing more complicated than a ruler and calculator.

Where space is critical, carry out the cast-off paragraph by paragraph. This provides the opportunity to check for widows (see opposite) which can be rectified by asking a copywriter or member of the editorial staff to cut the text to write fills.

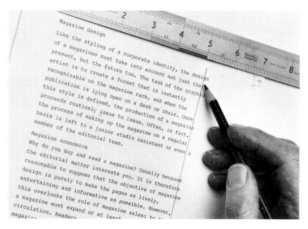

1 Find the end of a typical line of text – neither the shortest nor the longest – and draw a vertical line down through the typed copy.

Count the number of characters to the left of the line, and write it down: this is the average line length.

2 Next, count the number of lines on the page and multiply by the average number of characters per line. Write down the answer.

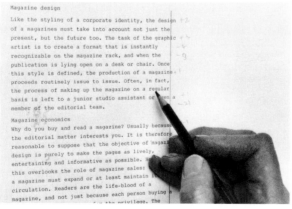

3 Now deal with short and long lines. Find lines that are shorter than average and count how many characters too short these lines are. Subtract this total from the result of the previous stage. Do the same for long lines, adding the extra characters to get the total number of characters in the piece of text.

4. Consult a copy-fitting chart to find how many characters of the chosen typeface and size will fit into the column width. Divide this into the total from stage 3 to find the number of lines filled by the text when it has been set.

Checking galley proofs

Typeset text is usually returned in the form of galley proofs (often referred to as just galleys) which must be checked for errors, and returned for correction if necessary, before being pasted down onto finished mechanical artwork. The word-for-word accuracy of the galleys is almost never the designer's responsibility: checks at the typesetter, by copywriters or editorial staff should pick up all typographical errors (typos or literals). The appearance of the set type, though, is the designer's responsibility, and problems here may not be picked up by either the client or the typesetter. So when galleys come back, examine them thoroughly, and carry out these checks.

Typography and and Typesetting

Many of today's printing methods do not require a raised metal letter to produce words on paper. All that is needed is a perfect copy of the text, precisely as it is to appear on the printed page. For some time, this was produced by setting type on a hot metal machine, making a proof copy, then pasting this into the appropriate space on the finished mechanical artwork – an elaborate and wasteful approach.

Today most galley proofs are created photographically without recourse to metal letters. This method of typesetting is called photocomposition.

Just as on a hot metal machine, the starting point is a keyboard. The typesetter enters the text for setting at the keyboard, and checks accuracy on a visual display unit. In addition to the words of text, the operator also enters the designer's setting instructions from the marked-up manuscript. These are typed as 'control codes', and appear on screen as a string of apparently nonsense words such as $SZ18.

When all the text has been typed in and checked, it will be justified if the designer has specified this, and possibly hypenated automatically, as well.

Second-generation typesetting machines do away with the photographic negative of the font.

First look at the general appearance of the setting, and make sure that the type is neither too small to be read easily, nor so large as to look odd even to the lay person.

Make sure that the type chosen is not too fancy or over-bold, and that the column width is not too long to suit the size and selection of typestyle. It may be better to get over-wide text reset as two columns.

Check that the text fits the space for which it is intended. If the text is overset (too much text) or underset, this indicates that: a miscalculation has occurred in the word or character count; the type has been set in the wrong size; or that copy has been duplicated or omitted.

Compare the setting with the manuscript, and make sure all the text has been set.

Check that all directions to the typesetter have been followed exactly.

Pay special attention to headline setting. It is often left up to the designer to order up headings, and when time is short, headline setting tends to be ordered by telephone, thereby greatly increasing the chance of errors. Don't just scan headlines quickly; read every word.

Examine the word spacing. Words should not be too widely spaced, or too tightly packed.

Look at the word breaks and hyphenation. Two consecutive lines ending in hyphens is acceptable. Three is not.

Look for 'widows' – paragraphs that end with a single word on the last line. These spoil the appearance of text set over a wide measure, though single long words in narrow columns do not look quite so bad.

If setting is not justified, check that the ragged edge is not *too* ragged – especially if the column is very narrow. If a new line begins with a long word, the previous line may be very short. Breaking the word over two lines will prevent this, and a sensible precaution when specifying unjustified text is to supply the typesetter the minimum acceptable line length. The closer this is to the maximum, the more words will be broken over two lines, and the less ragged the setting will appear.

Photography

Few designers can claim also to be talented photographers, but many nevertheless make considerable use of a camera in their work. This is particularly true of designers who do not specialize, and whose work covers the whole spectrum of graphic applications.

That said, good photographic equipment is not cheap, and like any other piece of studio equipment, a camera should be made to pay its way. This doesn't mean taking on photographic work that would normally be put out to a professional: rather it means looking for ways that photography can help make graphic tasks easier, cheaper or more effective. The following examples illustrate a number of ways in which this can be done.

Recording work This simply means setting up any design, whether it is a brochure or advertisement, and making a photographic record of the work. A set of colour photographs is a lot easier to post around to prospective clients than a portfolio, and photographic copies are invaluable when a client, printer or colour house misplaces work that has taken several days to produce.

Artist's reference On many jobs a line or colour illustration is required, and this means either sketching from life, or making do with reference supplied by a client. The illustration may be of something as simple as hands holding a variety of objects, or as complicated as a sophisticated piece of machinery. With a camera, it is possible to get precise reference which can then be processed and enlarged to the required size, to give correct perspective and accurate detail on which to base the illustration. With good enough reference to work from, many designers are capable of drawing perfectly acceptable sketches; whereas they would struggle if asked to draw the same subject from life.

This use of a camera should always be borne in mind when taking a brief at the client's premises, especially if these are some distance from home base. If the brief is for a specific job, make sure that sufficient reference is supplied – otherwise use the camera to collect your own reference.

Photography for visual use With just a little effort, it is not difficult to take photographs that are good enough to use in visual presentations to a client as shown opposite. Highly finished layouts always look impressive to the client, and there may be other benefits, too: clients often question the high fees charged by professional photographers, and a rough-and-ready snapshot of a product can quickly illustrate the specific photographic problems that the professional is required to solve.

FROM ANY ANGLE...

ALL ANGLES

THE MAIN COLLECTION

THE COLLECTION FROM ALCOA

LOCAL NETWORK...

THE BIG BIG 'A'

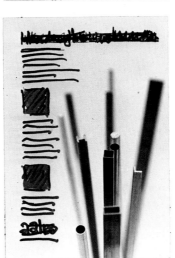

BAR TARIFFE

Equipment and film

For the majority of graphic applications, the most suitable camera is a 35 mm single lens reflex (SLR). These cameras can be fitted with interchangeable lenses, which makes them far more versatile than fixed-lens models. Additionally, the image in the viewfinder shows precisely what will appear on film, so composition is simple and precise. Even inexpensive SLRs are capable of producing professional-quality images if used with care, and most are now fully automatic, so that traditional photographic skills are not a prerequisite for reasonable pictures.

Lenses and accessories The standard 50 mm lens supplied with most SLRs is the photographer's workhorse. It is cheap, focuses quite close, and gives very good quality. Supplementing the standard lens with a 28 mm wide angle, and a 70-210 mm zoom produces an outfit that will cover 95 percent of the graphic designer's requirements. More exotic lenses for the popular makes of camera can usually be hired for about 4 percent of purchase price per day. No accessories can be fairly described as essential, but a sturdy tripod makes copying a good deal easier, and a flash unit prevents reference pictures from being marred by deep shadow.

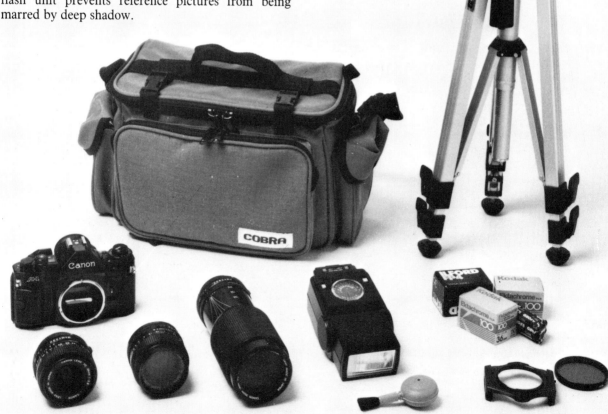

To make an undistorted view of a package using a 35mm camera, subject and lens must be level (far left) so the top is hidden. A large format camera, though, is capable of forming undistorted pictures even when looking down on the subject (middle left). Seen from the same viewpoint through a 35mm camera, the subject appears to taper towards the base (near left).

Film and format

Choice of film is of crucial importance, and has a considerable bearing on a photography budget. Even if the cost of film and processing itself makes up only a small element of the final bill, the format chosen can affect other costs. 35 mm film is very quick to use, so the photographer can take many pictures in the course of a day. This is an important consideration in AV presentations, for example, because pictures are on screen for only seconds. However, if a picture is to be printed bigger than about 8 × 10 inches (20 × 25 cm), this small format may not give good enough quality; a larger format of film may be required for other reasons, too. Roll-film cameras are almost as easy and quick to handle as 35 mm, and the film area is five times bigger, so the pictures can be blown up to a much larger size.

Sheet-film cameras generally make transparencies or negatives measuring 4 × 5 or 8 × 10 inches (10 × 12.5 or 20 × 25 cm) and the motive for using such formats is not just better quality. Large format cameras give the photographer more control over the image than 35 mm or roll-film models. For example, when photographing a square-shaped food pack, the camera must usually be above the pack, so that the top of the box is visible as well as two of the sides. To center the pack in the middle of the film, a 35 mm

camera must be pointed downwards, and this will cause the pack sides to converge alarmingly at the bottom of the frame. However, a large-format camera can be kept level, so that the pack sides remain parallel, and the subject is centered on film by lowering the lens – a 'camera movement' that is not usually available on smaller models. Use of sheet-film cameras is expensive: not only is the film costly, but the camera is slow to operate, so that the photographer may get through only two or three shots in a day. However, for some applications, particularly still-life, there is no practical alternative.

Choice of film stock is easier. Where a picture is to be reproduced in colour in a publication, transparencies (chromes) are preferable. However, if the required end product is a publicity photograph that will be handed out as a glossy print, a photographer may suggest using colour negatives. Black and white film rarely offers any financial advantage over colour, and the only reason for using monochrome is that the picture will eventually appear in black and white – perhaps as an advertisement in a daily paper. Even then, some photographers also shoot colour for their own portfolios, or to cover unforeseen eventualities: if a press campaign in black and white is successful, the client may decide to extend it in other media, and returns to the photographer for a colour re-shoot.

Location photography

Graphic designers often look upon the opportunity to art-direct photographic ideas on location as a pleasurable bonus, particularly when the location is far-flung and exotic. The reality, of course is often rather prosaic: the designer is as likely to be standing in the rain at the airport as tanning on a beach.

The client may be present throughout the location shoot, but the graphic designer or art director is usually responsible for the intensive organization that is necessary. It is therefore important to take the utmost care, and to anticipate all eventualities. Like all well-run and cost-effective exercises, a great deal of forward planning is required: models charge high daily rates, and transport and accommodation are required not only for models and photographer, but possibly also for lighting assistants, hairdressers, and other staff. All this makes location photography very expensive, and delays must be avoided at all costs.

Well before the trip is scheduled, decide on the main requirements. The client may have mentioned blue seas and skies, but is a *real* tropical background necessary? Could the picture be shot somewhere more mundane, then retouched? Remember that a sand pit can make a passable substitute for the dunes of Egypt and that with skillful photography, model pyramids ten yards from the camera are virtually indistinguishable from the real thing half a mile away. Is stock photography a practical alternative? After all these options have been ruled out, go ahead and draw up a list of locations. Possibly at this stage, the budget may be the deciding factor in the final choice.

The next step is to choose models and photographer. All the usual considerations apply, but compatibility and sound common sense are especially important. Setting up and completing a photographic session on location is one of the most unpredictable projects in the business, and when only a few days are available for photography, shooting cannot be interrupted because members of the team fall out, or because one of the models has large bags under his eyes after late night drinking at the local club. So try to pick people who have the right temperament, and who don't make waves. Look for good people with all-round ability who can cope with any emergencies as they crop up. If the photography is to take place in a very hot and sunny climate, make sure all models have good tans. If they are pale, they will quickly burn and become too red and sore to photograph.

At an early stage carefully check on all the props and equipment required. Some may be hired at the location, but this can be risky: promised items may not be available or in prime condition. Check and

For mundane subjects such as packaging, location photography makes a welcome and inspiring change from the studio. On location, the photographer can find a wealth of backgrounds and settings appropriate to the product.

double check equipment and materials that will travel with the team; the problems that arise when simple items are left behind or lost in transit assume major proportions, and add to the general turmoil. If a client's products are to be photographed, unpack them before leaving and check their condition before carefully repacking for the journey.

One major point that cannot be controlled is the weather. No matter how smoothly everything is planned and executed, lack of sun – or perhaps snow – brings the whole trip to a halt. All personnel therefore need to understand before leaving that they must take full advantage of the weather, since it can change at a moment's notice.

On arrival, and perhaps while others are recovering from the journey, it pays to do a little reconnaissance of the area. If there is a beach location on the list, check how the tide changes its appearance. Make a note of the point where the sun rises and sets, as this greatly influences the shots that have been planned. Shadows falling incorrectly can ruin an otherwise perfect picture. Be prepared to adapt the schedule according to the photographic requirements: always have alternative arrangements prepared, so that if it rains, for example, indoor pictures are substituted for beach pictures.

> **Draw up an administration checklist, including the following points:**
> - Hotels: to save travelling time, try to arrange for these to be near the location, or central if photography will take place at several points.
> - Dates of arrival and departure.
> - Vaccinations required.
> - Travel documents – passports, visas, work permits and vaccination certificates if required.
> - Insurance.
> - Transport for location work. On this topic, consider also where the models are going to change if the location is remote. If many changes of clothes are required – as on a fashion shoot – a large vehicle should be arranged when planning transport. This can accommodate a closet and a suitable area for models to attend to hair and make-up.
> - Foreign currency for general out-of-pocket expenses (remember to keep all receipts).
> - Check all personnel selected for the trip, and make sure that they know where they are expected to meet, and at what time.

In tropical regions the sun casts deep shadows that film records as empty and black. This location is rendered useless by the shadows at certain times of the day, as shown here, yet around midday the whole scene was sunlit.

Still-life photography

Photographers are rarely left to their own devices in the studio. Generally a designer will be present giving art direction during the shoot, and sometimes a representative of the client will go to the studio as well. Most designers get their first taste of art direction on a still-life shoot. Here, no models are involved, so costs – and risks – are lower.

Photographers are adaptable people, but vary in the amount of art direction they require. Most prefer to have the designer responsible for the shot in the studio while photography is actually taking place. The photographer may find the props, build the set, suggest the best lighting and prepare the backgrounds, but when everything is ready, responsibility is handed over to the graphic designer or art director. The photographer therefore takes the credit for the technical excellence of the shot, but nothing more. If as a result of a poor layout the pictures do not fit the page, the necessary re-shoot will be at the expense of the designer, not the photographer. So it should be fairly obvious that great attention to detail is the order of the day, and a good checklist is well worthwhile.

In the studio

If the photographer is efficient, everything should be ready when the designer gets to the studio. The basic set should be in position, the lights set up and tested, and the camera ready for the designer to get the 'feel' of the shot. Prepare or finish the set according to requirements and check that all the agreed props are there, and the client's products are up to date, the correct size and colour, and undamaged.

Proceed carefully, making sure that there is the correct amount of area as indicated on the agreed visual layout. Some designers like to use a wax pencil to sketch the final picture format on the camera's focusing screen as an aid in composition. If there is any doubt, remember that pictures can be cropped, so leave extra space around the edges of the frame.

When everything is ready, the photographer generally makes instant film test shots to check for correct positions and lighting. This is the last chance to make corrections and alterations. Remember, though, that instant film is only a guide and cannot match the colours of the final picture. In particular, shadows on a Polaroid look more empty, and highlights more burned out than on conventional film.

With a complicated shot, always process and evaluate film before dismantling the set and returning the props. This simple precaution avoids the expense of a re-shoot if a mistake has occurred, or if film is damaged in processing.

A photographer's role on a session varies tremendously – some contribute ideas; others simply execute the art director's wishes. Here, a preliminary sketch was sufficient to illustrate the principles of a new bottle closure. The photographer then used his skills to create the appearance of movement using a multi-exposure technique.

Carefully controlled lighting is the key to good still-life photography. In these four examples, the texture and tone of the subject have been radically changed simply by moving the light. No one picture is better than the other three; but each has a different mood, and would be suited to a different application.

To accommodate a room set, a studio must not only be physically big, but must also be well equipped. To light such large areas requires considerable amounts of flash power, particularly if the picture is to be shot on large format film.

Using a photo library

The alternative to commissioning a photographer to take pictures of a general nature is to use a photographic library. The key to using stock photography, though, is the word 'general'. As an example, imagine that a client requests a picture of a sunset, or of the Statue of Liberty, as part of the final artwork. The cost of commissioning such pictures is far greater than a library would charge for the use of existing stock photographs.

Libraries operate by encouraging photographers to supply a selection of their best pictures on a regular basis. Photographs are filed and indexed, and when a picture is supplied to a designer and published, a percentage of the fee paid goes to the photographer. Most libraries hold pictures of a very general nature, but some are stronger in particular areas such as travel, or nature subjects. The most specialized libraries are usually founded on the work of photographers who are experts in a particular field, such as insects or plants.

Pictures from these libraries normally carry very detailed captions. The accuracy of such captions is often important when choosing a picture for reproduction. Everyone knows what the Statue of Liberty looks like, but the appearance of a particular wildflower may be less well known, and there is always a chance that the transparency was incorrectly labelled. It is therefore a wise precaution to check the caption against a picture by another photographer in the same library, or against a reference book.

Library procedure
Many libraries allow their clients to sort through files themselves, or to send a picture researcher along, and this is generally the best way of getting the right image. However, some libraries insist that their own staff do the search, and if this is the case, it is important to provide as much detailed information as possible. A request for a picture of 'a couple in a park' will bring a deluge of unsuitable pictures, so be more specific. A city park or a National Park? What season and what time of day? Must the couple be young, or can they be senior citizens? The answers to such questions make the picture clerk's task easier.

Most libraries allow their customers two weeks to a month in which to make a selection and return unused material. Holding fees are incurred if pictures are kept for a longer period. There may also be a search and administration fee to pay if none of the pictures are used.

Reproduction fees vary from library to library, and before using the pictures, check up on the cost. This will depend on: how the picture is going to be used; how many transparencies the library is supplying; in what type of print or advertising material the pictures will appear; and what size they are. A really good photograph is often used many times by different companies, so always check that the picture selected for a client has not been used recently by a near competitor. Exclusivity of use costs extra, and covers only reproduction rights, never copyright.

When selecting pictures, choose the largest format possible. This does not mean discarding all 35 mm pictures, simply that the larger sizes give better quality reproduction. Check with a magnifier that the picture is sharp and correctly exposed; slightly darker pictures print better than those that are too light.

When borrowing pictures, take great care of them, and preferably take out insurance to cover loss or damage. If a mishap occurs, there will be a crippling bill. Even removing transparencies from their mounts renders the customer liable to a remounting fee.

Commissioning a close-up photograph of a flower is costly and pointless; specialist natural history libraries can almost certainly supply the picture you need from stock at a lower price.

Buying photography

Like most graphic skills, that of choosing and briefing a photographer improves with practice. Mistakes and misunderstandings can be costly, particularly on a location session where models and ancillary staff such as assistants and stylists are involved. So it is essential to choose the right photographer for the job, and to make sure that every detail is considered.

First, make sure that the photographer under consideration has a good track record in the type of work required. Look carefully at the portfolio, keeping in mind that it contains only a small proportion of a photographer's output, normally the best pictures. Remember, though, that photographers like to know what kind of work they are pitching for in advance of a visit to a designer; they can then add relevant pictures to the portfolio, and remove those that have no bearing on the job. On meeting the photographer, do not rely only on the evidence of the portfolio, but make sure that the photographer has the necessary social skills and tact. It is better to hire a merely competent worker who can take a brief and communicate with the client than to be burdened with an individualist who will not listen to what is required.

Having picked a photographer, provide the most detailed brief possible, and be prepared to listen as well as talking: the photographer will be aware of potential problems that may not be immediately obvious. Go and see the studio premises to make sure that they are suitable, with enough room – headroom as well – for the required shots.

Always discuss what will be required for the shot, and who will be responsible for supplying it. Once the picture session commences, every moment costs money, and time spent waiting for a vital prop from the other side of town can be extremely costly. Consult with the photographer about the time required to complete the photographic work, allowing enough time for preparing the set. Always allocate more time than you think you need rather than less, as things rarely run perfectly smoothly.

Finally, agree a fee, and establish precisely what the price charged will include. Practices vary, but usually the basic photographic fee includes only the photographer's time and that of one assistant (more than one if the photographer runs a large studio). Film and processing, proofs and prints, and other consumables are generally charged additionally, as are the services of specialists such as hair stylists or make-up artists. Rented items such as lights or studio space should be charged only when the photographer cannot reasonably be expected to need day-to-day access to such things. For example, rental of a smoke generating machine would usually be charged to a client, but hire of an ordinary instant-film camera would not.

When picking photographers, look for organizational skill as well as image-making talent. Even a simple shot such as this requires a great deal of coordination, and any delay in the shoot will inevitably lead to several highly-paid personnel standing idle.

Photographic models

Models of all descriptions are required for both studio and location photography, and the contribution that a model makes to a picture session is as important as that made by the photographer or the designer.

Professional models For important shots, it is best to work with full-time models. They will be used to relaxing in front of the camera, and therefore easier to work with. This in turn means a quicker shot, thereby cutting the cost of the session.

The stereotype photographic model is a pretty young girl, but models come in all shapes and sizes, from children right through to old people. The first step in choosing a model is to contact an agency, describe the type of person required for the picture, covering age, height, approximate weight, skin and hair colour. The agency will then send details of suitable candidates. From this short list select a few who seem to fit the specification, and arrange to meet them in advance of the photo-session. In the flesh, models may bear only a passing resemblance to their photographs: the camera makes everyone look fatter; makeup or hairstyles can totally change a face; and men grow or shave off beards. In choosing the model, be guided by the photographer, who knows what the camera will produce.

Booking Models are usually booked by the day or the half-day, and time booked must be paid for, regardless of whether the session finishes early. Don't arrange for a model to arrive at the studio at exactly the same time as the photographer, or there will be a lot of time wasted while lights are arranged and sets built. Equally, allow some extra time in the schedule for the model to get ready.

Unless other arrangements are made, the model will assume that all special clothing for the shot will be provided, and – for women – that a hair-dresser and make-up artist will be in attendance. If this is not the case, explain when booking what is expected of the model.

Very often young children are needed for a shot, and these infant models are amazingly able. However, they can easily become bored and irritable if kept waiting, often leading to floods of tears. Sessions in which children are involved should therefore last just long enough for the child to relax in the studio environment, and no longer.

Amateur models On low-budget sessions, it may be necessary to use amateur models. Often this works well: some members of the public are completely natural in front of the camera. However, others may be nervous and completely unable to relax in the allocated time, resulting in wooden expressions and wasted studio time. Check whether the chosen model can relax by doing a 'screen test' with an instant camera well before the session.

To ensure that amateur models turn up on the appointed day, use friends or local acquaintances who will have to provide explanations if they don't get to the studio. Total strangers have little incentive to turn up apart from the money they are offered, and on a tight budget, this may be small compensation for the inconvenience caused.

Model releases Always ensure that the model, whether amateur or professional, signs a legally binding release form. Without this, some publications will refuse to run the pictures.

Using pictures

Like other graphic resources, photographs cost money, whether they are supplied by a library, or commissioned from a photographer. So it makes sense to take care of them, and to use them intelligently. The first step is to go through all the photographic material, and select the best shots for reproduction purposes, putting aside all material that is too dark or too light, or unsuitable for other technical reasons. Look at transparencies on a light table or light box using a magnifier, and examine prints in good light. If the photography was commissioned, the difference between one frame and another may be slight, but these small variations can make pictures interesting. If the transparencies are mounted, make a pile of the best images; if they are in strips in acetate sleeves, use a wax pencil to mark the good frames. From this short list, it should be possible to make a final selection. The chosen image is now separated from the rest, and clearly marked to identify the area on the printed sheet where it will appear – a page number and position for a book or magazine. It is also wise to write down a description of the picture, the name of the photographer, and the size the picture will be used.

Unused commissioned photographs should be carefully filed so that they can be located later in case a picture change is requested. Itemize unwanted stock photography on a delivery note and return to the library by insured post.

Sometimes the choice of pictures is small and uninspiring, or there may be only one picture. Perhaps the client's products are a little uninteresting or just plain ugly, and using such pictures to make an attractive design can present very real problems. However, very often careful and thoughtful cropping can turn ordinary pictures into something quite dramatic when reproduced, and dropping a tint over a black-and-white image sometimes helps. When there are technical problems with the pictures, sort through the material supplied, this time including pictures that were discarded because they were too dark or too light. There may be some way to use these rejects – some perhaps have interesting lighting, or it may be possible to reverse type on the darker pictures. If there is no choice of image except what the client has supplied, improvisation is called for: try to turn technical problems to advantage.

Retouching and photocomposition

Occasionally a picture is salvaged by retouching. Prints can be airbrushed to remove blemishes from clients' products, or power lines from rural scenes. Likewise, transparencies can be touched up to improve on reality. Combining several different images in the darkroom creates a perfect illusion – this is known as photocomposition.

These services are expensive, and as remedial measures should be considered only when the alternative is a reshoot. As a planned and budgeted part of a job, though, photocomposition and retouching are valuable tools for the designer: composite photographs combine the imaginative strengths of illustration with the veracity of photography as shown below.

Three separate photographs were needed to create this image of Alice with an Old English Sheepdog (the trademark of the client). The room-set was shot on 8 × 10 inch film, and the other elements on roll-film. Skillful photocomposition and retouching united all three elements.

Illustration

The aim of all designers is to find the most appropriate graphic solution to the job in hand; it would be a very inflexible designer who used the same technique or treatment for each and every client. Most designers therefore soon accept that they can provide a better service for their clients by calling for the help of other specialists in individual areas.

This flexibility in approach opens the door to a group of people in the graphic industry whose unique talents are often needed to turn visuals into finished artwork – illustrators. In the strictest sense, photographers are illustrators, and indeed, photography is perhaps the most widely illustrative medium. However, a photograph is not always the most appropriate way of illustrating an idea: the camera records everything in a very matter-of-fact way, and often this is precisely what a client does not want. Equally, the subject to be illustrated may not yet exist – it is impossible to photograph a building when the foundations have yet to be laid. These are just a couple of reasons for calling on an illustrator.

Style and media

Using illustrations effectively means learning about the various techniques involved, understanding the limitations and costs of each, and recognizing how different printing processes modify and distort the original image. There is little point, for example, in commissioning a delicate ink-wash landscape as a newspaper illustration, because the headlines printed on the other side of the sheet will be clearly legible across the sky. A woodcut style is more appropriate for the robust medium of newsprint.

The very first illustrations were simple line drawings: no colours, no embellishments, just a simple line form scratched on a cave wall. Line is an immediate and direct form of illustration, and has other advantages, too: it reproduces well on even low-quality paper, and is the cheapest form of illustration to print.

Today, the basic line drawing in one colour is almost always worked in pen and ink. Though this sounds limiting, the pen covers a wide range of instruments from the simple steel nib, right through to technical drawing pens. The choice of pen type is dictated by the style of illustration you require. For strict line control on diagrammatic drawings with great detail, a technical drawing pen is difficult to improve on. When commissioning such work, you should specify line width – usually the artist will work with two or three line weights. For a freer, looser line illustration, more expressive lines of continuously varying thickness are needed, and for this most

illustrators use old-fashioned steel-nibbed pens. Virtually any instrument that can pick up and release black indian ink can be pressed into service for very free illustration styles: some artists even spatter ink onto paper with an old toothbrush, or lay it on with a brush or sponge.

You can turn photographs to line very simply using an office photocopier. A single exposure does not usually retain enough detail in all areas of the copy, so make several copies with the lighter-darker control at various settings. From the resulting series of prints, choose the best areas and paste them together. This creates coarse line artwork very quickly and extremely easily. Variations are possible by laying a coarse screen over the photograph before copying. This does not need to be a true halftone screen: it could be an unused sheet of self-adhesive mechanical tint in any one of a number of patterns. You may need to add a little detail on certain sections of the illustration – do this with ink, or by carefully scraping away the toner in dark areas. For a similar, though more detailed style of line illustration use PMT copies instead of photocopies.

Scraperboard/scratchboard This is the reverse of adding black ink to white paper. The special board used has a black surface with a white layer underneath: scratching the surface produces white lines on a black ground. Scraperboard illustrations look very clean and bold, and reproduce well even on newsprint. However, the technique is very specialized, and is undertaken by artists who have studied it for commercial purposes.

Schafline To improve on the poor quality of newspaper halftones, it is possible to convert black and white photographs into line artwork: one of the best known companies specializing in this work is Schafline. Though the result resembles a halftone photograph, the picture is actually a very lifelike illustration which uses a heavily-retouched photograph as a starting point. The highlights appear white, not grey, and the picture has more sparkle than a regular halftone. While this initial processing of the image is costly, subsequent copies are inexpensive, and can be enlarged or reduced without the picture breaking up.

Schafline conversions not only reproduce better – they also provide the designer with a wide choice of illustration styles, while retaining the realism of a photograph.

Adding tones Any printing method that can reproduce line illustration can potentially also print tone – though possibly only in a very crude form. For example by cross-hatching – ruling many closely-spaced parallel lines – you can add a tone effect to a line drawing. There are other similar mechanical methods of adding tone, such as filling in areas with tiny dots. However, these are very laborious and time consuming, and a more practical approach is to apply ready-made tones. The commonest way to do this is to use sheets of clear, self-adhesive plastic overprinted with halftone dots. The sheets are cut to fit the required area, then burnished down onto the artwork. Alternatively, you can rub tints down like transfer lettering. The choice of tints is diverse, including not only simple dots, but ruled lines of varying density, or even interesting patterns which appear as shades of grey except when viewed close-up.

Each type of tint is supplied in a range of sizes, and the size chosen must be matched to the printing method: newsprint and cheap 'instant-print' offset hold only very coarse tones, and if the dots are too small, the grey areas will fill in to black, or look blotchy and uneven. Remember too that if the illustration is reduced, the dots will get closer together, and may fill in when the picture is reproduced. If you are preparing a line and tone illustration half-up, it is best to complete all the line work, then reduce the image to its final size using a PMT camera before applying tone. This approach ensures that the dots reproduce well, and also gives you a completely flat surface to work on – so you do not have to apply tone onto several different layers of paper, or over rough areas of white opaque.

Halftone illustration If an illustration is to reproduce as halftone, there is greater creative potential. For example, you can soften the harshness of pure line work by adding an ink wash: put down the main line structure first, then add diluted ink with a brush. Keep in mind the fact that that tone is easy to apply, but difficult to remove or lighten.

You can also use the halftone process to create areas of flat tone on a line artwork: simply draw areas that are to print as tone on separate registered overlays, with an indication of the percentage grey required.

Pencil renderings Pencil drawings need to be clear and fairly contrasty to reproduce well: the clarity of the pencil line on the surface of the chosen paper, and the simplicity of structure and detail in the finished artwork all affect the appearance of the printed image. Soft pencil drawings lose all detail when printed in line, and generally speaking appear very much better when reproduced by the halftone process.

Colour artwork Book and magazine publishers use a wide range of artists to illustrate their chapters or articles. Increasingly, good colour illustration is commissioned for its eye-catching qualities: a good drawing livens up the format and stands out from the text and photographs that make up most of the graphic content on the editorial pages. On this type of illustration, colours are normally vivid and strong in presentation, and are chosen to react with one another, rather than blending in as do the softer tones of colour photography.

Line illustration (top right) is a cheap, clear medium for "how-to" drawings. To save money, these six were drawn in proportion, and originated as one subject rather than six. If an illustration is to run round text, as the painting on the far right did, always supply the artist with a layout showing type area. Delicate pencil drawings (near right) need halftone reproduction if they are to retain any subtlety.

Mechanical tints in these and many other patterns are the quickest and simplest way to add tones to line artwork.

Buying illustration

Just as when buying photography, choosing an illustrator is a matter of finding the artist who is best suited to the task in hand. An illustrator who can create excellent imaginative interpretations of an idea may have difficulty drawing a line illustration for an instructional publication. To make the job of selecting illustrators easier, keep a file of distinctive work in all kinds of media, and try to set aside time to look at artists' portfolios on a regular basis – perhaps for one afternoon a month. Many established illustrators use an agent to show their work to art buyers. The agent handles several artists, and when keeping an appointment, takes the opportunity to show the work of all of them, leaving printed examples of finished work. Meeting an agent is therefore a time-saving and cost effective way of seeing a number of different styles.

The briefing

This is a fundamental and important part of commissioning illustration: a hurried or inadequate brief leads to inappropriate or unsuitable work, expensive corrections and possibly a missed deadline. Before meeting the artist, draw up a list of illustrations required, assemble the layouts on which the work is to appear, and get together all artwork reference required. The amount and type of reference material needed depends on the subject of the illustration, and the style required. Step-by-step instructional drawings can be completed very much more quickly if you supply the illustrator with good black and white photographs, rather than a verbal description. On the other hand, for imaginative illustrations the rough or visual alone would normally be sufficient.

At the meeting with the artist, explain the brief carefully, preferably showing examples of other pieces of finished work in the required style. Cover deadlines and budgets, and make sure the artist knows whether the artwork is to be drawn same size (S/S) or at a larger scale – often "half-up" (50% bigger than the printed illustration) or "twice-up" (100% bigger). For simple pieces of work, most illustrators should be able to estimate cost at the briefing.

If the work being commissioned is complicated or detailed, it will need to be monitored at least once before completion. This generally means that the artist submits a rough or line illustration after the preliminary work is complete, to ensure that the style and content fit the brief. In the case of designs for products, or those where a specific colour treatment is required, you should be convinced that the illustrator has understood the brief correctly, and agree to the method of makeup to be sent to the printer.

Saving on illustration costs

Illustration work is costly, so think carefully before commissioning a drawing or painting. By running through the checklist below, you could save the artist time, and you may even be able to avoid the expense of an illustration altogether.

- **Would a photograph be better?** Make sure that you have a valid reason for commissioning an illustration; photography may be cheaper and more effective.
- **What is the picture doing?** Illustrations are used for decoration, for explanation, and to make existing information easier to understand. Ask yourself what the purpose of the drawing is, and you're well on the way to identifying the style and artist you require.
- **Do it yourself** Do you really need to hire an illustrator, or could you do the work yourself?
- **Get the right artist** Illustration is becoming increasingly specialized. Commission only illustrators whose portfolios already contain work of the type you require.
- **Consider using an existing illustration** Companies that commission a lot of illustration, such as some magazine publishers, retain the rights to the illustrations they buy. For some general subjects, there may be an existing illustration which you can use at a lower cost.
- **Cut out unnecessary detail** Detail costs money, and irrelevant, unnecessary detail can actually make an illustration more difficult to understand. Make sure that the illustration you buy contains just enough detail to get the message across.
- **Get the size right** Don't commission illustration until you have determined the area into which it will fit. Most illustrations work best at one size; reduce them too far, and lines and tones break up; enlarge them and they look empty and crude. This is especially important if you are using several pieces of illustration together. If you size any of them up or down after completion, the differences in line width will be obvious.
- **Cut down on colours** The fewer colours you use, the cheaper the illustration is likely to be.
- **Reference is essential** The more detailed the reference, the easier it is for the artist to give you what you want.
- **Keep text on a separate overlay** Unless the illustration is to print as line, it will be shot through a halftone screen. Text that appears on the illustration is then also screened, making it

less clear, but text on an overlay is shot separately to print as line. And if the printed work is translated, the overlay can be re-made with foreign language text.

- **Prepare detailed roughs** Much of the time spent in developing a drawing is spent in figuring out where each element of the picture should be placed. If you can sketch this out, you'll be saving the artist time, and yourself a series of annoying questions.

- **Supply the artist with typesetting** If annotation (call-outs) are to appear on the illustration, get these set in advance and supply them to the artist, who can then position them on an overlay. This is cheaper than having the printer position text and leader lines.

- **Anticipate changes** If there is a chance that details will change – perhaps to take in a modification at a later date – tell the artist this at the briefing. The information may affect the way the illustration is drawn.

- **Ask the artist's advice** An apparently insignificant change in illustration content or style can save the artist many hours of work. Don't be too proud to ask the advice of the expert who will execute the work.

- **Follow up** Monitor all but the simplest of illustrations, or you won't discover errors and inaccuracies until the last minute.

- **Plan for problems** Allow sufficient time in your schedule for dealing with problems and corrections that may arise.

The key to good illustration is good reference. If you can supply accurate and comprehensive artwork reference, you're more likely to be rewarded with an illustration that fits the brief without correction, delivered within budget and on schedule.

Selling Illustration

The skills of illustrator and designer are closely allied, and many designers who are adept at drawing soon find themselves earning more from their illustration work than from straight design. In business terms, though, there are differences between the two fields of activity. Perhaps the most important is geographical: the designer usually works closely with the client, whereas the illustrator may be based several hundred miles from the design studio, and may never meet the person commissioning illustration work. Illustrators must therefore necessarily be good self-promoters. If you plan to sell your illustration, you will need to invest time and money in making people aware of your skills.

Self promotion

To get work, you must let the people who are buying illustration see what you can do. The most economic way to make the initial contact is by mailing examples of your work to potential customers. You can then follow up with a telephone call, and possibly a personal interview with your full folio if the client expresses sufficient interest.

Before putting together a package to mail out, you need to make one fundamental decision: are you sending out expendable samples, or do you want your work returned to you? Each approach has advantages and drawbacks. Printing up non-returnable copies of your illustrations is costly, and limits you to displaying just a few examples, but enables you to leave the art-buyer with a constant reminder of your work. If on the other hand you send transparencies or tear sheets (printed copies taken from the publication in which the illustration appeared) you have to pay for return postage, but your presentation can be more lavish and comprehensive. A solution is to compromise, and print up a card with a single illustration typical of your work, adding your name, phone number and address. You can enclose this with a more comprehensive portfolio of photographs, so that the reminder is retained long after your portfolio is returned.

Making copies of your work

Your aim should always be to send the most lifelike possible facsimiles of your illustration work. Black and white line illustrations reproduce well on a photocopier, but other styles suffer to varying degrees when copied in this way. Colour illustrations can also be copied on office colour copiers, but like the black and white equivalent, these machines sacrifice subtlety. Unless you can afford the expense of making offset prints of your work, the best solution is to take photographs.

Use colour transparency film to do this, because colour prints usually distort the hues of your artwork, and sacrifice highlight and shadow detail. Colour transparencies (chromes) make a more faithful copy. The task of copying is best left to a professional photographer, but if you take the pictures yourself, take great care with lighting, colour balance, exposure, and focusing. Set the camera on a tripod to ensure that the illustration is square on to the camera, and to avoid camera shake. If you need multiple copies of the pictures, shoot many exposures of each piece of work: this is cheaper than having duplicate copies made, and the quality of original pictures is always higher than that of second-generation copies.

Mount transparencies in card or plastic, *not* glass mounts, and write or stamp your name on every one. Put the whole set of pictures in transparent plastic viewing sheets to protect the transparencies, and to make them easy to view.

Your package of work will be better received if you bind it together in some way, so that the contents do not fall in an untidy heap when the envelope is opened. Ideally, laminate tear sheets in plastic to protect them, and use comb binding to keep everything together. Send a *short* covering letter explaining who you are, where you have worked already, and perhaps a brief resumé of your career and education. Always send return postage and packaging if you want to see your work again, then label everything and pack the work very securely to prevent damage in transit.

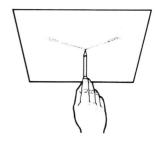

When photographing work, check for even illumination using a pencil – the two shadows should be equally dark. If they are not, move the lights back and forward until the lighting is more even.

The art buyer

Large companies that buy a lot of finished artwork and illustrations normally have a person directly responsible for choosing artists and commissioning work. This may be the art buyer at an advertising agency, or the creative head of a magazine or publishing house. This person's job is to evaluate the style of work required on each project, and to contact an artist who can best undertake the finished artwork.

Art buyers spend much time seeing these artists or their agents, who try to have their particular style of work put on file and therefore available for consideration. An experienced art buyer can usually pick out competent artists simply by looking at their portfolios. Some individuals have a particularly original way of working, or may be highly skilled in an area and the art buyer will try these people out with a small job. This provides an opportunity to time the work of the new face, and compare it with the piece from the same individual's portfolio. Few art buyers will risk putting out a major piece of work to a strange artist who has not been used before.

An important part of the art buyer's job is to cost the work. The price of a job depends on a number of factors: the standing of the artist or illustrator, the size of the work, how soon it is needed, and the style of illustration required. A simple line drawing would obviously be less costly than a large full colour technical illustration.

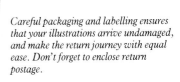

Careful packaging and labelling ensures that your illustrations arrive undamaged, and make the return journey with equal ease. Don't forget to enclose return postage.

Markets for illustration

The different markets for illustration work have different requirements. An obvious example is the collector plate: if you are trying to sell your work for reproduction on a plate, you must produce circular illustrations. The demands of other areas are less obvious to the outsider, but they are equally well defined. Make yourself aware of current trends by contacting the creative heads within the industry you are aiming to sell to, or by buying an industry guide such as Artist's Markets. These are the major buyers and key areas of interest:

Advertising Public relations firms and advertising agencies are more likely than other types of clients to seek a personal interview, and to commission local artists who can deliver work quickly. They use all kinds of illustrative work, in every conceivable shape, medium and style.

Collectibles, fashion and other products This is a highly changeable market, so monitor business trends and current products to see what sells well. Clothing in particular changes seasonally, so there is a constant demand for new printed motifs and patterns, and for fashion illustrations. Many companies will look for evidence that you have experience in designing for their section of the industry.

Design studios Here, as in advertising, local contacts are valued, so scan the yellow pages for names of design studios. Whether or not initial contact leads immediately to work, it is worth following up with a letter or telephone call twice a year or so, to remind the studio that you are still in circulation and actively seeking commissions.

Greeting cards and posters Sales of illustration to greetings card companies can generate a steady flow of royalties, rather than once only payments. However, to succeed in this competitive market, you must carefully match your work to the existing products of company that you are aiming to sell to. This isn't difficult – write for a catalogue of their cards and other paper products, or just look at them on display in a shop. Remember what makes people buy cards – weddings, birthdays, Christmas – and tailor your work to reflect the occasions and emotions. Card companies are happy to deal with artists by post, as work is commissioned well ahead of the deadline.

Most posters sold fall into the "unlimited edition" bracket, and as with greetings card ranges, catalogues are updated regularly. Posters are often bought to match the colour scheme in a newly decorated home, so when selling to poster companies it pays to read interior decor magazines which detail changing fashion trends.

Interior design and architecture Designers of buildings use illustrators primarily to create artist's impressions of finished jobs, so your portfolio should contain work of this nature. You should also have the ability to create realistic perspective drawings from architects' blueprints. Local contacts usually prove most fruitful, because some on-site visiting may be needed.

Book and magazine publishers The needs of this vast category of companies vary widely – the publishing industry is perhaps the largest consumer of illustration skills. Before sending off material, study the output of the publisher in a book shop, library, or on magazine racks. Some of the most unlikely publications use large amounts of illustration: computer publications, for example, need imaginative illustration to enliven otherwise visually uninteresting pages.

Markets for illustration are vast and varied, so don't start with any preconceptions as to who will buy your work. These four examples appeared in: an advertising brochure (left); on greeting cards (below left); in a newspaper (below) and a book (right).

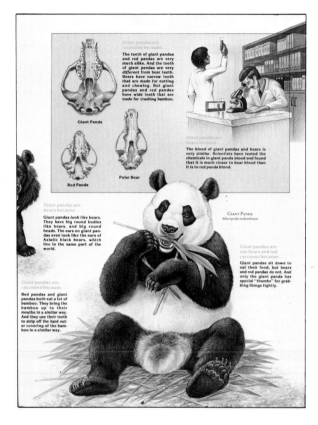

Newspapers Because of the restrictions imposed by newsprint reproduction, newspapers illustrations need to be bold and graphic. Newspapers normally use illustrations only for features and humour – explanatory news diagrams are always drawn in-house because of the pressing deadlines. Cartoons are bought unsolicited, rather than commissioned, and are one speciality where you may be asked to send original drawings rather than copies. This is routine because newspapers usually want first use of the drawing, and a policy of "originals only" enforces this.

The world of illustration is highly specialised. In order to succeed in any of these markets, you need to provide art directors and commissioning designers with a label that they can easily apply to your work. If you show potential clients a wide variety of different subjects, you will soon be forgotten. But take along several pictures on the same theme, and you will be remembered as ". . . that illustrator with the great outer-space scenes" – or whatever your favourite subject happens to be.

Print processes

The end result of virtually all graphic design jobs is a printed image, and the appearance of this printed image is the ultimate yardstick of your ability. Beautiful slick presentations may impress a client before the work is on the press, but if the finished job looks a mess, the appearance of the visuals, roughs, and even the proofs is not relevant.

There are three major print processes in use, and a medley of others can be considered for specific kinds of work. Each print process has its own unique characteristics and capabilities and the method of printing chosen for each job is of great importance. For example a piece of work that looks splendid when printed by offset lithography may look terrible when screen-printed. The section that follows therefore explains each process briefly and indicates how you can pick the process best fitted to the job in hand. However, printing technology is a complex subject, and further reading is advisable: there are many excellent books which explain the processes in greater detail.

Print problems that seem insoluble are rarely so: it is possible, though not always economic, to print onto almost any surface. However, before starting out on a design programme with perhaps an unusual shape or material, do think carefully about whether the method of reproduction chosen is appropriate, and consult the printer before making a commitment to a particular printing technique.

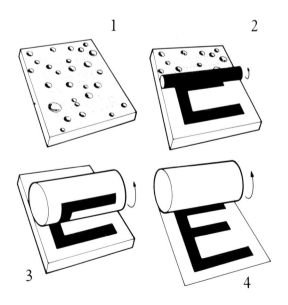

Lithography

Unlike the older letterpress process, lithography does not depend on a raised printing surface; litho plates are effectively flat. Ink is transferred from the rollers onto the printing surface by the principle of oil and water repelling each other (1): the areas of the litho plate that are to print are made greasy, and the ink sticks to them. Other areas of the plate are kept damp, and therefore repel the ink (2). When pressed into contact with the paper, an image of the greasy areas is transferred.

In the commercial litho process, the paper does not come directly into contact with the printing surface. Instead the ink is transferred from the plate onto a rubber blanket (3), which then presses against the paper (4). This system is known as offset lithography, or just offset, or sometimes simply litho.

Offset lithography is the most widely used print process for run-of-the-mill work such as illustrated books, leaflets, brochures and stationery. By far the majority of design work produced by the average studio will be printed by this means. Illustrations reproduce well, and low costs for all but the longest print runs make this a popular and growing print medium. Compared to letterpress, more of the preparatory work is done by the designer, and less by the printer: the finished mechanical artwork represents exactly what will print, with the exception of illustrations which are generally supplied separately.

From the artwork, the printer makes a negative or positive copy, on film the same size as the printed work. Black and white photographs and illustrations are at this stage enlarged or reduced to fit the spaces assigned to them, and made into halftones on film. The printer then strips-in (positions and fixes) the illustrations on the main piece of film, and lays this in contact with the light-sensitive metal plate. Exposure and processing creates the necessary ink-repelling qualities in the areas that are not to print. For colour printing, the procedure is more complicated, as explained later in the chapter.

Short-run litho printing or offset duplicating uses a virtually identical printing process, but the printing plate is made directly from the artwork, without the use of intermediate film. This process is adequate for cheap and simple printing jobs such as letterheads involving no illustrations or areas of tone. However, quality is not good enough for many design jobs.

On very long print runs, offset litho presses print on a continuous roll of paper – a 'web'. This is a cheaper method of feeding paper through the machine, but quality is not as good as sheet-fed printing.

Modern offset litho printing plants are highly automated and functional. In the foreground of this picture is an electronic console on which the operator controls the flow of ink. By comparing the proofs with the sheets coming off the press, the print technician can correct colour at the touch of a button.

Before plates are made, individual pieces of film are stripped together in the correct position using large light-tables in the planning room.

Letterpress

This is the oldest process, and was first used in the middle of the 15th century. As shown below, ink is picked up from the rollers only where the printing surface is raised. Areas of the sheet that are to appear as unprinted white paper are lower, and therefore do not get coated in ink. After inking, the paper is pressed into contact with the printing surface, and this transfers the ink onto the paper (bottom).

Text for letterpress printing consists of raised letters on a lower body. To print illustrations, a line or halftone negative is made and pressed into contact with a light-sensitive zinc or copper plate. After exposure to light, acid etching lowers the metal surface in areas which were not struck by light. Other sections of the plate remain raised, and therefore print.

From the design point of view, letterpress printing is rather inflexible. You can only specify where text

and illustrations are to be positioned on the printed page, and you therefore handle the print medium at arm's length. The actual letters that go to make up the text are solid metal, and must be locked into the correct position by the printer. This naturally limits the typographic possibilities.

Letterpress printing is used mainly for daily newspapers, mass-produced paperback books, and short-run printing such as invitations. All are examples of media that either have fixed layout requirements, or that do not demand a great deal of visual sophistication. For other types of printing, letterpress is not the ideal choice from the design point of view, and may not be economic, either. An additional consideration is that the quality of halftones and colour illustrations is not as good as those printed by the offset litho or gravure processes which are gradually replacing letterpress printing.

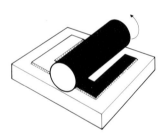

Gravure

Gravure plates are rather like letterpress plates in reverse: the areas that will print are depressed, rather than raised. The tiny depressions act as wells, retaining ink, and releasing it on contact with the paper. The depth of each well, its area, or sometimes both factors determines how much ink passes from plate to paper. Ink from the roller initially covers the whole plate (1); a "doctor blade" then removes ink from the raised parts of the plate (2) that correspond to areas of unprinted white paper (3).

Gravure is used mainly for printing long runs, such as colour magazines. It gives excellent results, particularly for illustrations, and gravure presses run at very high speeds. Because of high costs, gravure is used for short runs only if quality is of paramount importance, such as when printing fine art illustrations like the watercolour illustration shown here.

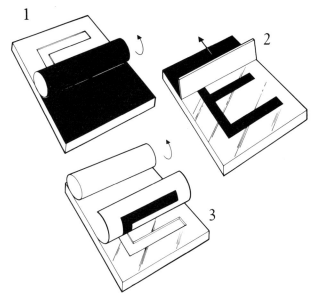

Printing in colour

overlay to print 20Y 20C

Rank green ref PMS 341

Rank Theatre

CUTIVE BRI

Everybody learns the basic principles of colour mixing in school: mixing yellow and blue paints produces green; yellow and red together make orange. In fact, the wide range of colours that is to be found in a paint box far exceeds the number needed to create pictures in lifelike hues. For printing in colour, you theoretically need only three different coloured inks: yellow, cyan, and magenta. Though it is possible to make perfectly acceptable full-colour pictures with just these three printing inks, a fourth, black, is always added to give greater detail and sharpness to the final result, and to provide richer, deeper shadows. Together, the four colours are known as the process colours, or the four-colour set.

Most print processes can represent only two shades – plain paper, or paper printed with ink. However, if the four process colours were printed at full strength the colours would be crude and brilliant, rather like a TV set with the colour turned full up. To get any sort of subtlety in the image, it is necessary to print the four inks in a range of different saturations, so that the paper carries a scale of tints running from very pale, right through to a richly-saturated colour. This is done in just the same way as when printing in black and white, by using halftones.

In practice, the manner in which this is accomplished is highly complex and technical, as indicated overleaf. The principles, though, are simple: the first stage is to determine which areas of the original colour

illustration are to print in which of the four process colours. This is done by rephotographing the original through three coloured filters, or electronically, using a scanner. Yellow areas of the original, for example, must print only with yellow ink; red areas must be printed with yellow and magenta inks; blue with cyan and magenta. This stage of the process is called origination, or colour separation, because the yellow, cyan and magenta components of the image are separated from each other.

The next step is to make half-tone copies of the photographic separation negatives. This is done in more or less the same way as for black and white printing, but with one important difference: the halftone screen is rotated to a slightly different angle for each colour so that the four dot patterns eventually print in different places on the paper, rather than lying one on top of the other. Failure to orient the screens correctly produces screen clash, where the various coloured dots overlap, interfering with proper colour blending, and producing a pattern of petal-like shapes.

The final product of the origination process is four sheets of film, each the same size as the printed image, and each carrying a record of one of the three colours, or of the black. The four pieces of film are handed to the printer, who makes colour proofs from them for checking and correction, as explained on pages 86-7. The individual images are then stripped into the large sheets of film from which plates will be made.

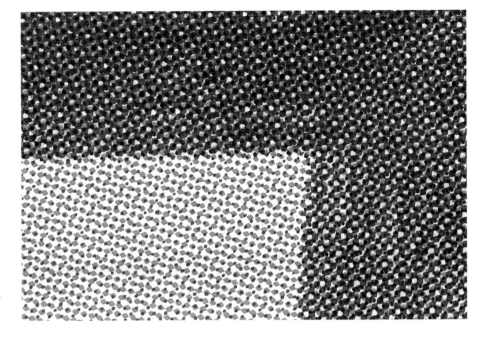

The halftone dots on a colour image are packed together at different densities for different printing applications. Posters (right) are viewed from a distance, so the dot pattern can be quite coarse (this illustration is 25 percent larger than life-size). Magazine illustrations printed on good paper have very much more tightly packed dots.

You can specify colour to the printer in two ways. One is to specify a percentage tint, using the four-colour set (far left). The other is to ask for a colour match (near left).

Origination methods

Colour originals can be separated into their yellow, cyan, magenta and black components either photographically – using a process camera – or electronically, by scanning the image and converting it into digital form. Both methods are widely used, but for origination from colour transparencies, scanning is rapidly replacing camera origination.

Camera origination The traditional method of making colour separations is to use a process camera – essentially an enlarged PMT camera. The original is fixed to the baseboard, and illuminated with powerful lights. Four black and white copies are then made of the original, each with a different coloured filter in front of the lens, so that the resulting separations record the images that will print in each of the four process colours. These separations are screened to make the halftone film that is supplied to the printer.

The colour scanner At the heart of the scanner lies a spinning drum, to which the colour original is fixed as shown overleaf. As the drum rotates, a beam of light is focused on the transparency or artwork, and light-sensitive elements then detect how much light of each of the three process colours is transmitted or reflected by successive points on the original. The scanning process begins at one end of the drum, and moves gradually along to the other, so that the originals taped to the drum are scanned in the manner of the lines on a TV screen – but with much greater precision. The

signals from the light-sensitive cells pass to a computer, which processes them into digital form. These digitized signals are now used to power four light sources so that the brightness of each corresponds to the amount of yellow, cyan, magenta and black ink that must be applied to the paper to build up the required image. The beams of light are focused on a piece of film taped to a second spinning drum which is synchronized with the first. As scanning continues, the four colour separations are thus built up on the sheet of film. Rapid processing of the film completes the procedure.

The computer at the heart of the scanner is what gives this system its flexibility. The digitized signals can be processed in a wide variety of ways to modify the original image.

Size Computer processing can enlarge or reduce the original, or even stretch it either vertically or horizontally. However, for each scanning process only one scale of enlargement is possible, so if several transparencies are taped to the drum, they are all enlarged to the same degree. For consistent results, they must all be of similar density, too.

Masking The dyes used in photography do not make perfect copies of the colours in the original scene; inadequacies in printing pigments add a further distortion. Electronic 'masking' can take account of these errors, and provide a much more faithful printed image.

Adding detail Remarkably, the scanner can actually improve on the image supplied for origination! More shadow detail may appear in the final printed image than was clearly visible on the original colour transparency, and it is even possible to make pictures appear sharper.

Colour correction A certain amount of colour correction and improvement can be dialled in at the scanning stage, but the results are often disappointing. By far the best way to get good colour is to supply good originals.

Picking originals for reproduction

Colour originals are divided into two groups. Reflection copy, such as watercolour illustration, is viewed by reflected light. Such originals are sometimes referred to as flat copy. Transmission originals, such as photographic transparencies (chromes or colour slides) are viewed by backlighting. Small examples of both types of original can be either scanned or camera separated, though extra-large or stiffened reflection originals will not fit into a scanner.

Colour transparencies should be absolutely sharp, particularly if they are on 35mm film, or if a small portion of a bigger transparency is being enlarged. Check for sharpness with a good magnifier, and try to minimize the degree of enlargement required by using large and medium format transparencies in preference to 35mm. Do not use over or underexposed images, but where there is no correctly exposed picture, it is best to use one that is slightly too dark, rather than a transparency that is too light.

Originals to be scanned are wrapped around a drum, shown stationary here. The keyboard in the foreground is used to set the scale of reproduction, and colour correction.

Broadly the same criteria apply for flat artwork – it should be neither too dark nor too light, and there should be ample detail. If the artwork is to be scanned, it must be on a flexible support which will conform to the shape of the scanner drum. Many illustrators prefer to work on rigid board, and you can accommodate this preference by specifying that artwork should be supplied on stripping board, which has a resilient working surface that can be stripped away from the heavy board backing.

Since the artwork must be bent for scanned origination, heavy impasto techniques are not acceptable because the paint surface will crack. When there is no choice, it is best to have the illustration copied photographically, and send this for scanning.

Flat colour (right) is a simple way to brighten up a low-budget assignment. This image is printed in black and process cyan, but a printer could mix virtually any colour to match your specification.

Printing solids

There is another way to print coloured images, and this is to mix ink which exactly matches the required hue. Such an approach is used when an absolutely precise colour match is required, and when the expense of printing in four colours is not justified – as on a simple two-colour poster.

To specify where a solid colour will print, the designer would commonly make an overlay in exact register with the basic finished mechanical artwork, and attach a colour patch to indicate the required colour of printing. If the main artwork is to be printed using the regular four-colour set, then this overlay will print as a fifth colour. This naturally increases print costs, so when a precise colour match is not essential, it makes sense to ask the printer to match the required colour from the four-colour set.

Buying print

The cost of printing a piece of design work usually far exceeds all other costs involved in the job, so mistakes made at this stage are especially damaging and expensive. In most large organizations, print buying is delegated to one person, whose job it is to place print and colour origination orders. This person may also secure paper supplies for the job, since the expense of paper makes up a large proportion of print costs.

As an individual designer, it is therefore likely that you will be expected to buy print on only relatively small jobs, and that you will be able to call on the expertise of others when placing large print orders. Nevertheless, you should know something about the expenses involved in printing, so that you can avoid some of the design traps that put print costs up.

Anticipating and avoiding problems

Many of the factors that increase the cost of typesetting have a similar effect on printing: for example, you are likely to get a better price from an out-of-town printer than from one round the corner. Simplicity affects print price, too. The simpler it is for a printer to execute a piece of work, the less that job is likely to cost you. Listed below are some of the factors that increase print costs, but these are really only indicators for the unwary. If you were to consider this a list of unbreakable rules, you would find your design work unduly restricted. So these guidelines should serve to make you aware that certain techniques and effects will push up the price of the print job. In some instances, there are two ways of achieving the same effect: this checklist helps you choose the cheaper option.

Extra work for the printer This is a catch-all: many of the points that follow fall into the same category. Always remember that work which the printer does is going to cost money, so if the result is the same, it is cheaper to do the work yourself. For example, on line artwork you can create areas of tone yourself using sheets of self-adhesive half-tone dots. The alternative – to put on the artwork overlays which the printer must shoot separately to create tone simply adds to the cost of the job.

Messy boards Finished mechanical artwork that is covered in dust specks creates negatives covered in pin-holes. The printer then has to touch out each hole with a paintbrush – a time-consuming and costly activity. Keep artwork as clean as possible, and after you finish pasting up, remove all traces of stray adhesive with lighter fluid, so that there is nothing for dirt to stick to. Knife cuts and stripped-in lines create shadows that show up as clear lines on the negative. These too must be painted out by hand, so try to keep artwork elements as large as possible.

Poor planning Plan your work in cooperation with the printer. The direction in which the sheets pass through the machine affect the printer's ability to correct colour on press, and coloured tints and boxes in particular sometimes create problems. If you discuss your plans well in advance, the printer may suggest simple changes that could save a great deal of money, and improve the appearance of the printed work.

Bleed and grip If you plan to bleed pictures off the edge of the page, consult your printer. The printing press needs a strip of blank paper for gripping along the edge of the sheet, and pictures must not bleed into this margin.

Unusual shapes and sizes Unusually-shaped brochures and books create impact, but unless you plan carefully you could waste a lot of paper. Find out the maximum paper size that the press can accommodate, and plan your design work to make best use of the whole sheet. Always remember that trimmed paper is wasted money.

Extra colours Every extra colour adds to the cost of a printed job, so here again, planning pays off. If you are printing a brochure, you can often save money by putting colour illustrations on alternate spreads or pages. Depending on the imposition – the arrangement of pages on the press – this may enable the printer to run 4-colour printing on one side of the sheet, and black on the other side. Other details of imposition are explained on pages 84-5. If you are

printing in full colour throughout try to get all tints and tones from the four-colour set (see page 74). If you specify a colour which cannot be matched from the 4-colour set, you will have to print a fifth colour at extra expense. This cost is usually justified only when a sample of a company house colour must be matched precisely by the printer.

Reversed-out and outline text Reversing text out of a solid or a picture always involves extra work, and therefore higher costs. Outline letters filled with colour similarly cost extra.

Difficult registration Thin rules in colour, narrow keylines around pictures and vital elements near the sheet edge create difficulties on press or during print finishing. Remember that paper stretches as it passes through the printing press, so that even if colours are exactly superimposed at one side of a large sheet, they may be misregistered at the other. You can easily avoid problems by keeping keylines round colour pictures broader than 1/25in (1mm), and coloured rules thicker still. Trimming is never as accurate as printing, so leave a margin of error at the edges of your design – don't run important credit lines up the exact edge of the page, or they could disappear when sheets are trimmed.

Cut-outs Cutting out the subject of a photograph from its background involves mechanical work by the printer. If you want to isolate the subject, tell the photographer this so that a pure white background can be created using studio lighting.

Unsuitable originals If you send the printer less than perfect original photographs to work from, you can expect only imperfect results. Corrections can be made to the colour and density of transparencies, but the results are better and cheaper if you start with a good original.

Large areas of tints Unbroken areas of tints create inking problems for the printer. Keep tinted areas small and pale if possible.

Metallic inks Use metallic inks with discretion. They look good on certain types of paper, and may need varnishing to prevent scuffing – this counts as an extra colour.

Corrections Try to make all corrections on finished mechanical artwork. The longer you leave the corrections, the more they cost.

Proofing methods Colour proofs with each image in position on the page are expensive. You can save money by requesting 'scatter' proofs: the printer proofs as many images as possible on a single sheet, irrespective of where they appear in the book or pamphlet.

Hand operations All print finishing operations that must be carried out by hand are very costly. If any hand assembly is involved, find out whether a small change to your design would allow a machine to take over the task.

Die cutting Die-cutting and embossing are costly operations: reserve them for long print-runs and prestigious, high-budget projects.

Die cutting (left) is essential for some products, but the cost of making the die is high. When the budget is tight, look for a design solution that avoids this operation.

Scatter proofs (right) are invariably cheaper than proofs on which each image appears in the correct position.

Print finishing

Print finishing turns untrimmed, printed sheets of paper into the final article as you designed it. At the simplest level, this means trimming off unwanted edges from the sheet, and cutting to size. More often, though, other manufacturing operations are needed, including folding, collating, and binding.

On all but the smallest jobs, several pages will be printed together on each sheet of paper. The printer positions the negatives made from your finished mechanical artwork in such a way that after folding, each page is in the correct position relative to the other pages. By trimming two or three of the edges, it is then possible to open out the brochure or pamphlet. The arrangement of pages on the press is known as the imposition, and is discussed later in the book.

There is a restriction on the size of publication that can be produced from a single sheet of paper. Usually, the limit is 16 pages at a time, but on larger presses it may be 20 or 24. If you require more pages, several sheets are printed, folded, and bound in order. Each folded and trimmed sheet is then called a signature.

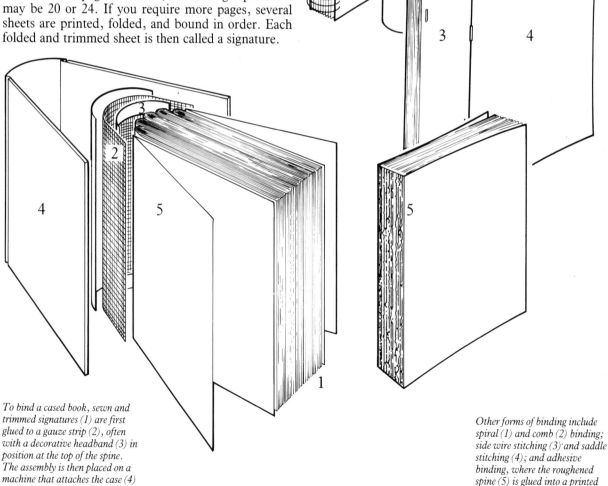

To bind a cased book, sewn and trimmed signatures (1) are first glued to a gauze strip (2), often with a decorative headband (3) in position at the top of the spine. The assembly is then placed on a machine that attaches the case (4) and end-papers (5).

Other forms of binding include spiral (1) and comb (2) binding; side wire stitching (3) and saddle stitching (4); and adhesive binding, where the roughened spine (5) is glued into a printed cover.

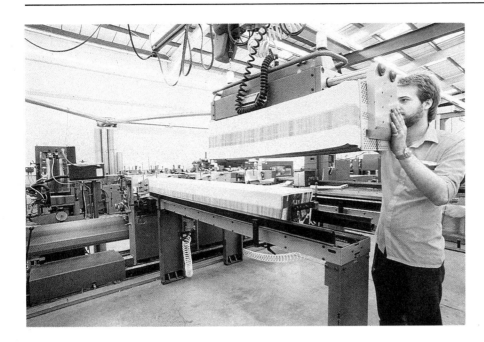

Binding methods

Pamphlets, brochures and other publications longer than 4 pages (6 or 8 with gatefolds) must somehow be held together. The simplest form of binding for short pamphlets is stapling, or in printer's jargon, wire stitching, or wire binding. Pamphlets up to ⅛ in (3mm) thick bound in this way open flat if the staple passes through the spine and is crimped in the centre pages (saddle stitching). However, for publications thicker than ⅛ in, the staples run from the front cover and are crimped at the back, so the pamphlet will not open flat; this is called side wire stitching.

Wire stitching is not restricted to single signatures. Indeed, if you are printing more than one signature, you can add variety to your brochure by printing sections on two different papers, and stitching them into a single cover. This approach is popular for company reports where annual financial results are printed on cheap coloured paper stock, and combined with glossy coated sheets carrying colour photographs of company activities.

Adhesive binding

Pamphlets, magazines and books thicker than about ¼ inch (6mm) can be held together at the spine with adhesives – a method sometimes called 'perfect' or threadless binding. The folded edge of each page is trimmed off and the surface roughened before applying glue to hold the pages together. Bound in this way, though, the publication does not open flat, and a wider margin is required at the gutter. Adhesive bound books do not stand up well to wear, so the technique is used largely for paperbacks and magazines. A slightly more durable method of adhesive binding is to sew the sections together, and glue them into a separate cover without cutting at the spine.

Cased books

Hardback books are case or edition bound. Here, each individual signature of the book is sewn together and the signatures are gathered (put in order). The gathered sections are glued to a piece of fabric, and a ready-prepared cover is fixed to the free edges of the fabric strip. This very brief description conceals a wealth of variations on what is now a highly mechanized form of an ancient craft. For example, the sections may be sewn to each other for extra strength; the book may be finished with a fabric covering; or the spine and covers may be blocked (embossed).

Mechanical binding

Books that need to lie open on a desk or work surface are frequently bound mechanically. The signatures are trimmed on all four sides, and punched or drilled at the spine. The pages are held together with a metal or plastic spiral or comb. Mechanical binding is a hand operation, so books bound in this way are more costly to produce than case-bound books.

Other print processes

Letterpress, litho, and gravure printing make up the enormous majority of all printing work. However, there are a number of other processes which, though marginal, are of importance in certain specialized areas of design.

Screen printing

This is a stencil-based printing process. A stencil of the image to be printed is stuck to a screen of stretched fabric, and a squeegee forces ink through the open mesh of the screen and onto the surface being printed. This need not be paper – it could equally be glass, wood, metal, plastic, fabric or practically any other smooth surface.

Screen printing applies a thick layer of ink which covers very well, so it is suited to printing light colours onto dark stock. Set-up costs are very low, so short runs are a practical possibility, and for this reason screen printing is often used for exhibition stands and point-of-purchase displays. However, the texture of the screen itself imposes some restrictions, and reproduction of halftones in particular is not good.

To produce screen prints, only very simple equipment is necessary – anyone can start a print workshop in their basement, literally overnight. At the other end of the scale, commercial screen printing machinery operates at high speeds, and prints on to virtually anything – even bottles.

Stencils for commercial screen printing are made photographically, and the design stages leading to stencil making are virtually identical to those required for litho. A film positive made from the finished mechanical artwork is placed in contact with light-sensitive film and exposed; areas struck by light harden and are stripped away before the stencil is stuck to the screen.

Flexography This is an ideal method for printing flexible packaging in hard-surfaced materials such as cellophane, foils, and plastic. The printing plates are made of low-cost rubber, and changes in the size of items to be printed or in the copy required can be handled easily by insertions on the original rubber plate. The inks used are highly pigmented and opaque, so that their brilliant colours make this the most suitable process for printing gift wrapping paper. The main problem is that the artwork has to be produced by a qualified person who is familiar with the process, because the rubber plates tend to distort and fill-in.

Thermography Mostly used on business stationery, thermography gives a raised appearance to the image printed on the paper. Special slow-drying inks are used, and after printing (by letterpress or litho), the paper is dusted with a resinous powder. A vacuum sucks excess powder off the sheets which are then briefly heated to expand and fuse the resin. The result closely resembles embossing, but costs are far lower. However, unless the work is done with great care, the type begins to spread, giving an uneven edge.

Copperplate engraving This process is rightly regarded as archaic, but is still in use for invitations and announcements. The plate itself has to be hand engraved by a skilled engraver, runs are very short, and costs high.

Screenprinting applies a heavy layer of colour, so it is an ideal medium for printing metallics and fluorescent inks, which sometimes look dull when printed in other ways.

Short run printing

Conventional print media have high set-up costs, making the printing of short runs relatively expensive, particularly in colour. If you need to print small numbers of a brochure or hand-out, it makes sense to look at alternatives to mainstream processes.

The most frequently overlooked alternative is the humble office photocopier. For black and white printing, some of the larger office copiers can now closely rival offset for quality. However, many copiers cannot reproduce solids well, so avoid large black areas: use narrow rules and light display faces in your designs. Bold faces tend to appear with a strong black outline, fading away to grey in the middle of the letter. Modern, well-maintained copiers do not suffer from this problem, and can reproduce even heavy rules and extrabold type as rich blacks.

Electrostatic copiers turn continuous-tone photographs to line, but cope well with halftones, so if your artwork includes illustrations, get these screened before pasting into position. Keep artwork elements large, with few changes in level: the moving light-source on the photocopier reveals scalpel cuts and strip-ins very clearly. If shadows do show up when copying, try turning the artwork and paper feed through 90°, so that the cuts and changes in level run parallel with the direction of movement of the light-source. This often eliminates shadows.

Colour photocopiers are not a replacement for offset colour printing, but they can be used to make simple colour facsimiles on paper or acetate, and can generate colours from black and white line artwork. Most copiers of this type are optimized for just the additive and subtractive primaries – red, green, blue, and yellow, cyan, magenta. These six colours are copied cleanly and quite faithfully, but other hues, particularly pastels and earth colours, are degraded by the copying process.

For best results with a colour copier, restrict your artwork to the six primary colours in varying degrees of saturation. Keep important artwork elements away from the edges of the sheet, as some machines cannot copy right up to the paper margins.

Photography

For high-quality full-colour printing in runs of about 50 to 250, photographic prints are frequently the most practical and economic option. Artwork preparation is little different to regular printing: you make up finished mechanical artwork, and indicate positions of pictures in the usual way. A photo-lab that specializes in this kind of work then makes a photocomposite of your pictures and artwork, to create a single negative which is printed on an enlarger to the required size. Text and other artwork elements can appear in any colour, but reversed-out body text has a tendency to fill in.

Photography also provides a useful method of producing multiple copies of dummy packages and presentations. Your full-colour artwork is shot using a specially-adapted copy camera, to make a direct positive print. Size changes are quick and easy, and the process is cheaper than most of the other methods outlined on pages 26-27.

This poster was printed in a run of under 100, using the photographic processes described above.

Imposition

A printer preparing work to go on press arranges your finished mechanical artwork very carefully. Pages of a booklet, for example, are not printed individually, but grouped together to save press time, and make optimum use of materials. The chosen arrangement of pages on the press is called the imposition.

At first glance, there may seem to be countless different ways of arranging pages on the plate, but in reality, the number is limited by the fact that when the printed sheet is folded, the pages must appear in the correct order. To understand how this works, take a sheet of paper, and fold it in two. Then fold it again. What you now hold in your hand is an eight page booklet – or it would be, if you slit along one of the folded edges so that pages could open flat. With the folded edges at the top and left, number the pages from 1 to 8 at the free corner, and unfold the sheet.

You can now immediately see one way in which the printer could arrange the pages on a press that is big enough to print four pages of the booklet simultaneously. Two plates would be used, one printing pages 2, 7, 6 and 3, and the other, 1, 8, 4, and 5. One

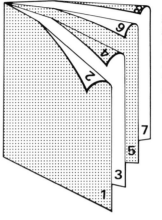

To print an eight page self-cover pamphlet using a single plate, the pages would be arranged on press as shown below. Folding, wire stitching and cutting along the short edge yields the pamphlet with pages in correct order, as at left.

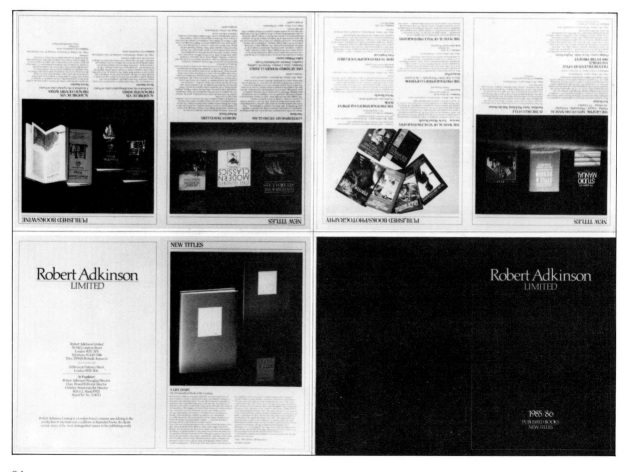

side of the sheet is printed, then the plate on the press is changed, and the other side is printed. This is called sheetwise imposition, because all the pages that are to print on one side of the sheet are imposed on the same printing plate.

If the printer has a press that is big enough to accommodate eight pages at once, there is another option. The plate now carries all eight pages, arranged as shown at left. After running the sheets through the press once, the printer turns them over, and runs them through the press again. So now the work can be cut in two before folding and trimming, to yield two booklets per sheet. The number of impressions (printings) is halved, as is press set-up time, and the number of plates. For obvious reasons, this imposition scheme is called work-and-turn.

Each of these two schemes has drawbacks and benefits. Sheetwise imposition allows you to limit costs by printing four colours on one side of the sheet, and one or two colours on the reverse. On the other hand, if you are printing four colours with work-and-turn imposition, colour is available on every page, even if you do not take advantage of it.

Even if you are planning to print in just two colours, sheetwise imposition frequently gives you more options. You could print black with blue on one side of the sheet, and black with red on the other. Instead of black and red on every page, your brochure now has red and blue available on alternate spreads for very little extra cost.

Imposition does not just affect availability of colour, it also affects your ability to correct and control colour. If a picture goes across the gutter and the two sides print from separate plates it can be difficult to match colours across the fold. Printing the job so that both pages are on the same plate would make colour matching easier.

The direction in which the pages move through the press is important, too. The printer can adjust the flow of ink across the width of the press in order to make last-minute corrections to colour. However, correcting the colour of a photograph by reducing the flow of ink at one side of the press inevitably changes the colour of all the pages "downstream" and "upstream" from the illustration being corrected. For similar reasons, a heading printed in colour "upstream" of a colour illustration removes ink from the roller, so that a shadow of the heading appears on the illustration.

For simplicity, these examples use a sheet which carries just 4 pages on each side. However, large presses may print 16 or more pages at once, and the imposition becomes correspondingly more complex.

Imposition is easier to understand if you actually fold and trim pieces of paper. Try photocopying and cutting out these three examples, then fold each along the dotted line and paste the unprinted sides back to back to simulate printing on both sides of the sheet. If you then fold along the solid lines and trim, you'll create 6, 12, and 16 page brochures.

Evaluating proofs

Before proceeding with any piece of work, a printer supplies proofs which indicate how the final job will look. It very often happens that a design or a piece of artwork which you undertook with great care returns in proof form with a number of problems and errors, and these must be picked up and corrected immediately. So before giving the go-ahead for the printing of any item, always study the proof carefully. The larger and more complex the job is, the more care you must take in checking the proofs. Checking of proofs is always carried out in cooperation with the client. Never authorize a printer to proceed without the client's signature on the proof itself.

If you have produced and checked finished mechanical artwork, there should be no problems about the relative positions of type and pictures on the page. However, if the printer has pasted up the mechanicals, this is the first thing to check. Always read the copy again, as type often moves out of alignment and small corrections can easily fall off the boards.

Text and colour proofs are usually separate. Put both sheets in register on a light-box, check that the pictures are positioned correctly, and that they have the correct captions. When there is a specific house colour, check this against a colour patch supplied by the client.

Very often the work is not proofed on the paper chosen for the final run, so check this carefully, and look for signs of show-through. If there is evidence of this, point it out to the priner. Proofs usually arrive from the printer as flat sheets and if folding of any sort is part of the job specification, as it is for a package design, then cut and fold the proofs to size. Check on any problems such as the graphics being too near the edge of the paper, or graphic material becoming distorted over the folds.

A printed sheet of paper can never be an exact replica of a colour transparency, but in checking colour proofs, your job is to ensure that the differences are minimized. At proof stage, some colour correction is possible, but if there is real cause for concern ask for a revised proof.

Some proofs arrive as progressives. These are prepared by the platemaker, and show each colour printed separately and then in combination. However, it is the combination proofs that give the best guide to how the final colour set will look. Along the edge of most colour proofs there is a colour bar; this is a reference for the printer, showing the four process colours and allowing measurement of colour fidelity.

When checking colour, always compare the printed image with the original, ideally with controlled lighting conditions such as a daylight-balanced light box. Check also that every picture is the right way round (right-reading). This may not be obvious with subjects like landscapes and portraits, but will soon be spotted by anybody who knows the area or the person depicted. The cause may be a mistake by the printer, or perhaps the transparency was incorrectly mounted. If the problem arises, check with the client whether the subject needs to be reoriginated. In instances where the fault is totally unacceptable, such as letters in reverse, simply mark up the proof accordingly.

Look for bad reproduction, over-inking or a lack of sharpness, and where there are large areas of even tone, such as a blue sky or a colour printed as a solid, look for an uneven mottled effect. If this is bad at the proof stage, it is likely to get worse on the actual print run, and any sign of this bad inking must be dealt with early on. Screen clash on the colour proof may be an error in origination, but the problem also occurs when making half tones from originals which were themselves screened.

If there are proof problems, the first stage is to discuss corrective measures with the printer. Record the corrections requested on a set of proofs, and supply these to the printer, but keep a duplicate set in case there is a dispute about failure to carry out corrections when the work is on press.

Other types of proof
Not all proofs are made by actually inking up the plates and taking pulls. There is a growing tendency for printers to supply dry proofs, such as Du Pont's Cromalin. This is a photographic proof from the film, not from the plate, and is made up of a series of coloured tones, each applied to a sheet of clear film. When the sheets are accurately superimposed, a full colour image is built up. Cromalins cannot be folded, and they do not have the true feel of ink on paper. They are expensive, too, and a printer will normally supply just one or two for approval. By contrast, it is not unusual to receive six or ten copies of a conventional colour proof.

Ozalids, blueprints and bluelines These are final proofs showing type and illustrations stripped together in their correct positions, but reproduced in just one colour: usually blue or brown on white. This is the final opportunity for checking the job, and changes should be avoided, as they are extremely expensive.

Proof sheets are rarely backed-up (printed both sides) so show-through is not usually apparent. Check for it by placing behind the proof a piece of text printed in bold type. It the proofs are printed on the paper which will be used for the run, the type should not be visible.

Bad registration is the easiest proof error to spot: look for coloured fringes around pronounced changes in tone, and tell-tale coloured strips down the edges of the pictures.

PART 2 – GRAPHICS IN ACTION

The advertising campaign

The word "advertising" covers a whole spectrum of activity, ranging from a hand-lettered card on a bulletin board announcing 'kittens for sale' through to a national television and press campaign costing millions. Graphic design is an integral part of *all* advertising – even a well-lettered card sells kittens quicker – and the advertising industry is possibly the biggest employer of designers.

In all but the most limited forms of advertising, the client makes some decision about how and where to promote the product, and this is the essence of an advertising campaign. Even a local charity organizes an advertising campaign when it announces a fund-raising gala by placing a single advertisement in a local newspaper, and delivering handbills to local homes.

The way a campaign is planned depends on many factors, including the budget available, and the catchment area in which the target customers live. However, there are some general marketing pointers which apply to every campaign and every product, and it is easiest to understand these pointers by considering a particular example. Let us suppose that you have been asked to prepare a campaign to boost the sales of a step ladder called "Step-Hi". How do you go about it?

Get to know the product The ladders are made of metal sections, and though they superficially resemble other makes of ladder, Step-Hi ladders are manufactured to a higher standard. They are easier to erect and position than cheaper competitors, more versatile in use, longer yet much lighter, and have proved to be safer and less susceptible to accidental damage. Sales have been growing steadily over the past three years, but the product is more expensive than the competition. The problem is therefore one of convincing the market that the benefits of a Step-Hi ladder outweigh the price disadvantage.

Identify the market Market research shows that Step-Hi ladders are mostly sold to people who own their homes. The extra length enables users to reach the upper parts of the house, but makes the ladder difficult to store easily, so a garage or shed is usually necessary. Since the ladder combines stability with light weight, it appeals to older people; these consumers also have higher incomes and are therefore more able and willing to pay the premium price for quality.

Locate potential buyers The owners of newspapers, magazines and TV programmes know their audiences well. They have to, because advertisers always ask who reads the publication, or who watches or listens to the show. Through market research, media owners break down the audience into standard classifications which are understood by everyone in the advertising industry. The divisions are made by analyzing the social group, occupation and spending power of the head of each household. Then the viewers, readers or listeners are divided up approximately as follows:

Category	Description
A	Higher managerial, professional and administrative
B	Intermediate managerial administrative and professional
C_1	Supervisory or clerical and junior managerial, administrative and professional
C_2	Skilled manual
D	Semi-skilled and unskilled manual
E	Casual labourers, state pensioners and unemployed

A, B, and C1 consumers are of most interest to the manufacturer of Step-Hi ladders. A and B groups are unlikely to do their own repairs, but may employ a casual handyman who requires a ladder, or the family may use the ladder for gardening. C1 groups often carry out repairs and redecoration themselves. All households need ladders for a few everyday uses – in larger houses high ceilings make ladders necessary even for changing light-bulbs.

Assess the client's budget The advertising budget for Step-Hi ladders is not big enough to pay for costly TV campaigns, so the client naturally looks at print media, such as local and national newspapers, and specialist publications dealing with home improvements and gardening. The ladder is made of unpainted metal, so colour availability in the publication is not an issue.

Schedule the campaign Step-Hi ladders will get most use in the garden and on the outside of the house in the spring and summer, so the campaign would probably be most effective in March or April. Since step ladders are not usually considered gift items, the Christmas period would be an unfavourable choice. Timing may also be influenced by the cost of placing advertising, which fluctuates seasonally in certain media.

Decide on the sales pitch It is difficult to show the versatility of the ladders in a single advertisement, so the best choice is a series of press advertisements each highlighting a different use. By illustrating an older woman using the ladder, the designer puts emphasis on easy handling, light weight and stability.

The advertising agency

Most companies have little idea about how best to advertise their products or services; a designer may be equally ignorant about the marketplace, and about the most cost-effective way of getting the message across. What both advertiser and designer require is the help of people who understand the message to be put over to potential customers; people who know how to research the market, and who can turn the advertiser's message into an advertising campaign.

This is the role of the advertising agency. In the agency, people with the necessary skills are grouped together in the form of a team. A client approaching an agency will be assigned an *account team* who deal with the product or service to be promoted. The make-up of the team varies from client to client, but there is always an *account executive*, who takes care of the client account on a day-to-day basis. At a more senior level, the *account director* or *account manager* handles major decisions concerning how the campaign should run, and oversees its planning.

After taking a brief from the client, the agency prepares a marketing strategy. This may entail some market research to check the client's facts: is the product right, or are changes needed? will the product sell? does the competition have a superior product? who does this product appeal to? This information is collated, and the creative team develops a rough idea of the type of approach that is most likely to succeed – or perhaps several approaches.

The creative team normally comprises just two people: the *copywriter* and *art director*. Sometimes there is also a *creative head*, who acts as principal to the agency's total creative output. The ideas put forward by the creative team go to a studio to be brought from rough form up to presentation standard, and these presentations are then shown to the client for approval before proceeding.

If the client approves the presentation, then other specialists move in: the typographer, photographer and paste-up artist make the artwork ready for reproduction. The agency may have its own in-house art studio, but specialist photography and illustration are usually purchased by the agency's art buyer. Once the client has passed the artwork, a *production controller/manager* dictates how the material is produced for newspapers and magazines.

Though these are the principal characters involved with an account, there may be other professionals involved, too. The *media department* chooses suitable publications in which printed adverts should appear, and buys air-time for TV commercials, all in conjunction with the account and creative teams. The *traffic controller* or *progress chaser* ensures that the right material arrives at the right media on the correct date. The *print buyer* chooses printers and colour houses for brochures and advertising material that needs to be reproduced independent of other publications. *Proof-readers* check for accuracy and *research sections* check facts before and sometimes after campaigns, assessing effectiveness; and of course there is the usual financial back-up from an *accounts department*.

The advertising industry is a complex one, but agencies differ in size and in the level of service that they offer. Although agencies at the top of scale offer a total in-house service to their clients, there are also many graphic companies who can offer a partial agency service, buying in specialist skills as and when needed. This approach is very cost effective, and therefore particularly well-suited to the advertiser on a low budget.

The agency family tree *Areas of responsibility and job titles may vary slightly from one company to another, but this chain of command exists in a roughly similar form in almost all advertising agencies.*

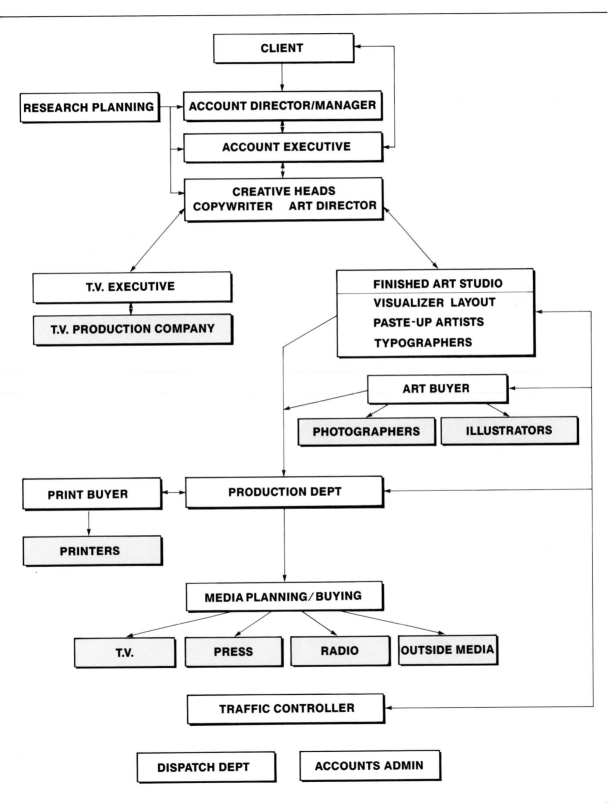

Working with a copywriter

Creative copywriters are the graphic designer's best friends: though strictly speaking they are responsible only for the words of advertisements, copywriters are used to thinking in visual terms, and often come up with exciting ideas for visualizers to follow up. Copywriters frequently head the creative team, relying on designers to interpret their ideas into visual form for clients to see.

When you are presented with headlines or body text by a copywriter, the priority is to understand the thinking and visual idea behind the words. This is made easier if the copy is accompanied by even the crudest of line drawings, indicating how the graphics are to be projected. The responsibility for communication does not lie exclusively with the copywriter, though: you are expected to be able to evaluate the sentences in a literate way, and interpret them in a manner that reflects the copywriter's initial ideas.

You will usually be working from a typescript with headlines, subheads, and main text all indicated. If there is any doubt as to emphasis, clarify this before proceeding. If you are visualizing a TV storyboard or an audio-visual presentation, the copy will be supplied frame-by-frame in two columns: in one column is a written description of what appears on screen; alongside are the words of the soundtrack.

Starting from the material supplied by the copywriter, produce some simple rough layout ideas, approximately indicating the size and position of copy and pictures. Don't always assume that the heading goes at the top; in fact, don't make any assumptions. Try a number of variations before going back to the copywriter to review the ideas. If at this point you both agree on a positive approach, continue with this in a more finished style, expanding the chosen idea while still remaining within the context of the joint creative approach. Naturally, you will have your own ideas; put them forward, but never at the expense of your partner's ideas. Integrated copywriting and graphic design make an exciting combination – but when the two members of the creative team are pulling in different directions, the result can be disastrous.

Solving copywriting problems

The two most common difficulties with copy are that the text is too long; or that when interpreted into visual terms, the copy pushes the campaign over-budget. The solution to both these difficulties is to talk to the copywriter, and request changes in the copy; the copywriter may in turn have to talk to the client, suggesting that the ideas are too wordy or ambitious. Don't try to get around the problem by reducing type size, as the reader will often turn the page rather than tackle a long piece of text set in an unreadable face. Spectacular campaigns on shoestring budgets are equally misguided: better to persuade the copywriter to adopt a lower-key approach, and do it well.

Highly technical copy always presents problems, but here the solution lies in the hands of the graphic designer. Often the copy is supplied in the form of a sheaf of typewritten pages, and the sheer quantity of text bears no relation to the space available. The first step is to read the copy and make sure that you understand it. If the advertisement is aimed at a non-specialist audience, you should be able to grasp the meaning of the text without further explanation; but if the material is to appear in specialist publications, you may need to consult the copywriter or a representative of the client for a simple explanation of the workings and benefit of the product. If there are complex diagrams or flow charts, ask where these should appear in relation to the copy. Don't start visualizing, though, until you are quite clear about the points that the client wants to emphasize.

To make the copy more readable, look for ways to break it up. If a paragraph of text refers to certain parts or functions of a machine, see if these paragraphs can be used as annotation or call-outs on a diagram or photograph. Can any of the text be separated out in a box or as a sidebar? Can the most highly technical details be moved to the last page of a brochure or pamphlet? Perhaps the copywriter can sum up large sections of text in a few sentences: these can then run in a much larger face, with the unedited text alongside the body copy.

Media and graphics

On your way to work one day, count how many advertisements you see. In a city, you'll soon lose count – a city commuter may be exposed to over 1,000 selling messages in the course of a one-hour journey. To stand out against this background, your advertisement must not only be eye-catching; it must also be positioned where potential buyers are most likely to see it. Placing advertising where it has most effect is the job of a media buyer.

Most agencies run their own media buying departments. This reflects the importance of media buying in the success of a campaign, and also the fact that most of a client's budget is spent on buying advertising space and air-time. However, there are also specialist independent media companies who will buy for a smaller agency, or even place advertising for low-budget clients of a large art studio.

Good media buying is about experience, financial muscle, and creative sense. The skill lies in choosing the right mix of media, and then being able to negotiate for the maximum possible coverage within the budget. The choice of media is very broad: obvious places for a client's message are space in the press and 'slots' (chunks of air-time broadcast at specified dates and times) on TV or radio. There are also poster sites and direct-mail shots to be considered, and other more unlikely places such as the backs of parking meters.

To create effective advertising graphics, you need to know where, how and when your advertising design will appear. Media selection is part of the creative process: sizes and shapes of advertisements are as important as the number of colours and the message that is to be put across to the market.

Unusual shapes

In certain instances the media buyer and art director design a campaign that uses a variety of unusual shapes, and the choice of these unorthodox spaces is no accident, but is the result of a positive creative strategy. However, to create a campaign using odd shapes and sizes requires a media buyer with some influence. A newspaper or magazine is unlikely to revise the page make-up to accommodate a designer's whim unless the media buyer is placing a lot of advertising. Even if the spaces are negotiated, costs remain higher than for standard shapes of comparable area such as full, half or quarter page. It is therefore wise to clear unusual shapes with media department well in advance of the campaign, and to monitor the budget carefully.

Campaign strategy

The creative team of copywriter and art director usually initiate the campaign ideas and present these to the client. The campaign strategy, though, is planned with the cooperation of the media team who draw up a media schedule. The easiest way to understand how this works in practice is to consider an advertising campaign, and see how the graphic and media teams make the best possible use of money available for production and media costs.

The products are for gardening enthusiasts, and a selection of garden magazines were chosen to carry introductory advertisements. The designer initially visualized one single whole-page advertisement, but the media buyer suggested breaking this into four quarter-page spaces in a single issue of each magazine. This ensures that as the reader turns the pages, the client's message appears repeatedly in key positions (below left). The drawback of this approach is that it is harder to make an impact with these small spaces.

How do the media buyer and creative team cooperate to tackle the problem?

First, the media buyer negotiates to place the advertisements on the inside of facing pages, and since they are joined in the middle (bleeding off at the gutter), the magazine has little choice but to put editorial matter in the remaining space. The graphics stand out from the surrounding type, and the advertisements dominate the page. The media buyer has achieved almost as much impact as two full pages, but at a fraction of the cost (below middle).

The media buyer also negotiates with the magazine so that the editorial text on the page covers topics that complement the advertiser's message. This too helps to make the small space dominate, because the reader's eye travels naturally between similar editorial and advertising copy.

Finally, a small but important point is that the rest of the spread is printed black and white. This too gives the colour advertisement more impact.

Promotions and competitions

Many advertising campaigns aim to keep a brand name in the public eye, or to introduce a new product. However in a highly competitive market, even the most successful products sometimes need extra promotion to maintain or increase market share.

One popular way to promote a product is to use special promotions or competitions which run over limited periods of time ('below the line' activities). These promotions are normally used for consumer products that face tremendously aggressive marketing from opposing brands: mostly branded goods in food and tobacco products; drinks, especially alcoholic beverages; and petroleum products where high turnover is essential for profit.

Types of promotion
To the consumer, there seems to be little difference between one type of promotion and another. For the advertiser, though, there are considerable differences. Some sorts of promotion are very costly; others virtually pay for themselves. Some provide a temporary boost to sales; others have a less immediate impact, but develop long-lasting brand loyalty.

By far the most common promotion technique is a 'money-off' message printed or stuck on the package. A similar, though slightly less used alternative is the 'extra value' promotion offering the consumer more of the product without a price increase. Variations on

this basic theme include 'Buy two and get one free', and vouchers which the consumer collects and exchanges for cash, a gift, or free samples of the product. Gifts work especially well if they have some association with the product or can be used in conjunction with the brand offering the gift. For a cereal manufacturer, for example, breakfast bowls are more suitable than glasses.

The characteristic of all these promotions is that they are comparatively short-term measures, and after a period of weeks the price and package are restored to normal marketing conditions. When designing graphics that will be used on a label or package for such an offer, always make sure that the additions you make do not overwhelm the label: your message should in no way alter or obscure the overall look of a generally accepted brand identity.

Gift sets The short time-span of 'money-off' promotions and their variants can be extended by offering gift sets. The gift is selected so that one or two have little value but by continuing to purchase the same brand the consumer collects a 'complete set'. For instance, one or two pieces of cutlery are practically worthless but with each place setting that is added, the perceived value increases. This type of promotion is fairly long-term, enabling the consumer to collect a 'set' of items, and promoting brand loyalty.

Lottery promotions These promotions appeal to the gambler in us all, and can be very effective weapons for overcoming brand loyalty. Lotteries are presented in many forms but typically have top cash prizes large enough to literally transform the lifestyle of the winner. Most competitors win less significant amounts of money, or token consolation prizes. Nevertheless, these should be large enough to keep even the unluckier ones in the game. When planning lottery promotions, take legal advice because some countries, cities and states have laws prohibiting them.

Competitions With the exception of lotteries, all competitions require the entrant to exercise skill and judgment. Competitions cover every age group but there is a particular bias towards women with children: market research shows that the competitions that have widest appeal are those featuring food and drink products and cosmetics, which are mostly purchased by women. More often than not competitors enter on behalf of all the family and purchase the promoted products when family shopping; so the prizes of the large competitions tend to be those which can be enjoyed by the whole family.

Prizes and competition formats vary widely, but for any competition the entry form must be easy to complete, and the tasks required of the entrants should be within the capabilities of the market you are selling into. Other aspects of the graphic presentation also affects the response to a competition: the more appealing the prize appears to be, the more people take part. The designer must therefore create an exciting image, capturing the imagination of the entrant by showing to best advantage the result of winning; if the prize is a luxury cruise to Sri Lanka the entry form could perhaps show a couple relaxing on deck against a tropical background. If the prize can be linked with the brand, so much the better. For instance, an active holiday such as a ski trip would make a good first prize in a competition to promote a health food product.

Children's competitions These must be structured so that a parent's approval for the child to enter is guaranteed. This often means using the child's talent in some way, like drawing or painting or some other educational slant. Graphics for children's competitions must be carefully focused on particular age groupings. Children will ignore or reject a competition which they perceive as aimed at those even a year younger than themselves. They respond to graphics that are exciting and dynamic, and that have novelty appeal.

The specialist competition

These are found in sports or hobbies magazines and normally the prize is directly connected with the magazine content, such as a trip to the Grand Prix in a motor sport publication.

Here, the most important factor is to create graphics that stand out from the editorial content. For instance, your 'Win a ski trip' design showing a large picture of a skier looks good in isolation on a layout, but the image will disappear among the mass of other similar pictures on the magazine page. So it is important to get the feel of the magazine in which your advertisement will appear, and consider carefully the graphic approach chosen. If most of the editorial pictures are photographs, consider using an illustration for the competition entry form, to make it stand out from the rest of the page.

Special promotions

Regular advertising ensures that a brand-name is familiar, and sells products by reason of their superiority over the competition. Promotions may have this function too, but what sets them apart from other advertising is that they offer the consumer a supplementary incentive – a free gift, a saving of money, a chance to win a fortune, or some extra reason for buying. So for a promotion to be successful, it must fulfil two criteria: first, the identity of the product or brand must be clearly projected. Second, the consumer must understand why it is worth changing brands, or buying a product that is new to the market. In other words, the selling message must reach its target. The first criterion is easy to fulfil: when designing a promotion, you simply make sure that the product identity always dominates, and that the promotional graphics do not obscure the client's trademark. Fulfilling the second of these two criteria provides more of a challenge.

The task is made easier by the fact that most promotions run simultaneously in several media: often the selling message reaches the consumer primarily through TV commercials, but posters and press advertising provide back-up. Not all media are equally well-suited to communicating sales messages: the side of a small package offers little scope for promotional graphics; point-of-purchase advertising is in view for far less time than, say, a newspaper advertisement. For the consumer to be repeatedly reminded of the product and promotion, the whole campaign must have a unified corporate look. This is most easily understood with reference to a specific example as explained on the facing page.

The promotion aims to boost the sales of red kidney beans. Research indicates that the product is rarely consumed alone – more often as part of a family meal. So the promotion must appeal primarily to a family market.

Canned beans are not a terribly exciting product in themselves, so a major function of the campaign is to make them seem more exciting and less ordinary. The creative team decides to exploit the fact that this type of bean is widely used in Caribbean countries, so the island of Barbados is used as a backdrop for the graphic story.

Barbados is a colourful, exciting island, and the graphics for the packaging and advertising reflect the island's character: blue sea and sky, palm-fringed beaches, calypso music and colourful clothing. Since the product is food, the overall theme of the campaign becomes 'Caribbean Food Carnival'.

The focus of the promotion is a competition – the first prize of which is a luxury trip to Barbados for the winner's family. To reflect the island theme, entrants are invited to find buried treasure.

The selling message itself must be delivered by someone who is clearly an expert on Caribbean cookery. So a dominant yet motherly female character is created to front the promotion, and her face appears on all promotional material.

The campaign runs as press advertising in women's magazines, with point-of-purchase displays and special packaging.

Children's advertising

There are special requirements and restrictions when the advertising campaign is aimed at young consumers. Children and adults respond to different kinds of advertising, and if you are designing a campaign that is aimed at children, you must take pains to understand your customers and the way they think. Never underestimate children's perception, intelligence, imagination, or their capacity to evaluate and select items or products that are offered to them. Children are very price-conscious, and count their small change with care. The youth market is further complicated by the fact that many children's products are actually bought by adults, so the designer is faced with the task of selling to customers from two different age groups.

Graphic guidelines

The age of the child at whom the campaign is directed is clearly a consideration when designing a promotion of this sort. For younger children, a colourful presentation is all-important; text plays an insignificant role. As the child gets older, so the graphic presentation must grow up in parallel to reflect the child's changing interests. However, the following themes appeal to children of most ages:

Collecting Children love to collect and hoard things, and exchange them with their contemporaries. This provides the advertiser with good opportunities for repeat purchases, or, when the adult is buying, for developing brand loyalty.

Clubs Membership of a closed society makes a child feel special. This is a harmless form of elitism, because any child who saves the requisite number of coupons can join the charmed circle. The paraphernalia of the club is largely graphic output: badges, membership cards, posters, magazines and stickers must all be coordinated with the advertiser's corporate style.

Education Children's advertising that is informative or educational obviously has some positive benefit besides profit for the advertiser. This makes it attractive to parents and kids equally. Educational campaigns must be particularly carefully targeted, though, since the interests of growing children change quickly.

Fantasy Children lead a richer fantasy life than adults. They quickly identify with heroes and villains, and much children's advertising is built around this theme. Comic-strip characters are very effective at getting an advertising message across: merchandising rights to many existing characters are available, but a less costly option may be to establish a completely new cartoon character.

Packaging for children's goods can serve a dual purpose: the toy shown above was constructed from a shoe-box. A cutting guide and the masonry details were printed on the inside of the box.

Children love the excitement of travel, and are captive consumers for the duration of a flight. This package of literature keeps them occupied, and, carried off the aircraft, serves as a lasting reminder of the airline for the child and parent.

Precautions

Strict rules govern the graphic presentations of children's products. This is perfectly reasonable: no other section of society is more vulnerable to misrepresentation than children. National, city and state rules are widely published, but regulations vary from one place to another, so clearly it makes sense to take extra care when a promotion crosses administrative boundaries.

Fantasy and reality The child must be able to distinguish between real and imaginary attributes of the product. For example, a toy train could be advertised with a drawing of a speeding express – which is seen to be imaginary – or with a realistic photograph of the toy. A photograph of the real train would not be acceptable in this context, because it could deceive the child.

Food Don't encourage bad nutritional practice: make clear that the product is just one part of a balanced diet. Never show overconsumption.

Misinterpretation Only the exact product or parts of it should be shown – it is misleading to show on a package more sections or pieces of a toy than the box contains. Products that are supplied in kit form should be shown in the course of assembly, and if any accessories are needed – such as batteries – this must be clear, too.

Size Always indicate the size of a product by including the child's hand or some common object.

Other children Advertising graphics must not imply that by the use of a product, a child could become superior to others; nor should the advertising demean other social groups.

Safety Never show the child in an unsafe situation, such as walking alone in a street, or close to an unguarded fire. (These rules obviously do not apply to public service promotions which aim to heighten the child's awareness of the danger.)

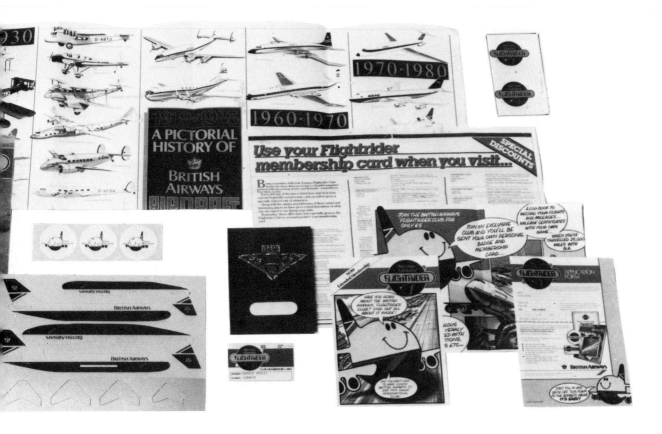

Designing for direct mail

Direct mail is a very cost effective way to advertise when your client has a good list of prospective customers who are all known to share a special interest. Unfortunately, the converse is also true: we all receive 'junk-mail' from time to time; however well designed this advertising is, we immediately discard it if we are not remotely interested in the product. Most often, though, the mail-shot falls somewhere between these two extremes: the product has general appeal, and the challenge is to capture and hold the customer's attention for long enough to get the full selling message across.

Before attempting to put together a direct mail design, it's worth reminding yourself that the cost of mailing and distribution can be higher than all the design and production costs put together. Furthermore, for every 100 envelopes mailed out, there are on average only about two responses. So while a good mailing can be very successful, a bad one will cost the client dearly.

There are some practical considerations when designing for direct mail – these are dealt with later on. From a graphic point of view, though, it is best to start without any preconceptions about practicalities. If the budget is big enough, there is no end to the type, style and complexity of ideas suitable for a direct mail design. Let your mind run riot over all the possibilities, because the object of the exercise is to catch people's imaginations, and make them respond. This won't happen unless *you* use *your* imagination.

Success depends on the image that the consumer sees on opening the envelope. If this is a strong enough statement or message the recipient will read on, and hopefully respond. It is not necessary to start with a picture of the product. Indeed, when selling life insurance, this is impossible anyway; in other instances it may be possible but undesirable. Put yourself in the position of the managing director of a small engineering firm who opens the envelope over breakfast and is faced with a photograph of an anonymous-looking machine. However good the copy, it is unlikely that this mail-shot will be successful. Eye-catching graphics, though, could show that this machine can make money for its purchaser: showing a stack of money would be more attractive than showing the product itself.

How much information should go into a direct mail shot? This is largely for the client to decide. Many large companies like to present the potential customer with a mass of detail, interwoven with different buying opportunities. For complex products, though, or where the consumer is making a considerable financial commitment, it is often better to simply arouse interest – a salesman can then make an appointment to call on people who return the reply-paid card.

It is important to remember that personally-addressed mail shots always receive more attention than general ones. An envelope marked 'The Office Manager' is rarely even opened – but one addressed to 'Mr. John Jones, Office Manager' will reach the right desk.

The envelope is the most important part of any direct mail promotion, so it needs to have immediate appeal. Unless you capture the imagination of the addressee at this stage, all the effort spent on styling the rest of the mail shot is wasted.

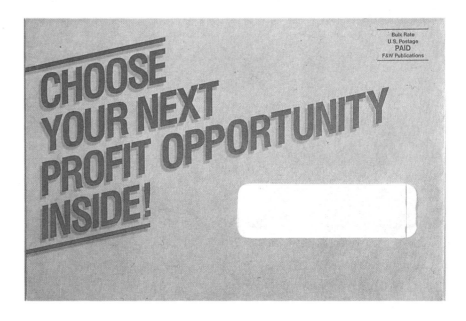

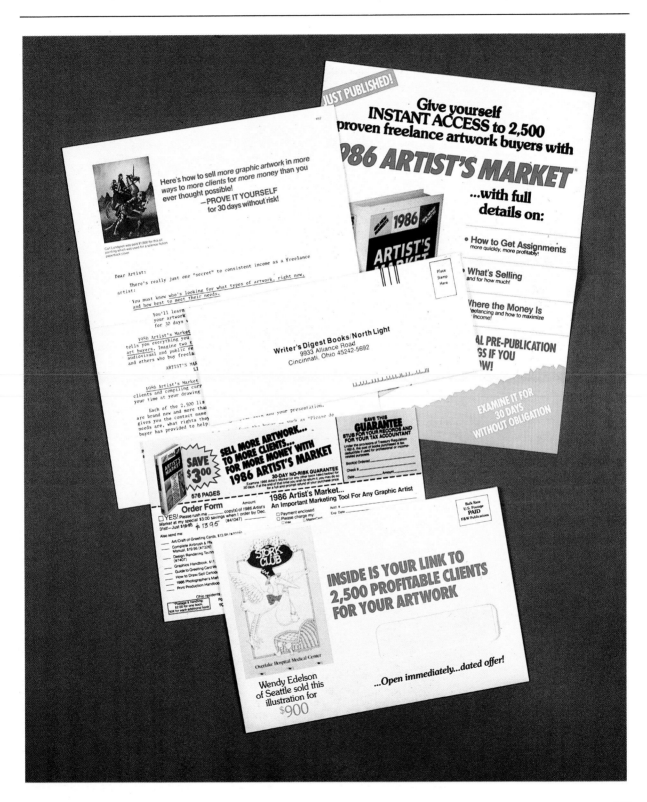

Practical considerations

Small differences in weight can create considerable savings in postage for the advertiser who uses this medium. Similarly, some sizes and shapes of envelopes are more costly to make than others. Final decisions about envelope details should be made in close cooperation with the company that is manufacturing but these guidelines apply in most instances:

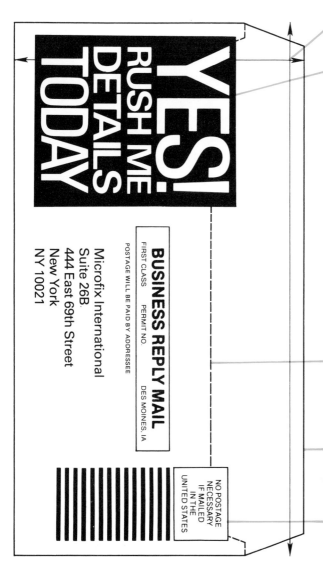

Stock or custom? Stock envelopes are cheaper, and easier to obtain. They can be overprinted with your design, but there may be some limitations on this as explained below. Bespoke envelopes can be made in any size and shape for added impact, but are economic only for very large runs – a practical minimum order is 100,000.

Weight Look very carefully at the weight of the completed mail-shot. If it is just a fraction over one of the Post Office weight steps, ask yourself whether you could cut the dimensions of the mailing by a fraction without reducing the impact of the client's message. This is especially important if the mail is to be sent to an overseas destination.

Size and proportions the Post Office can supply a list of preferred envelope sizes on request. Mail in these standard sized envelopes reaches its destination faster.

Overprinting If you are printing onto ready-made envelopes, bear these constraints in mind. First, try to keep printing away from envelope seams, where there are two or three layers of paper. Second, do not create a design which would suffer from inaccurate registration – keep all printing away from the envelope edge. Third, keep the printed area small if possible to avoid set-off (wet ink from the front of one envelope rubbing off on the back of the next).

If you are mailing more than 50,000 or so items, it is usually more economic to have envelopes printed before assembly. This provides more flexibility in design. However, die-cutting and assembly is not as accurate as the printing that precedes it, so the comments about registration still apply. There are Post Office rules about how much of the envelope can carry an advertising message, and where this can appear: the details vary according to the envelope size. Printing must not be so bright and glaring as to cause eye-strain or irritation when the mail is hand-sorted.

Flap and throat Banker style envelopes with a pointed flap are unsuitable for use with mail-insertion machines. Wallet-style envelopes with a straight flap and high throat are preferable. The shape of the flap corners is important, too – certain machines will only work if the corners are rounded.

Robustness Before finalizing the design, make up some dummy envelopes and mail them to yourself. Check that the finish is not damaged or marked by postal handling machinery and – more important – that the envelope does not split at the seams.

Reply-paid cards and envelopes Again, there are strict rules about the size, weight and design of these. Contact the Post Office for detailed information.

When personalized with the recipient's name, mail shots such as those shown above are more likely to be read than messages addressed to "The Occupier".

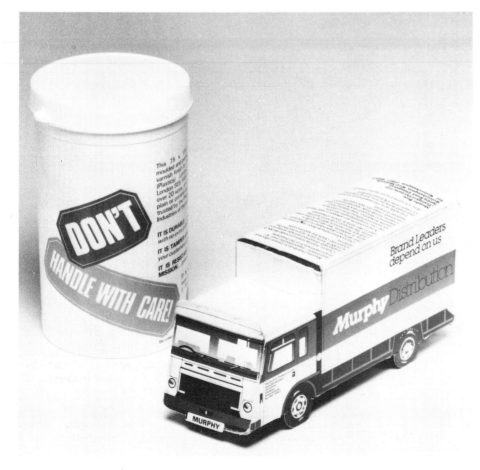

Direct mail promotions don't have to arrive in envelopes. These two examples use a three-dimensional form to add impact and interest.

Outdoor advertising

The poster presents the designer with problems and opportunities that are quite different from other media. The main concern is to visualize how a design on the drawing board will look when blown up to 20 feet across or larger. If the design looks untidy on the drawing board, it will look progressively worse when enlarged to poster size. Scale is not the only consideration: posters are seen by people in motion, and this inevitably affects the length of message that you can comfortably put across.

If posters form part of the larger campaign, take special care in adpating the graphics from other media. In contrast to other small scale adapts (see page 39) it is not usually wise just to enlarge a press ad to bring it up to poster dimensions. Think of how the poster will look in an urban context, with traffic passing in front of it, and surrounded by clutter and distractions. Contrast this with a full-page newspaper advertisement, which virtually fills the reader's field of view, and you will see the problem. Poster graphics must be bold and have a focal point – without this the poster becomes confusing and is overlooked. Posters lend themselves well to single giant photographs; short typographical statements work equally well.

With a good site and a high enough budget, posters can be the most exciting and invigorating of all media. The top three pictures show how a designer has cleverly used a moving display to promote a brand that "refreshes the parts other beers cannot reach". And the image at right makes a witty trompe l'oeil joke.

Posters are often seen as the poor relation in the advertising family – simply as back-up to heavyweight campaigns in other media. This rather narrow-minded attitude overlooks some of the major advantages of the poster as an advertising medium. Perhaps the most important of these is geographical: the media buyer knows exactly where each poster is going to be seen, when it will appear, and when it will be taken down. The advertiser's message can thus be aimed at any geographical level, from a few streets right up to a nationwide campaign. For the designer, the size is another advantage. No other medium provides so much scope for thinking big: the massive scale of highway billboards is now a graphic design legend. Finally, posters are an inexpensive way to advertise, which makes a poster campaign particularly suitable for a client with a low budget.

Messages in motion
At one extreme, a poster on a large roadside hoarding or billboard may be in view for just a matter of a second. The message on these posters must be short and to the point. At the other end of the scale railway,

bus and subway stations offer the designer a captive audience. Here the message can be much longer and more complex, because the passenger has time to spare and will read almost anything to relieve the boredom. Even if the bus or train interrupts, the reader will probably be back the following day and – if the graphics are sufficiently good – will seek out the poster to finish reading. Posters on the walls of escalators add a narrative dimension to advertising: cunning graphics make a story unfold from frame to frame as people move past. Posters on vehicle sides are themselves moving, and this ensures that the advertisement is seen over a wide geographical area at relatively low cost.

Poster sites
Outdoor sites are usually owned by groups of companies that offer considerable flexibility to the media buyer, both in terms of the scale of the campaign, and the location of individual posters. Transport authorities control poster sites on public vehicles and stations, and sometimes in other property owned by the authority, such as on railway bridges.

One way to isolate the poster from the city street is to use a large white area, with small areas of type. Large posters are not printed in one piece: they are pasted up as individual sheets of a standard size, and the size of the poster is usually specified by the number of sheets used. Typical posters are 16, 32 or 48 sheets, though some are as big as 96 sheets.

The small wall poster

This has a high copy content, and is designed to give the passing public a list of forthcoming events, or outline information about exhibitions or theatres.

Because of their informational function, such posters are principally typographic, and are printed as short litho runs or even using letterpress. Reverse type works extremely well.

The one-off poster

One-off posters for short term use are not difficult to create with transfer letters. However, if they are to be displayed outside, the surface must be protected with self-adhesive film or plastic lamination. Avoid using photographic colour prints on outdoor posters for long term display, as the colours quickly fade.

At street level, a giant close-up on a 48-sheet poster creates surreal juxtapositions which the designer and media buyer can use to gain a creative edge over the competition.

Specials

For extra impact, and when the client's budget is sufficiently high, the poster can even leap beyond the boundaries of the billboard.

Brochure design

One piece of graphic work for which there is a constant demand is the brochure; even small businesses that do not advertise in any other way often require brochures to describe their products.

The size of the brochure needs careful consideration, for the economic reasons outlined on page 78. Additionally the brochure may have to coordinate with a range of other similar pieces of printed matter, or perhaps there are existing point-of-purchase display stands into which the brochure must fit. Envelope sizes may also have some bearing on the choice. Having picked a size, remember that an oblong format can be used either upright (portrait) or landscape. Landscape format brochures are more unusual, but most clients prefer an upright format for mailing.

The use of colour on a brochure depends entirely on the material selected for inclusion by the client. A typical problem is that colour material available is a combination of transparencies, colour prints, and odd pieces of flat artwork (reflection copy). Before proceeding, explain to the client that such mixtures will affect the cost and reproduction quality of the job. If the material supplied is simply of low standard, it is best to tell the client this (tactfully) rather than carrying on in silence, only to have the printed job rejected. Sometimes the client insists that you use an assortment of pictures and other miscellaneous information not relevant to the main selling purpose. Try to confine this material to the back pages, while retaining it within the overall design theme. This leaves you free to place the selling story on the bulk of the pages. A common format for a brochure is an upright oblong, with a gatefold. The front page should be kept simple and eye-catching, though directly related to the pages that follow. This is the place for a simple, bold selling message. On opening the brochure there are two main design considerations: the reader sees pages 2 and 5, so these to pages must work well together from a design point of view; yet when page 5 is lifted, page 2 is juxtaposed with pages 3 and 4. Try and solve these problems by careful placement and division of copy, and by giving some thought to the use of the pictures. A very positive design theme gives a feeling of continuity, and is especially necessary when a range of complex copy and illustration is involved. You can provide the necessary integrated look by running coloured bands across the top of each page, or perhaps by leaving a large area of white space before starting the type and pictures lower down the page.

If there is a mass of technical information to be included, try to box this off as a tinted panel. Good use of typography and alignment can make sense of jumbles of figures. Complex flow diagrams or obscure tables of figures benefit from the same sort of tidying-up treatment.

A brochure such as this does not present any special production problems, apart from the gatefold: remember that to fold in properly, page 4/5 must be a little shorter than the other two pages.

Don't abandon a good design idea just because you've used it once. In these brochure designs, you can see the same multi-picture idea used repeatedly, yet small changes make each example look fresh and different.

Creative and self-confident use of white space is perhaps the test of a good designer. Unprinted paper can make as much of an impression as text or pictures. In a six-page brochure, the principal opportunities for using space creatively occur on pages 2, 3 and 4. If copy is sparse, don't attempt to fill the space on the page with oversize body type or large pictures, but instead consider using wider margins, a simple tint over part of the brochure, or a major heading.

Packaging design

The designer's task when styling packaging is the same as with any other advertising: selling the client's product. A package, though, is placed alongside other competing packages on the supermarket shelves, and the consumer is making a straight choice between brands – or between your work, and the work of another designer. While it is certainly true that the choice is also influenced by experience and by press and TV advertising, it is the packaging itself a lot of the time that convinces the customer to buy one brand and leave another on the shelf.

Packaging design is a very specialized part of the graphic arts business, and much of the work is carried out by just a handful of companies. The reason is straightforward: packages are costly to produce and are manufactured in very large numbers; unless the designer understands the process fully, there are sure to be some expensive and embarrassing mistakes. Most large companies therefore employ only designers with a proven track record when commissioning a new package for a major product. Small design studios should take care when approached for a package design: there are many pitfalls.

For the inexperienced designer seeking work in this field, the safest way is to start with a less sensitive package, such as the large cardboard outer case that holds domestic electrical equipment or large numbers of smaller packages. The principles are the same, but the sums of money at stake are lower.

Maintaining brand identity
Frequently a new product is launched under the umbrella of a well known brand: Speedy brake linings, for example, might branch out into oil filters. The packaging must therefore coordinate with an existing graphic house style. If the job you are tackling falls into this category, find out first how strongly the corporate image is to feature on your package. If the company logo is to be relatively small, are there other aspects of the house-style that nevertheless need to be echoed – perhaps a tyre tread pattern overprinting the whole package? Does the client want this pattern in the same colour across the entire product range, or can each product category have a new colour scheme?

Much of this groundwork will already have been done for you if you receive a comprehensive brief. If you have had little guidance, ask for the company's graphic arts manual, ask for samples of existing packaging, and above all, ask questions.

Find out what graphic elements need to be included on the package, including the statutory requirements listed on the next page. On food packages there may be preparation instructions, or, on large packages, a recipe. Determine which broad range of materials are suitable for the packaging: dry goods such as breakfast cereal could be packaged in almost any material, but the range is of course more restricted for liquid products such as brake fluid. Do some research into similar products on the market, and find out why various materials such as foil, film, cardboard, plastic and steel have been used. The material chosen may reflect the shelf life of the product. For example, certain food products can be packaged in clear cellophane, but a foil package keeps out ultraviolet light, ensuring that the product stays fresh for longer.

Ask the client or agency where the product is to be

sold or used: products sold through a garage or service centre, for example, need a different presentation to those sold in supermarkets or department stores. Packaging design also follows the same guidelines as other advertising with regard to customer profile: find out the age, gender and social class of the consumer who is expected to buy this product.

When you start work on the design, by all means make preliminary sketches on a pad, but make the move from two dimensions into 3-D as quickly as possible. In the long run, it is far better to work on assembled dummy packs than on a drawing board. The actual 3-D shape must guide your graphics, and if you work on the flat, you may overlook an important feature of the package. Pay special attention to colour. Extra colours always add to the cost of the package, but don't hesitate to suggest printing further colours if you feel this will make a significant difference to sales. This is particularly important when a house colour – part of a corporate identity – cannot easily be printed from the four-colour set.

When a package is displayed on a shelf, only one side of the container faces the consumer. Some packages, such as soap powder or jars of jam, have just one "face", and are always arranged in such a way that this side of the pack is prominently visible to the customer. When designing these packs it is most important that the brand identity is very prominent on the main face, and also on the top, in case the package is displayed on a low shelf.

Certain products, though, such as boxed reams of typing paper, may be displayed either upright, or in piles, in which case it is possible that the consumer will see any one of five or even six sides. These packages must feature the brand identity prominently on all faces. Packages that are displayed loose in a dump bin must have an even clearer identity, because they are viewed from every angle, even upside down. When working on a round container, bear in mind that the whole face is visible only when the package is viewed from the front. A good design is one on which important aspects of the package such as the brand name remain in view as the consumer walks past the product in the supermarket aisle.

At these early design stages, don't be too concerned about how the package is constructed, filled or sealed, as these considerations can be dealt with later. Concentrate on the graphics.

Most large corporations are justifiably proud of their trade marks, and will scrutinize your interpretation of the symbol very carefully indeed. You will probably find that the image is available as a bromide print sized to fit your artwork. If you have to create the image, though, take special care not only that you use the right typeface, but also that the line weight is the same. Photographic copying of a fine-line logo can cause parts to fill in, and lines to thicken.

You may be asked to design packages for a whole range of products simultaneously. Bear in mind that the manufacturer cannot control how the packages are displayed once they leave company premises, though point-of-purchase displays help in this respect. The consumer may therefore see just one product displayed at a time, or the whole range. This is why the corporate identity is so important – it helps the consumer differentiate between your client's range of products and those of the competition. The brand image must not be too strong, though, or the consumer will not be able to pick out the required product from the range on display.

This box of tissues can be stacked so that any one of five of its sides faces the consumer, so the manufacturer's brand identity appears prominently on all these five surfaces.

Legal constraints

A whole mass of legislation has been passed to protect consumers from misleading packaging practices. Laws are constantly updated, so it is impossible to say precisely what can go on a label and what cannot. However, some practices are clearly outlawed, and common sense rules out some others.

Product names The name on the package must identify the product as fully and accurately as possible. A can of rice with chicken pieces is "Rice with Chicken", not "Chicken with Rice". Descriptive terms must be accurate: cod, not fish; basil, not herbs.

There are exceptions to this rule: pizza, for example, is a well-known dish, and need not be described as "savoury open pie on thin dough base". Some food items are created, and therefore have no generic name. For example, a potato-based product called "Twisters" could be labelled as such on the package, but below the brand name, should appear the words "a crunchy potato snack with cheese flavour" and a list of ingredients should appear elsewhere.

Statutory information Most countries have laws which oblige the manufacturer to list certain facts on the package. These include: weight or volume; country of origin; fibre content (clothing and furnishing fabrics); active ingredients and dosage (pharmaceuticals); ingredients and nutritional value (food). Often the information must be presented in a specified way to satisfy local laws; some countries dictate only that ingredients are listed in order of weight, while others require the actual amounts in grams, or the nutritional value per serving. If the product is harmful, like tobacco, this must be stated on the package; products that put children at risk, such as medicines, or the plastic bags of the packaging itself, must be printed with health warnings.

Bar codes Supermarket chains may request that you print a bar code on the package, usually at the bottom left-hand corner. Once again, there are regulations governing where this must appear, its size, and the information encoded.

Misrepresentation Your design must clearly represent the substance, nature and quality of the contents. Photographs or illustrations must show what is inside the package – and no more. If a package containing frozen chicken pieces shows them cooked on a plate and surrounded by vegetables, the words "serving suggestion" should appear on or close to the picture. If there are two chicken legs in the package, there must be two on the plate, not three.

Information about all these statutory requirements, and which apply to the package you are designing, can be obtained from the relevant government department. If the design work is for a large company or for an advertising agency, ask the legal department for more information. The important point is to be aware of the legal aspects of the design, and to leave sufficient space for any necessary text. Your work will almost certainly be vetted by legal experts before printing.

Packaging is such a specialist area that you are likely to need help in specifying for manufacture. These bottles, for example, all feature a security closure, either to prevent tampering, or to protect children.

Cosmetics packaging

Budgetary considerations usually constrain the packaging designer's imagination, but budgets on top cosmetics packaging jobs are very high, making this is a rewarding and exciting area for the graphic designer. Packaging has to be good, because cosmetics appeal to a fickle, fashion-conscious area of the market, and because of the tiny quantities of the product that the package contains. Stripped of their packaging, some cosmetics are more costly, weight for weight, than a precious metal.

The client always wants a positive and unique package that cannot be confused with any other, and therefore usually provides a very comprehensive brief as to the market segment at which the campaign is aimed, and the required sales strategy.

The designer's main objective is to produce a package which reflects the value and quality of its contents, and the care which has been taken in their manufacture. This is done by subtle use of colour a nd metallic finishes, and careful choice of materials. The manner of construction of the package is important, too: try to create a package that complements the cosmetics in much the same way as a well-made ring complements a small but precious stone set into it: the setting increases the grandeur of the stone without actually giving a false impression of its true size.

Packaging design – case history

ICI is an international group of companies with a product range that serves almost every sector of industry, commerce and medicine. The company is one of the largest chemical concerns in the world, with nearly 150,000 employees working at major manufacturing facilities in the USA, Canada, Latin America, Europe, and elsewhere. Some of the company's output is supplied as bulk raw chemicals, but consumer products are of course packaged. Here and on the following pages we look at how ICI styles packaging for one of its many divisions – garden products.

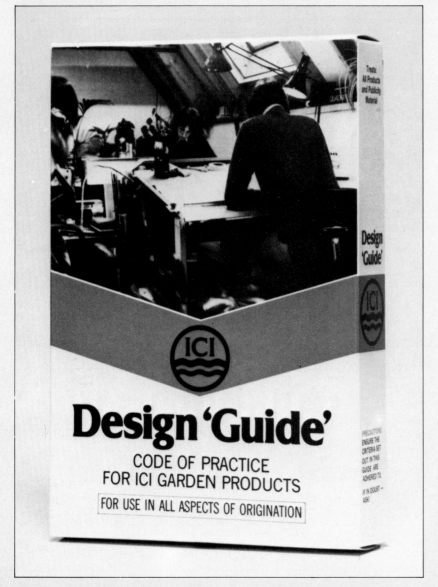

This box of index cards provides an overall guide to packaging for the garden division. Many of the guidelines, however, apply to all ICI products, and are repeated in the design guides for other divisions. Turn the page to see how this scheme is implemented in practice.

Outer Case Format

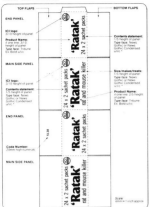

TOP FLAPS	BOTTOM FLAPS
END PANEL	
ICI logo: 3/10 height of panel	**Contents statement:** 1/5 height of panel Type face: News Gothic or News Gothic Condensed u/lc.*
Product Name: if one line: 3/10 height of panel Type face: Tribune Ex. Bold u/lc.	
MAIN SIDE PANEL	
ICI logo: 3/10 height of panel	**Size/makes/treats:** 1/5 height of panel Type face: News Gothic or News Gothic Condensed u/lc.*
Contents statement: 1/5 height of panel Type face: News Gothic or News Gothic Condensed u/lc.	**Product Name:** if one line: 2/5 height of panel Type face: Tribune Ex. Bold u/lc.
END PANEL	
Code Number: 20mm high numerals	
MAIN SIDE PANEL	

Scale: 1cm = 1 inch approx

* Use open type face; only use condensed if necessary.   Continued overleaf.

Use of the Roundel

When using the ICI Trademark, (the Roundel) there are certain rules which must be observed.

a   The Roundel should be reproduced photographically, and not by drawing. Master negatives are available for this purpose. Dry transfer sheets of Roundels in various sizes are available in black or white.

b   The Roundel may only be all white or all black.

c   The Roundel can be used against any solid background colour providing the blank areas inside the Roundel are the same as the background surrounding it.

d   It is not general to allow the ICI logo to be embossed into objects, but exceptions may be made on reference to Secretary's Department, Millbank.

Usage of Garden Products Name

a   Where the company name is used on any printed material it should be presented in the following ways:—

For Garden related Products
Imperial Chemical Industries PLC
Garden Products
Farnham
Surrey GU9 7UB

For Household related Products
Imperial Chemical Industries PLC
Household Products
Farnham
Surrey GU9 7UB

b   When the Roundel is combined with the Garden Products title, the formats above are the only layouts permitted.

Note
All printed Publicity material designated for the export market must also carry the phrase 'Printed in England'.
Imported packets will need to state country of origin, ie. Made in Belgium.

Critical Dimensions for Standard Packs

Standards for package design and print layout to be used for products packed in identical size containers. (All measurements shown below are in millimetres)

PACKAGE	FRONT LABEL AREA WIDTH × HEIGHT	THICKNESS OF ARROWHEAD	POINT OF ARROWHEAD TO BASE OF LABEL AREA
50ml glass bottle	38 × 53	7	15
100ml glass bottle	44 × 69	9	18
200ml glass bottle	63 × 97	13	27
2 sachet Weedol et al	139 × 90	17	26
4 sachet Weedol et al	90 × 138	18	46
8 sachet Weedol et al	140 × 115	20	38
16 sachet Weedol et al	140 × 190	29	53
32 sachet Weedol et al	190 × 200	29	57
1kg Fertilizer	127 × 190	25	50
3kg Fertilizer	235 × 430	40	100
6kg Fertilizer	305 × 570	52	118
12kg Fertilizer	360 × 620	62	145
4 sachet 1 pint grains	58 × 81	12	20
8 sachet 1 pint grains	121 × 81	12	21
4 sachet 1 gal grains	81 × 121	18	30
8 sachet 1 gal grains	121 × 162	18	32
150g Puffer bottle	180 × 130	17	33
300g Puffer bottle	205 × 170	23	43

These dimensions do not necessarily follow the 1 : 7.2 rule, but the arrowhead device must be consistant with the 16° angle.

Methods of using Trademarks

The current range of product trademarks and product names (in correct type face) are listed below. They should always be used in this typeface.

Trademarks

'Clean-Up'	Super 'Verdone'-G	'Forest Bark'
'Rose'Plus'	Super 'Verdone'	'Keriroot'
'Lawn'Plus'	'Rapid' GREENFLY KILLER	'Keristicks'
'Compost'	'Abol'-X	'Picket'
'Kerimure'	'Kerispray'	'Picket'-G
'Liquid Tomato Plus'	'Waspend'	'Ratak'
'Kergrow'	'Abol' Derris Dust	'Abol'-G
'Kerishine'	'Sybol'2	'Nimrod'-T
'Pathclear'	'Kericompost'	'Roseclear'
'Weedol'	'Cutlass'	'Couchban'
'All Seasons' Lawn Food		

Other Product Names

Mosskiller for Lawns	Lawn Spreader	Plant Pots
Sodium Chlorate	Thin Clear Sheet	Capillary Matting
Club Root Control	Thick Clear Sheet	Weedkiller Sprinkle Bar
Slug Pellets	Tunnel Cloche	Lawn Tonic
Antkiller	Green Sheet	Liquid Growmore
Triple Length Sprinkle Bar	Black Sheet	Growing Bag
Root Fly and Wireworm Dust		Weedkiller Applicator
Tunnel Cloche Replacement Sheet		

Points to Note

a   Whenever trademarks are used on packaging, display material or in subsidiary text they should be in quotation marks. eg. 'Weedol', with the first letter in upper case and the rest of the trademark in lower case. Wherever possible a statement should be made indicating that the product name and others listed in the text are Trademarks of Imperial Chemical Industries PLC.

b   The quotation marks for trademarks should always be in the following form – ''

c   Certain product names consist of a trademark and further text. In these instances it should be ensured that only the trademark is placed in quotes eg. Super 'Verdone'.

Continued overleaf ...

'Lawnsman' Outer Case Format

(inc. provision for cut case display)

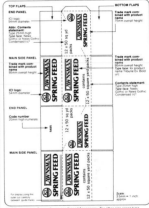

* Use open type face; only use condensed if necessary. For other size cases type sizes should be proportionalised.

ICI Garden Products Corporate Image

All Garden Products packaging should comply with the basic design rules shown below.

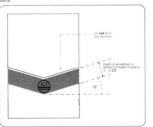

a   The face of the pack should be split by an Arrowhead device. When aesthetically possible, the ratios shown above should be used. The ratios are not suitable for all pack sizes. The angle should never vary.

b   The area beneath the Arrowhead device should have a white background and be used only for the product name and descriptive text.

c   The area above the Arrowhead device should be used for the illustrative element of the pack and subsidiary text as required, always ensuring that there is a white space between the Arrowhead device and illustration. The width of the white space should be 1mm for all sizes up to 1 kg/1 litre; 1.5mm for all sizes up to 3 kg/5 litre; and any pack above 3 kg/5 litre should be 3mm.

d   The height of the Arrowhead device is flexible and depends on the amount of information needed to be given above and beneath it. But there must be consistency for similar size packs.

There are restrictions on the use of typefaces, colours etc., which are detailed in further sections of the manual.

Type Faces

a   TRIBUNE EXTRA BOLD N

ABCDEFGHIJKLMNOPQRSTUVWXYZ
abcdefghijklmnopqrstuvwxyz

b   NEWS GOTHIC

ABCDEFGHIJKLMNOPQRSTUVWXYZ
abcdefghijklmnopqrstuvwxyz

c   NEWS GOTHIC and NEWS GOTHIC CONDENSED

ABCDEFGHIJKLMNOPQRSTUVWXYZ
abcdefghijklmnopqrstuvwxyz

ABCDEFGHIJKLMNOPQRSTUVWXYZ
abcdefghijklmnopqrstuvwxyz

d   NEWS GOTHIC BOLD

ABCDEFGHIJKLMNOPQRSTUVWXYZ
abcdefghijklmnopqrstuvwxyz

a   Whenever product names are used by themselves or as part of a display line or heading, the product name will appear in upper and lower case Tribune Extra Bold N.

b   Whenever a product description is used as part of the display line or heading e.g. Rapid 'Greenfly Killer', the descriptive element Greenfly Killer should appear in ordinary News Gothic Caps.

c   Whenever text is used, the correct type face is upper and lower case News Gothic or News Gothic condensed.

d   For Precautions, subsidiary headings and content declaration, News Gothic Bold should always be used.

Contents

Introduction

The object of this document is to broadly outline some of the major criteria which should be remembered in the design of products for the ICI Garden Product range. In most instances the image will incorporate the arrowhead device and ICI roundel. Specific exceptions will exist for some products but such exception will be determined as part of general marketing policy and not by individual design.

Display Material
Although this area has a great deal of flexibility in design content, it should nevertheless use the basic elements in the manner as described in the manual.

Packaging
Within this area continuity is extremely important. The link within the ranges will generally be the arrowhead device and the Roundel. Although striving to keep an individual product identity, there should nevertheless be an underlying range/group image using all the basic elements as set out in the manual.

117

These products from ICI's garden division are all concerned with lawn care. The chemicals are supplied in both solid and liquid form, so the designer has had to tackle packaging in several different media. Additionally, the range includes a piece of hardware – a lawn-feed spreader – and the protection of this equipment from damage during transit presents design challenges quite different from the rest of the range. As shown on the opposite page, the design solution includes not only packaging, but point-of-purchase advertising supplied directly to the retailer.

Three distinctive features provide a unified livery for the whole range. First, the ICI wavy line symbol appears on every product, usually (but not always) at the point of the company's red chevron. Second, the product range itself has an individual trademark, with the name set consistently between broad and thin rules, and printed in green. Finally, the individual product description always appears prominently set in Tribune Extra Bold and printed in black.

Within these broad guidelines there is considerable variety of approach and media. The spreader packaging is simplest: it carries a graphic two-colour line illustration which reproduces well even when printed using the fairly crude flexographic system. Other products makes greater use of colour. Boxed products in particular are printed offset litho using the full four-colour set to show a healthy lawn.

Several of these products were launched in the spring, with a major advertising campaign, and you can see how the designer has resolved the problem of putting a simple promotional message on the packs (just the word "new") without affecting the overall brand identity. The colour and diagonal slant of the promotional strip draws the eye, yet it does not cross any area of type or illustration.

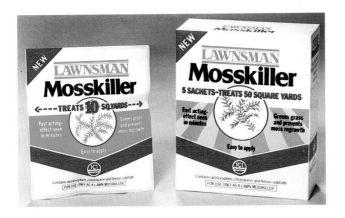

These two mosskiller packs show how design can be adapted to suit printing methods. The Inner sachets are printed using flexography, and use only areas of flat colour. The outer, printed offset, uses half-tones to suggest a neatly manicured lawn.

Display design

TV, press, radio and poster campaigns are almost always supported by a promotion at the point where the customer actually buys the advertised product. This is called 'point-of-sale' or 'point-of-purchase' advertising. The form that the promotion takes depends on the size, shape and weight of the package on display; on the environment in which the product is sold; on the expected life-span of the display; and, of course, on the budget available.

The marketing department
Competition for space in a supermarket is intense. Space at eye-level is particularly valuable – this is where products sell best. The designer has little control over how point-of-purchase material is used: this is entirely a matter for the management of the retail outlet, and even the best-designed point-of-purchase display will not boost sales if it remains in a store room. Convincing retail managements to use the display material, and to put out more of the product on the shelves (more 'facings') is just as important as persuading the customer to buy. For this reason most point-of-purchase promotions are accompanied by advertising in the trade press. Trade advertising stresses the overall campaign spend, and aims to persuade the retailer to buy extra stock, and to make full use of the display material provided by the manufacturer's representative.

Shelf talkers (far left) and dump bins (near left) generally carry very little graphic information. Often just the brand name or logo is sufficient to catch the eye.

Displays that have a community function – such as this message board (near left) – are more likely to be allocated precious wall space than those displays that have a purely commercial function.

A corner store shows how acute are the problems facing the designer of point of purchase displays (far left). Here the many different graphic schemes conflict, and only the largest of selling messages stands out clearly.

The display stand

This may be a permanent feature in the store, but it is often introduced only during a short promotional period, after which the products go back onto the shelves to be sold in the normal way. Permanent displays usually have a more generous budget, and are made from more durable materials than temporary stands. These are some of the material options open to the designer.

Cardboard This is a popular material for short-life stands. It is cheap, easily fabricated and printed, and can support remarkable heavy loads if construction – creasing, cutting and folding – is carefully designed. Cardboard is not the best material for long-life displays, though.

Corrugated plastic sheet This plastic material shares many of the qualities of cardboard, but is stronger, has a longer life, and is very much more suitable for outdoor displays.

Wire Displays made of painted wire are ideal for large numbers of small products. The display may be free-standing, or hung on the wall, and is inexpensive, remarkably sturdy and light in weight. An enormous range of designs can be made to suit most applications, but fabrication is best finalized in close cooperation with the manufacturer. If you outline your requirements in a simple line drawing, wire display designers will translate this into a practical, cost effective display. Graphic messages are added by slotting a cardboard panel into grooves.

Vacuum-forming and injection moulding Plastic is perhaps the most versatile of materials for display stands. It can imitate other materials, such as wood, and is widely used by the cosmetics and pharmaceutical industries. The cost of a counter display in plastic can be considerable, so this material is usually used for permanent displays. Vacuum-forming is economic even for short runs, but set-up costs for injection moulding are much higher, making the process suitable only for long runs. Again, design detailing is best left to experts.

Wood Fabrication costs for timber displays are high, but wood has a warm, traditional quality that no other material can match. Wood displays are therefore sometimes used for prestigious high-value products such as cosmetics.

Cardboard is perhaps the most versatile and widely used material for display design. All three examples shown above are constructed from die-cut and folded cardboard.

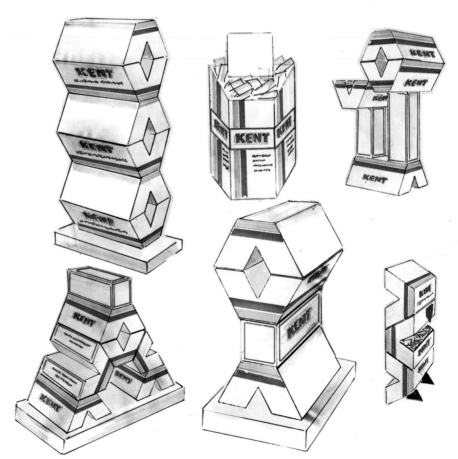

Modular displays that slot together are often slightly more expensive to produce, but save money in the long run. This unit can be assembled into a wide variety of configurations to suit different retail premises.

Exhibition design

Exhibition stand design – like packaging and point-of-purchase design – gives the graphic artist a rare opportunity to work in three dimensions, instead of two. However, stand design shares a less welcome attribute with these other two media – the potential for disaster. A designer who is not familiar with stand design can easily make expensive mistakes.

Visualizing for exhibitions

Design ideas for an exhibition stand are usually presented either as artist's impressions, or in the form of a model. Whichever form of presentation you choose, the first step is to study the brief thoroughly. This will probably include: the dimensions of the area that the client is hiring; the position of roof supports; a list of services available, and where they are routed in relation to the stand; and the rules and regulations governing the show. These details are practical constraints on your ideas, but they can also be starting points for your imagination. A roof support need not be an obstruction; it could be integrated as a focal point for the stand. Within the framework of the space and facilities available, rough out some ideas, and evaluate which of them looks most promising.

From these early sketches, work up the idea in more detail. If you are preparing sketches, the client will want to see the stand drawn from several angles. Models should not be too elaborate – don't forget that the job may go to another design studio if your work is rejected, and if this happens, all your preparatory work will have been wasted. Consider scale carefully: make the model big enough to include a reasonable amount of detail, but not so big that it won't go through the door.

This is the time to think about budgets, and discard ideas that are obviously over-optimistic. Don't get obsessive about money, though, as detailed estimates can be prepared only later once you have quotes from

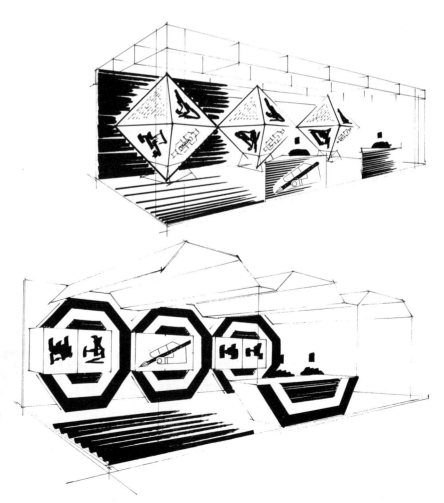

If you are doing two-dimensional visuals of an exhibition stand, you'll find it helps to first sketch in the overall volume of the space with which you're dealing. Then you can draw in seating, boards, and other display elements.

contractors. These are some of the points to bear in mind when planning the stand:

Visibility and accessibility How will visitors find the stand? Long distance graphics draw people in – use light, height, colour and movement to attract attention. Check where the entrances are, and make sure that the stand is visible from the main doors.

On-stand graphics These do not need to be as bold as the long-distance graphics, but once the visitor has arrived, on-stand graphics are very important. They must be sufficiently concise to make the product's major selling points immediately clear; but there should also be supplementary information for the browser. Try not to fill the entire wall area with photographs and odd pieces of text – this looks messy and confuses visitors. A better approach is to concentrate all the graphics – text and pictures – into a compact area which is not obscured by people walking past, or by the exhibits themselves.

 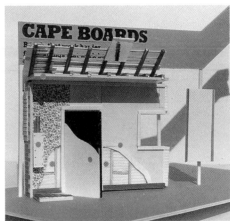

For a lavish and expensive stand, you may be required to submit very detailed models. Specialist model-making companies can create these three-dimensional interpretations of your visuals if you are not yourself sufficiently skilled at construction on a small scale.

Seating, storage and surfaces How much seating does the client require? Is a reception desk needed? Work out how much space the stand furniture will take up, bearing in mind factors like space to open doors (sliding doors take up less) and leg-room around chairs. Make sure there is space to store coats and brochures – nothing looks more untidy than toppling stacks of printed material.

Space and blind spots Is there room to move around the stand and inspect or operate the exhibits? Does the client want a private area in which to entertain important customers? Will activity on one part of the stand interfere with what people are doing elsewhere? AV presentations in particular can be especially irritating to staff if the recorded cycle is repeated every four minutes throughout the day. Are there any pieces of furniture or graphics that will obscure one part of the stand? Blind spots are wasted space, so eliminate them. All these problems are easily sorted out on preliminary models; if you are just drawing elevations, plot the stand to scale on squared paper to highlight difficulties with clearance.

Flooring If there is no heavy machinery on display, a raised platform floor simplifies the routing of services, and acts as a visual boundary for the stand. Think about what will cover the floor: for custom stands carpet tiles are a good choice, because damaged tiles can easily be peeled up and replaced. Vinyl flooring is better if there is a lot of water on the stand – perhaps the client's machinery needs to be washed down.

Catering Most stands need a water supply and bowl for washing glasses and coffee cups.

Lighting Don't forget that some on-stand lighting is essential; without this the products will look very gloomy. Exhibition contractors supply lights on custom stands, but on low-budget shell schemes, you may have to organize this vital aspect of the stand.

Services Three-phase electric power, hot and cold water, drainage and compressed air supplies are laid in trenches that criss-cross large exhibition centres. It isn't necessary to fix the exact routing of services until a final plan is drawn up, but you should be aware of the client's requirements, and bear them in mind when visualising. This is particularly true when the client is showing equipment that draws and discharges water continuously. All services are expensive to lay on, and this may affect the budget for the stand.

Contractors and exhibition spaces

Once you have worked out a fairly detailed scheme, contact two or three contractors, brief them in writing, and get quotes for constructing the stand. Bear in

mind that contractors who are based close to the exhibition hall have no travelling and accommodation expenses, and are therefore usually cheaper than out-of-town businesses. You will need to supply drawings with reasonably accurate dimensions, and to indicate the position of all services and lighting required. The basic quotes may vary tremendously, but if they do, check the specifications on each one. Items that are included on one quote may well be an additional expense on another.

The shell scheme

Smaller exhibitors cannot usually afford the luxury of a custom-built stand, and therefore buy a 'ready-to-use unit' at the show. These 'shell scheme' stands are the exhibition equivalent of the off-the-peg suit. The geography of the unit varies according to size and site, but generally your client will be supplied with a back wall, two side walls, a front and a name panel. There is no choice of carpet colour, but there may be optional extras such as muslin ceilings, lighting, counters, cupboards and shelving (right).

As designer, your role is more limited than when the stand is custom-built: your task on a shell scheme is really to dress an existing stand. On the other hand, an exhibitor on a low budget will probably expect you to play a major role in the production of the graphic material, rather than hiring a contractor.

Although all shell schemes supply a front with the exhibitor's name and stand number, this is of standard size and typestyle, and will not reflect your client's corporate image. To establish the brand identity clearly, you can use a simple banner, with the company image running like a border around the stand, or one or two dominant graphics on the walls. Choice of materials is crucial, because on many shell schemes, nails, screws and tacks are strictly forbidden. The panels therefore have to be either free-standing, or sufficiently light to be held in place with adhesive tapes. Foam-filled board is ideal – it is rigid, but very light. Mount all photographs onto board, so that there is no loose matter flapping around.

When you are designing and ordering boards, think very carefully about the size of each graphic component. It is difficult to grasp the scale of a display panel on the drawing board, and all too often the finished graphic is too big to fit into the truck that has been hired to transport the client's products. Very large panels should be constructed in sections, and assembled on site.

If the client has a series of exhibitions to attend, see if the graphic material can be reused. Foam-filled board is easily damaged, but company logos can be stuck in the middle of large sheets, then peeled off when the show ends: fresh, clean board is used for the next show.

All exhibition stands – whether purpose built or shell scheme – need to be constructed and dressed in a very short space of time. The apparent chaos of construction gives way rapidly to an elegant well lit display just minutes before the public are admitted.

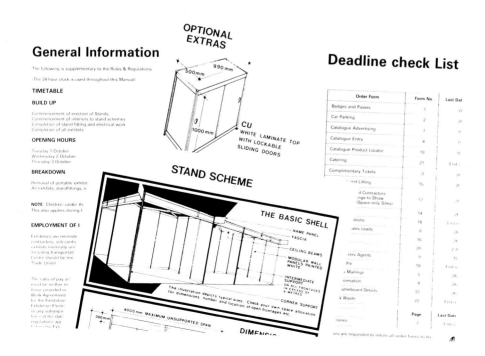

Design for business

As a graphic designer, you are already aware of the importance of presentaiton. The portfolio that you take round to potential employers or clients is arranged to show off your abilities to advantage, and to illustrate the confidence with which you can handle a range of graphics. The portfolio is your shop window, and is frequently your first point of contact with a potential client.

Many organisations, though, make their first contact through a letter, or a piece of printed material. So it is important that the graphic presentation of a company's printed matter should reflect the same standards of confidence, ability and market performance that you seek to project in your portfolio. The function of a corporate graphic style is to ensure that the company projects a positive, integrated image of itself at every possible opportunity.

Many organizations – particularly small businesses – feel that the company letterhead is all that requires a designer's attention. They allow jobbing printers with no design experience to print up untidy and clashing selections of business cards, invoices and compliment slips. Other companies grow quickly, and are unable to control the proliferation of stationery styles. Either way, the result is a weakened company identity.

The design advantage
Conversely, good design and a totally integrated graphic style not only shows the company in a better light, it also makes sound business sense. Smart invoices tend to rise to the top of the pile for payment; a crisp, efficient-looking business card has a way of opening doors. So in the pages that follow we examine the best ways to evaluate a company's requirements, to create an integrated corporate identity, and to apply it to all aspects of a company's graphic output.

The Coca-Cola logo is perhaps the definitive example of the design advantage. The red and white logo is universally recognized as a guarantee of quality and authenticity. Remarkably, the characteristic style of the company letterform is so distinctive that it is unmistakeable even in a foreign tongue.

128

Company stationery

The most widely-used piece of stationery is undoubtedly the main company letterhead. It is often the first opportunity that a potential customer has of assessing the company, and therefore merits special attention. All aspects of a letter influence the impression it gives: the way the company symbol is used with the typography; the appearance and weight of the paper; the typist's layout; all play an integral part.

There are no rules for the positioning of graphics on a letterhead: the variations on this centuries-old theme are limited only by your imagination and budget. You might choose to put the company name across the bottom of the sheet or up the sides, and if the client does not object, such a design could well create a very striking piece of stationery. However, before presenting your more outrageous designs consider these rather mundane, practical points.

First, business people who receive a letter from your client may be quite conservative, and will instinctively look for the sender's name and return address at the top of the sheet. If this information is elsewhere, it must be especially clear and easily located, or your design will cause irritation.

Second, a letterhead is for writing on: there is no point in designing a very elegant piece of stationery if the typist's work spoils the overall impression. You can avoid this problem at the outset by typing a typical letter and copying it onto a piece of clear acetate. As you work through various designs, lay the film over each one, and to check if the design lacks balance. The fault may be the spacing on the page, or the relationship of the design or colour to the mass of black typing.

Third, only personal stationery carries just the sender's name, address and telephone number. To comply with the law, the letterheads of incorporated or limited-liability companies must carry specified details as explained overleaf, and these details may run to several lines. Ideas that start out very crisp, smart and spartan in concept frequently look untidy when all the legal requirements have been added.

A positive step when researching a letterhead is to gather examples of the uses that the current letterhead is put to. You may get some surprises. For example, at a briefing, the client tells you that the name of the individual sending the letter appears only at the foot of

the page, typed below the signature; by collecting existing letters, you discover that in practice, things are not quite this simple. Secretaries to some of the directors type the sender's name in the top margin above the company name. Company directives, however strongly worded, rarely break long-standing habits, and this may influence your design. In this example, you might choose to add 'Please reply to:' underneath the company address.

Always keep the desired company image in mind, not just as creative inspiration, but as a force of moderation. If the letterhead you are creating has a self-consciously 'Designer' look, it will say more about your own personality than about the image of the company that's paying you.

As a general rule, a design centred on the page is difficult to balance with typing aligned on the left. This problem can be avoided by allowing a larger area around a central design, or by keeping the whole concept very simple. Positioning the main area of graphics on the right or left may well be a more comfortable solution, but you can also combine several different alignments in a single letterhead.

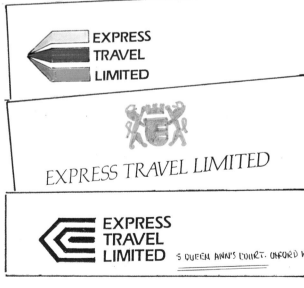

The company letterhead

When taking a brief for a letterhead, find out *exactly* what information is required – there's a checklist below – and make sure that you are given correct, double-checked information. If director's names and qualifications are listed, for example, be sure that the person concerned has approved the form of entry. Don't accept 'I think that's right' as an answer.

1   The company symbol must appear on the letterhead, along with the full company name, address, and postal or zip code.
2   A company trading as 'Microfix' may actually be registered as 'Microcomputer Repair Corporation Incorporated' and both names must appear.
3   The registered office and company registration or incorporation number are required in some areas.
4   Separate letterheads may be required for each company subdivision.
5   A market description is sometimes appropriate: should the company name read simply 'John Brown', or is 'John Brown Advertising and Marketing' more appropriate?'. Often the client requires a slogan, as well, such as 'David Smith, Landscape Gardener – flowers are our business.'
6   Registered trademarks often appear on the letterhead – does the client wish to include them on this job? Likewise, if the company has won an award for exports or business achievement, or is a member of a trade confederation, corporate pride may require that these details appear.
7   Telecommunications: these do not stop at the telephone number. Ask about telex, facsimile (fax) machines, cable addresses and electronic mail. If each senior member of management has an individual telephone number, there should be space for this in addition to the main switchboard number. Figures and codes should be used in brackets, not with the cross-slash symbol, which is open to incorrect interpretation: (0938), not /0938/.
8   Abbreviations: avoid them whenever possible, as they can easily be misleading. Numerals should always be Arabic, not Roman, and letters combined with them should be capitals, not lower case – '21A East Street', not '21a'.
9   Directors' names must appear on company letterheads. Spell out in full their positions in the company: 'Managing Director', not 'MD'. Letters of qualification may be written in various ways: ASTD and A.S.T.D. are equally correct. However, from a typographic point of view, the former looks less untidy particularly if further punctuation such as a comma or semi colon separates the abbreviation from the next name.
10   Directors working in a country which is not their normal place of residence should have this clarified: (FRG) would follow the name of a German director, for example.

4 **A division of Microfix International**
Services to the computer industry worldwide 5
A member of the Computer Service Engineers Confederation

8 **Microfix** 1

74A Lordship Park
London N16 5UB
Telephone (01) 487 4893 7
Telex 295030 MicFixG
Electronic Mail Prestel 938273051

6

Mr Richard Platt
Suite 26B
444 East 69th Street
New York
NY 10021   USA

Date: 14 February 1986

Your ref: -

Our ref: BB/RJCP/JD

Reply to: Bert Braham

PAGE LAYOUT OF TYPING ON COMPANY NOTEPAPER

Dear Richard

This letter illustrates the preferred style for correspondence
on company stationery. The aim is to create a neat letter with
the minimum of fussy detail. For this reason, we have abandoned
all punctuation marks in the address except where commas or full
points are essential for understanding. The position and length
of the address is also important, not only for stylistic
reasons, but also because the company has now adopted standard-
sized window envelopes. For the entire address to be visible
through the window, the first line of the must be level with the
date, and must be aligned with the end of the rule above; the
longest line of the address must not extend beyond the end of
the line "A division of Microfix International"; and the address
must be no longer than five lines.

The topic of the letter should be typed in capital letters, and
must appear no less than twelve lines below the lower rule--if
it is higher than this, it will be visible through the envelope
window. The salutation appears after a line space, and must not
be followed by a comma.

Paragraphs are separated by a single line space, and the first
line of each must not be indented. All text must be left-aligned
to ensure consistency: although the electronic typewriters and
word-processors that we use in head office can justify text,
this is a facility that is not available on the older
typewriters used in branch offices.

I hope this summary provides you with the information you need,
and I am grateful to you for drawing my attention to the lack of
consistent style in company correspondence.

Best wishes

Bert Braham

Bert Braham

2

3   Microcomputer Repair Corporation Ltd Registered Office:
23 Camden High Street London NW1 4ED Registered in England No. 145329
Directors: Bert Braham BA (managing) Richard Platt BSc (USA) 9   10

Other stationery

Few companies require just a letterhead; even the smallest business generally needs invoices, compliment slips and business cards, and there's an endless list of other stationery. Commoner items include monthly statements, small letterheads, purchase orders, overprinted envelopes, despatch labels and internal stationery such as memo pads.

As with a letterhead, content needs to be considered carefully for each item, but there is some specific information that you need to know before starting.

Compliment slips Does the client require a blank area for writing brief remarks? Should there be a simple map on the back to guide visitors to company premises? If a map is required, it should be printed in pale ink to avoid showthrough.

Business cards There is a growing movement to standardize the size of these at 2 × 3¾ inches (50 × 95 mm) to fit into wallets. Business cards can fold though, along either the short or long edge, and this allows more space for information.

Invoices and statements These present special design problems which are shared by most forms used in accounting and dispatching departments. The text describing conditions of supply and payment often runs to hundreds of words, and there must be space on the form for a great deal of typed information. To overcome these problems, stick rigidly to the chosen house typeface, using different weights and sizes to give emphasis to the main details of the form. If the conditions are really long, put them on the back of the form in small type. Try to standardize the thickness of the column rules, and check that adequate space is left for typing in details.

If the company uses multi-part carbonless forms, find out how many parts are needed, and which colour sequence is preferred. Normal business practice is white for the top sheet, then pink, blue and green. Top and bottom sheets are usually heavier than intermediate forms. Multi-part forms are supplied as individual sets, in pads, or as continuous stationery, so ask about this, too. When the forms are to be fed through a computer printer as continuous stationery, line-spacing is crucial, and is dictated by the accounts program software. More information is available from the client's data processing department. Continuous stationery requires special printing methods, so check that the printer you plan to use on the job has the appropriate machines.

Continuous stationery

Increasing numbers of companies use word processing equipment and computer printers. Though this does not affect design of letterheads, it does have some impact on production. Three options are available to a computer user: *a sheet feeder* attached to the printer can feed ordinary letterheads of virtually any paper thickness; but for faster printers, a continuous strip of paper is needed, with holes punched at ½ inch centres along the sides of the sheets. Since this paper is supplied in continuous form, folded like a concertina or fan, it is often called *fan-fold* paper. Letterheads are printed directly onto the paper, with perforations along each edge so that sheets can be separated, and the punched edges removed. If the paper is *microperforated*, the edges are almost as smooth as regular cut sheets. However, if perfect cut edges are required, the fan-fold paper is used just as a carrier sheet, and ordinary company letterheads are attached to it with a low-tack adhesive. This is the most costly of the three options.

The section on direct mail (page 104) details the special precautions that are necessary when designing for envelope overprinting.

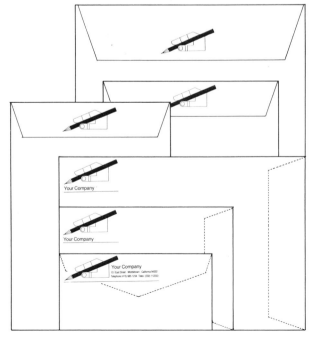

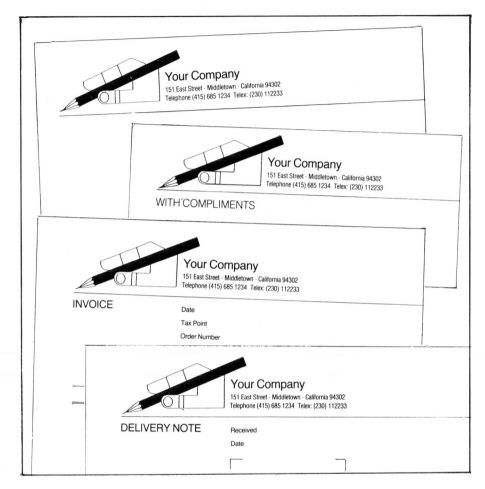

Blind embossing gives stationery a prestigious feel, but adds considerably to print costs. For a small business, a practical alternative may be a hand operated embossing press, though this produces a slightly less highly finished result, and is suitable only for small designs such as this monogram (shown life-size).

Saving time and production cost

Creating a whole range of company stationery can be time-consuming and when expanding a corporate design from one item to another, you will find that a photocopier is a great help in visualizing. Use this to make a number of photostats of the basic symbol, placing the main design in the middle of a large sheet of paper. You can then cut away the unwanted paper to leave the logo positioned as required for each business form.

For example, you decide to place the main graphic grouping at the bottom of the compliment slip. Take one of the photostats and cut across slightly below the symbol, leaving it at the bottom of a smaller sheet. Trim left and right to centre the symbol, and cut the top of the sheet to the required size. Now you can strip in the required type above. If you photocopy the

rough paste-up, you'll get a passable presentation of the finished printed item (without colour of course) and you can repeat the procedure for other items. A photocopier with enlargement and reduction facility makes the process even more versatile.

The cost of printing a symbol in a second colour on business stationery can be greatly reduced if the symbol always appears in the same position and size on every item. A single plate for the second colour is used to print every sheet with the company logo. Individual stationery items are then just overprinted on this basic stock in black, and trimmed to size.

Doubling-up artwork is another way of saving, too: trimming half-size letterheads from full sheets wastes 30 per cent of the paper. You could print compliments slips on this area.

Logo design

It is hard to overstate the importance of a company logo. This symbol has to be immediately recognizable wherever it appears; it must evoke the company image the instant anyone sees it; and it must be capable of reproduction in every conceivable size and medium.

Creating a logo that fulfils these requirements is neither easy nor cheap, and many clients comment that they cannot see the need for a corporate logo. A common argument is that nobody even recalls the symbol. For a small company trading only locally, this argument perhaps has some merit. However, small businesses don't always stay small; when trading expands to a regional, national, or international level, a recognizable trademark not only identifies the company, it also guarantees the quality of the goods which carry that symbol. In recognition of this, major companies go to great lengths to stamp out abuse of their trademark. For example, the Swedish engineer-ing company SFK employs an 11-strong legal team specifically to prevent other manufacturers endorsing shoddy goods with a counterfeit SKF logo.

How do you go about designing the company logo? Start by looking at the existing company symbol. If the client has been using a purely typographic letterhead without a strong identity, then you have *carte blanche* to create a new corporate image. Often, though, there is a symbol already in existence. If this is well-known, discarding it could be a mistake, rendering the client's publications and stationery virtually anonymous. You may thus decide that a gradual change would suit the company best, and therefore create a series of logical revisions which would give customers a three or four-year period to adjust to the new image. Alternatively, you could work around the main shape and colours of the current logo, simplifying it and giving a more contemporary look.

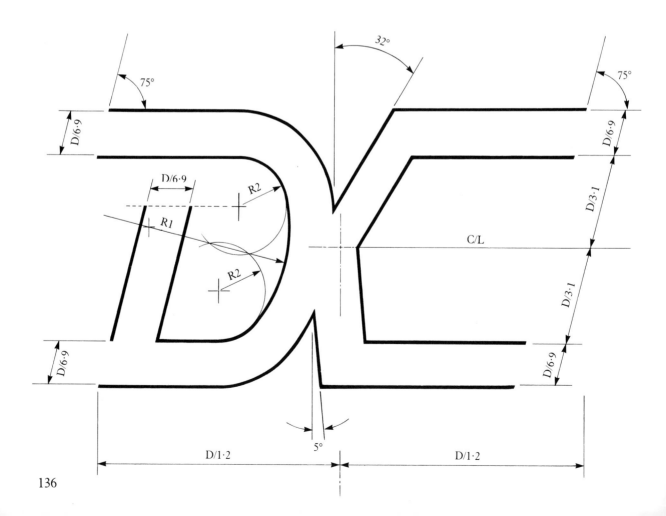

New logos

When starting from scratch, there are five principal routes to a good logo:

- Use the full name of the company, and present it in a unique way. This is obviously more practical if the company name can be abbreviated: "ManPressCo" is more easily crafted into a logo than "Manchester Pressing and Manufacturing Corporation".
- Take the company initials and form them into a symbol. This can work well with conservative companies that reject the first approach as bastardization of the company name. Many corporations – particularly those with long names – are already known to customers by their initials.
- Put forward a graphic symbol that represents the company's market or products. Beware of graphic clichés, though, such as the wire hanger for the clothing manufacturer.
- Design an abstract symbol that is strong enough in graphic terms to be eye-catching and memorable in the company's market. A hazard here is that establishing the logo in the public eye requires a massive commitment on the part of the client. Usually only major corporations can afford the advertising spend this entails.

- Combine a symbol with a typestyle.

Just as when visualizing any other design application, initial sketches should quickly narrow down the field to just a handful of possibilities. At this point, start to think of a few practicalities. First of all, printing: your design must reproduce well in black and white on a small scale, and on the cheapest paper. Think carefully before using halftones or mechanical tints as these have a tendency to fill in when reproduced. Avoid many fine lines or small type reversed out from black for the same reason.

A logo will always be seen in context: on a letterhead, on the side of a vehicle, on an invoice. So at this preliminary stage, it is a good idea to sketch out possible stationery designs, to see how the symbols look on the page, and how they interact with areas of type. Crumple and fold the symbol: this is how it will appear on a flag flapping in the breeze. Try to picture the emblem twenty feet high on a poster: does it look ridiculously heavy? If the managing director wants the symbol cast on gold cuff-links, will it still read? Remember that you are designing not only for the client's needs and graphic applications in the present, but also in the foreseeable future.

From your short-list, you may eliminate several otherwise good designs on the grounds that they cannot be translated into other media.

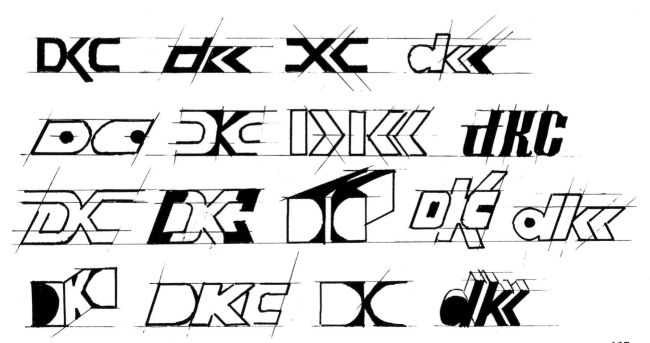

House colour and typeface

Most companies specify at least one extra colour as part of a corporate identity: even conservative clients such as banks and other financial institutions have to choose a paint colour for their vehicles. The use and choice of colour as part of a corporate programme is not as simple as it appears at first sight: just as the logo must be sufficiently adaptable to look good in many different forms, so too the house colours are used on stationery, outdoor signs, posters, and perhaps packaging as well.

Check first of all whether there is a second colour in use already, and whether the management have any strong views – positive or negative – regarding house colours. At the same time, it is wise to investigate the corporate colours of other companies in the same market segment. The client knows the market better than you, and will be quick to criticize if you have picked the same palette as a rival uses.

International corporations often do not limit their house colours to black plus one other. They may use two or three extra colours or even the full four-colour set. However, extra colours are costly, and businesses may rule out more than two colours for this reason. Remember though, that you can add a second colour simply by printing on coloured paper. Extra colours can be made to pay for themselves: a small company that depends on direct mail for most of its business may find that extra colours bring a better response. Don't feel tied by convention when choosing colours. Hues that appear to clash badly can, with skill, be used to great effect. A deep colour that can be printed as tints will invariably provide more versatility for the future than a pastel colour that disappears when printed as a 50% tone. Once you have chosen house colours, these should be included as part of the corporate manual (see page 144).

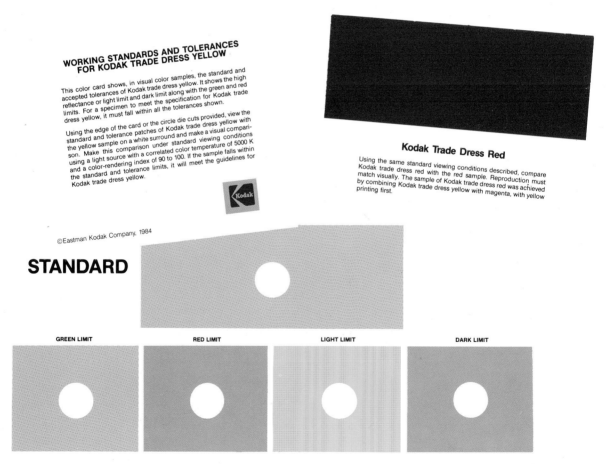

WORKING STANDARDS AND TOLERANCES FOR KODAK TRADE DRESS YELLOW

This color card shows, in visual color samples, the standard and accepted tolerances of Kodak trade dress yellow. It shows the high reflectance or light limit and dark limit along with the green and red limits. For a specimen to meet the specification for Kodak trade dress yellow, it must fall within all the tolerances shown.

Using the edge of the card or the circle die cuts provided, view the standard and tolerance patches of Kodak trade dress yellow with the yellow sample on a white surround and make a visual comparison. Make this comparison under standard viewing conditions using a light source with a correlated color temperature of 5000 K and a color-rendering index of 90 to 100. If the sample falls within the standard and tolerance limits, it will meet the guidelines for Kodak trade dress yellow.

Kodak Trade Dress Red

Using the same standard viewing conditions described, compare Kodak trade dress red with the red sample. Reproduction must match visually. The sample of Kodak trade dress red was achieved by combining Kodak trade dress yellow with magenta, with yellow printing first.

©Eastman Kodak Company, 1984

STANDARD

GREEN LIMIT   RED LIMIT   LIGHT LIMIT   DARK LIMIT

The house typeface

The selection and correct use of type in a corporate identity programme is almost as important as the logo itself. The main difficulty is often in convincing the client that this is the case. The subtleties of typography are lost on the untrained eye, and a client who sees flaws in an existing logo may be quite happy with the jumble of badly-chosen and ill-sized type that is combined with it. An effective way to convince such an unwilling client of the need for uniformity is to assemble the worst examples of the company stationery. Presented with the extremes, even the most visually illiterate people can be made to see that there is a problem.

For all basic graphic applications, pick a family of typefaces that matches the image the client is trying to project; collecting samples of stationery from other companies in the same business often helps you to do this. Insurance companies, for example, wish to appear stable, financially sound and trustworthy, yet approachable and welcoming

of new business. For such clients you might wish to pick a typeface from the Classical range to reflect the company's traditional side, yet use the type in a contemporary manner as a reflection of their up-to-date approach to business.

Contrasting typefaces can be most effective if used sparingly, but make sure that the company name is not obscured: specify a bolder face or a second colour to make the name stand out.

Type specification and choice should be included as part of the corporate manual. It is not enough to specify just the face or faces to be used. You must also cover the size and weight of type for each application, bearing in mind the relative size of the logo. Explicit details of line width, letter spacing and leading are all part and parcel of a full corporate type specification.

If you choose to specify just one family of faces for corporate use, pick a face such as Times or Helvetica: both are available in many variations, providing maximum versatility in the future.

Vehicle livery

One of the most satisfying sights must be to see your work passing you by, larger than life, on the side of a client's vehicle. Apart from being a moving advertisement for the company, it is also a very public announcement of your skills – though regrettably, you'll never get a credit. Styling vehicle livery combines the challenges of package and poster design: like packaging it takes the corporate image into the third dimension: and translating a letterhead into a truck side requires a rethink comparable to that of changing press-ads into posters.

Vehicle livery is in some respects an uneasy mixture of corporate identity and advertising: a vehicle is seen by many more people than a letterhead. The client therefore quite correctly views trucks and other vehicles as free advertising. However, changing the appearance of a vehicle is not as simple as changing a poster, so when considering the appearance of a company vehicle fleet, it is important that you and the client strike the right balance between simple corporate identity and selling message.

Once this has been done, find out what vehicles make up the fleet, and check whether any new models are being considered. From the vehicle manufacturers, obtain detailed photographs or drawings of all vehicles (brochures will do) and enlarge the outline details, painting over all extraneous detail except main doors, windows and trim. You will end up with outline drawings of left *and* right sides, for the front and back, and perhaps for the top, too. This is the canvas onto which you will paint your client's company identity.

As likely sites for graphics, look for areas of the vehicle that are unlikely to be obscured by mud thrown up from the road, or scratched by constant handling and wear. Try various sizes of graphics, not just large logos and lettering; a quiet, confident statement sometimes makes more of an impression than a shout. Think how the lettering will look on double doors, and whether the half-message created by opening them will create an undesirable impression. Should illustrations be used, and is there the budget to cover this option? Is this part of the vehicle solid, or is it a fabric blind? If it is a blind, does it roll up? Vehicles used in cities are seen from above: is it worth painting a message on the roof? Should the message on the front be reversed, so that it can be read in a rear-view mirror?

Since vehicles are in motion much of the time, the length of message that they can carry is limited by the time that the truck is in view; so, much like roadside posters, vehicle panels need to carry short, crisp slogans. The back of the vehicle is the exception. A motorist may follow one of your client's fleet for many miles, so this is the place to put detailed information such as telephone numbers.

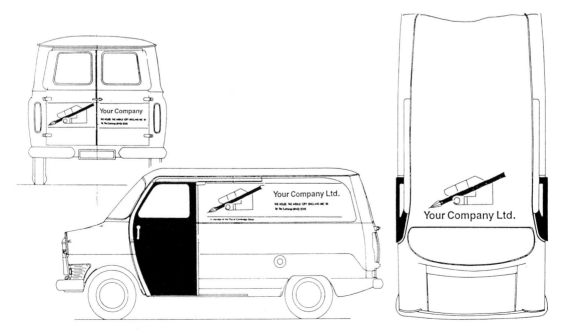

Big, bold graphics work best on vehicles: if your client has a well-known logo, here's your chance to use it on a grand scale.

Corporate image: case history

Garotta Garden Products is a small but highly successful British company which had for many years concentrated on one product, a compost accelerator. Spread onto garden and kitchen waste, Compost Maker helps turn the rubbish into rich fertilizer that could be dug back into the ground to improve the soil. This product is a brand leader – Garotta sell more compost accelerator than any other manufacturer.

Garotta commissioned an in-depth market research programme which confirmed the company's excellent reputation, and revealed that the brand name was well known by gardening enthusiasts. So when Garotta prepared to launch three new products, they wrote a brief that emphasized the importance of taking full advantage of the company's high market profile.

The company called in two graphic companies and an advertising agency, asking each to put forward their individual approaches for a complete new corporate identity programme, covering not only packaging for new and existing products, but also for all the company's stationery requirements. There was also to be an advertising campaign to introduce the 'new look' Garotta to the wholesalers, the retail outlets, and, of course, to consumers.

After all three graphic concepts had been presented, a small graphic company was chosen to take on the work. They in turn approached a specialist media buying company to submit a media schedule incorporating the advertising suggestions. These were for a media mix that best suited the market previously identified by market research.

Here, then, is a unique opportunity to see how a total corporate identity programme is carried through for a small company.

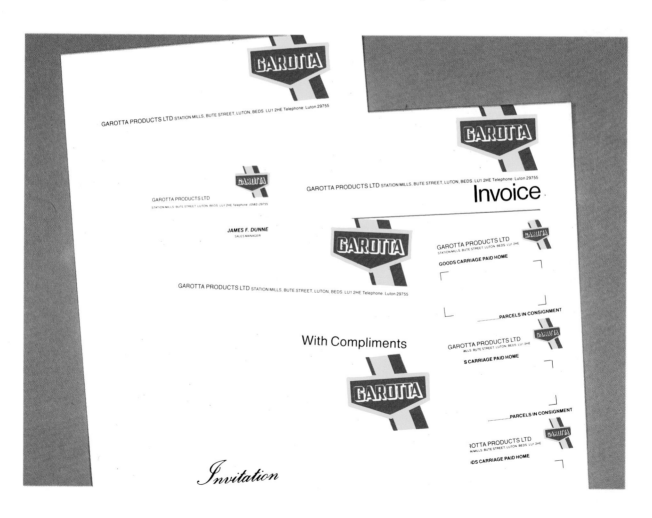

Simplicity is the key to the Garotta corporate identity. The diagonal strips of colour and reversed out sans-serif name can potentially be adapted to virtually any graphic environment as these examples show. The scheme is very cost effective – the yellow is regular process yellow, with a magenta overprinting to produce the warm red.

The corporate manual

Once a corporate identity scheme has been completed, the designer usually relinquishes control over the client's graphic affairs. At this point, the top level of management who commissioned the new look are usually very enthusiastic about it, and discard old graphic material in favour of the new. Further down the corporate pyramid, enthusiasm tends to be more muted, and old material remains in use until stocks are exhausted.

The change takes place more quickly if you make clear the concept behind the new identity, and the reasons for adopting it. This is easily done with the aid of a corporate graphic manual. The manual is made available to all heads of department, and to others who have a direct interest or influence in the project. Don't forget that the lowliest typists have more responsibility for the appearance of a document than the manager who dictates the letter, so your corporate manual must involve people from the top of the company hierarchy to the very bottom.

The form that your corporate manual takes should reflect the needs of the company, and the budget that can be allocated. In large companies, the corporate manual is totally comprehensive, covering every situation in which type, logo and pictures are used. To understand the need for such detail, think about the structure of a franchise business. Here the umbrella company provides national advertising and some supplies, but local franchise holders organize everything lower down the scale, from shopfitting through to local press advertising. These people need a guide which they can hand to local designers, so that the company look is the same nationwide, from major city outlets to small village branches. At the other extreme, a small local company employing 40 people needs only the most general type of guidance. If tomorrow the smaller company requires further graphic work to coordinate with the corporate identity you created a year ago, they will probably call you up and give you the job, to avoid having to brief a new designer.

Few designers get the opportunity to create elaborate and comprehensive manuals, so it is more appropriate to consider the contents of a less ambitious version. This should contain the following.

1. A general introduction explaining why the changes have been made.
2. A cross-section of the new stationery – letterhead, compliment slip, business card, invoice, statement.
3. A page of type showing the new house typeface in various sizes and weights.
4. A letter typed on the new letterhead, showing the recommended style. This should indicate the ideal paragraph spacing and the amount by which the first line of each should be indented; the standard tab settings if these are to align with any part of your design; the correct position for the date, the sender's name and signature, and the typist's initials; and all other relevant information.

Where the manual will be used by others to put your graphic guidelines into practice, you should also include the following information.

5. Line copies of the logo at a range of sizes.
6. Swatches of colour to enable printers to match house colours.
7. Detailed guidance on typefaces and their size, weight and position relative to the logo. This is very important if the company does not have its own design studio. Often a printer who does not hold the exact face specified will substitute a similar face, with varying degrees of success. A corporate manual should specifically rule out such substitution in order to impose uniformity.
8. Advice on the use of the logo and type style on outside or indoor boards.
9. Guidance on company livery for vehicles, and large blow-ups for exhibition purposes.
10. Instruction in the use of the corporate style on brochures and advertisements.

Design for publishing

Publishing provides a more diverse spectrum of opportunities for the designer than any other area of employment. At one extreme, there are book publishing companies that continue much as they have for centuries; at the other, designers working for software publishers are performing tasks that did not even exist ten years ago.

The easiest way to come to terms with this vast, constantly-evolving industry is first to consider publishing at one of its simplest levels: the internal company newsletter. All companies know the value of good staff relations, and strong management/employee communications. To encourage this, many companies produce some form of printed literature for distribution as an internal news-sheet or newsletter. Sometimes these are lavish publications printed in colour and distributed on a monthly basis; just as often they are typed sheets of paper pinned to bulletin boards and notice boards.

Whatever the format, these internal fact sheets serve basically the same purpose. They are there to inform the work force of the direction in which the company is moving, plans for expansion, retirements and new appointments, promotions, and any kind of personal information of general interest. They are in every sense of the word *news*papers.

When you work on a company newsletter, you will almost certainly be cooperating with another person who collects, collates and edits all the required information. This person generally has wide contacts in the company, and is therefore able to sort out which pieces of material are of greatest interest and importance to the staff. In broad terms, they play the role of editor. Your job is to ensure that each picture and piece of writing with which the editor supplies you gets the prominence it deserves.

This usually means borrowing many of the typographic conventions of the daily newspapers in the wider world, and putting them to work on your more humble publication. In this and other respects company newsletter design reflects a much wider and more ambitious sphere of publishing.

The first task is to fix a format for the publication. The size and the number of pages are usually dictated by the budget available and by printing constraints. However, there are other aspects of the format that give the newsletter a positive identity and make each issue immediately recognizable. These are the front page name and logo, the body typeface and setting style, the display faces used for headings, the column width, and the use of second colour. You should make sure that these style points remain constant once you

have chosen them, in order to reinforce the identity of the publication.

The distribution of different types of news and information throughout the pages of a newsletter also gives it a very distinctive flavour. With the editor, put together a list of events that are likely to occur regularly, and decide where each will be featured. The front page is almost always reserved for major items of company news, such as export results, new products, increased sales, major departmental changes, and other company activities. Assign a fixed position for social and personnel items such as retirements, engagements, weddings, births, company sporting fixtures and results, and social gatherings such as dances and dinners. Set aside a column for correspondence, too, and make sure this always features in the same place.

Once you have all the copy in for the issue, do a rough cast-off to determine how much text there is in relation to the space available. A certain amount of

variation in text length is inevitable, and can be accommodated by changing the size of headings and pictures. However, if an edition has far too much text, you must ask for articles to be cut in length, or dropped altogether. At other times there is likely to be a shortfall of copy, and to be prepared for this, you should keep a file of non-topical articles that can be used as fillers in virtually any issue of the newsletter. In newspaper parlance, these are 'features' – guaranteed copy that can be used regardless of how little genuine news there is to report.

Before sending text out for setting, break up long columns by adding crossheads between paragraphs. These may introduce sub-sections of each article, but many designers use them simply as an aid to legibility: in articles with subheads the reader is faced with a few shorter pieces of text, rather than one long indigestible block of words.

When body text returns from setting, you can lay the newsletter out with greater precision, size photo-graphs and other visual material, and assign space for headlines. On a small-scale publication, headlines are best set using transfer lettering; the cost of photoset headlines is rarely justified.

The priorities in any company newsletter are pace, topicality and interest. Some of the information which appears is inevitably dry and fairly dull, and your role as designer is to entice employees to read the publication from cover to cover. You won't do this if you try to win design prizes – aim instead for a busy, 'newsy' look, and don't worry too much about imperfect type spacing; if the newsletter is too sedate in appearance, it will begin to look more like an advertising brochure than an up-to-the-minute piece of journalism. Try to use pictures of the staff wherever possible, because people like to see their own faces and those of their friends in print. And keep production schedules short, so that people read company news in your publication well before they hear it by word of mouth.

Newsletters for client mailing

The function of a newsletter for internal company use is to foster a close family relationship between employees and management, and perhaps to encourage friendly competition between individual divisions. Newsletters are often read by visitors to a company, though, and some are mailed out to clients, whether or not this was the intention of the team that put the publication together.

People outside the company are unlikely to be interested in personal news about employees and management, or about the inter-departmental football championship; so many companies produce a different newsletter for mailing to favoured clients or potential customers. These client mailings are not always regular. They appear when enough new material has accumulated, perhaps quarterly or twice a year. The emphasis and editorial slant needs to be more general than that of an internal newsletter, and the publication should be written and designed to depict the company in the best possible light.

Your graphic design work should therefore project the company identity clearly: a good eye-catching design for the title helps in this respect, perhaps together with a strapline (a brief slogan or statement of company aims). Since the publication will circulate externally, you need to take special care with graphics, typography and illustration. If you run a photograph of company products in operation, make sure that they are being used correctly and safely, and preferably have pictures vetted by specialists within the company.

The actual page format for a client newsletter can closely resemble that of a publication for internal distribution, but if anything, articles need to be shorter and more immediate. Aim for a strong start to the story, perhaps using bold type over two or three columns for the introduction, dropping back to a single column of bold text for the first paragraph, then reverting to normal setting for the remainder of the piece.

Look for background features on behind-the-scenes aspects of the company, such as general maintenance of products, or profiles of the company representatives who are the first line of contact with the clients.

Magazine design

Like the styling of a corporate identity, the design of a magazine must take into account not just the present, but the future too. The task of the graphic artist is to create a format that is instantly recognizable on the magazine rack, and when the publication is lying open on a desk or chair. Once this style is defined, the production of a magazine should proceed routinely.

Why do you buy and read a magazine? Usually because the editorial matter interests you. It is therefore reasonable to suppose that the objective of magazine design is purely to make the pages as lively as possible. However, this overlooks the role of magazine sales: to thrive, a magazine must expand or at least maintain its circulation. Readers are the life-blood of a magazine, and not just because each person buying a copy pays a sum of money for the privilege. The number of readers, their life-style and spending power is of great importance to the advertisers who buy space in the magazine and the reader profile is therefore promoted as shown here. Advertising revenue pays a large proportion of the cost of printing and salaries on a magazine, often much more than the cover price. Some magazines are free, and paid for entirely by their advertising revenue.

The more exciting the contents of a magazine, the more readers it attracts, and the more the publisher can charge for advertising. This in turn provides revenue which is used to improve the magazine still further. Unfortunately, the opposite is also true: a magazine that has a shrinking circulation will also lose advertising. Advertising and editorial departments of a magazine are thus mutually interdependent, and the initial design of the publication needs to take both sides into account.

When a totally new title is launched, the design of the cover and editorial pages is heavily influenced by advertising sales. The magazine's publisher reacts to a gap in the market, and decides that a certain group of people has a common interest that is not currently served by a magazine. In order to finance the publication, advertising space must be pre-sold, and advertisers convinced that the projected magazine will be a good showplace for their wares. The publisher therefore draws up a profile of the projected readership, using the criteria explained on page 88. The designer's principal task is to give the magazine a distinctive image that appeals to this target group of consumers.

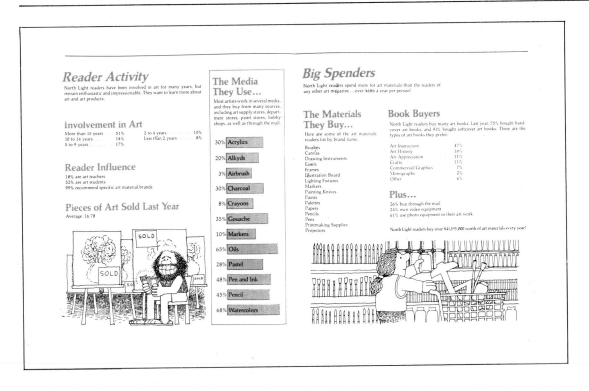

Reader Activity

North Light readers have been involved in art for many years, but remain enthusiastic and impressionable. They want to learn more about art and art products.

Involvement in Art

More than 15 years	51%	2 to 4 years	10%
10 to 14 years	14%	Less than 2 years	8%
5 to 9 years	17%		

Reader Influence

18% are art teachers
52% are art students
99% recommend specific art material brands

Pieces of Art Sold Last Year

Average: 16.78

The Media They Use...

Most artists work in several media, and they buy from many sources, including art supply stores, department stores, paint stores, hobby shops, as well as through the mail.

30%	Acrylics
20%	Alkyds
3%	Airbrush
30%	Charcoal
8%	Crayons
35%	Gouache
10%	Markers
65%	Oils
28%	Pastel
48%	Pen and Ink
45%	Pencil
68%	Watercolors

Big Spenders

North Light readers spend more for art materials than the readers of any other art magazine...over $686 a year per person!

The Materials They Buy...

Here are some of the art materials readers list by brand name

Brushes
Canvas
Drawing Instruments
Easels
Frames
Illustration Board
Lighting Fixtures
Markers
Painting Knives
Paints
Palettes
Papers
Pencils
Pens
Printmaking Supplies
Projectors

Book Buyers

North Light readers buy many art books. Last year, 75% bought hardcover art books, and 91% bought softcover art books. These are the types of art books they prefer:

Art Instruction	47%
Art History	16%
Art Appreciation	11%
Crafts	11%
Commercial/Graphics	7%
Monographs	2%
Other	6%

Plus...

26% buy through the mail
24% own video equipment
61% use photo equipment in their art work

North Light readers buy over $41,195,000 worth of art materials every year!

Artist's Magazine Reaches Entire Range of Artists...

Your advertising message in **The Artist's Magazine** will reach established artists, plus a growing number of new and active artists. **The Artist's Magazine** helps increase your sales by putting you in touch with this flourishing market segment.

...ced fine artists

...arkable 14% of ...readership. ...sing habits and ...fluential readers ...tents every year.

...of 127 students ...r 2.5 million

...hic Artists

...of our readers work in graphic arts, and half of them have direct ...onsibility for annual art supply purchases totaling more than ...million...yet two-thirds don't read any graphic art magazine ...can reach them all in **The Artist's Magazine**

...are some of the products graphic artists told us they'll be ...hasing in the next 12 months:

...ate
...sives
...ushes
...hes
...rasels
...ting Equipment
...Supplies
...ving Tables

Erasers
Fixatives &
  Spray Coatings
Illustration Boards
Inks
Knives & Knife Blades
Lamps
Layout Paper
Markers

Paints
Paper Cutters
Pencils
Pens
Transfer Lettering
T-Squares, Rules &
  Triangles
Wax Coating
  Machines & Wax

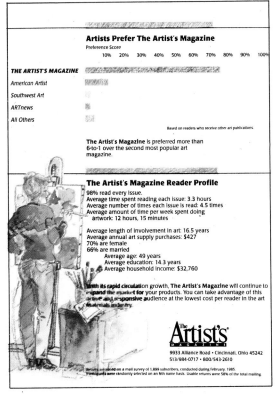

Artists Prefer The Artist's Magazine

Preference Score

	10%	20%	30%	40%	50%	60%	70%	80%	90%	100%
THE ARTIST'S MAGAZINE										
American Artist										
Southwest Art										
ARTnews										
All Others										

Based on readers who receive other art publications.

The Artist's Magazine is preferred more than 6-to-1 over the second most popular art magazine.

The Artist's Magazine Reader Profile

98% read every issue.
Average time spent reading each issue: 3.3 hours
Average number of times each issue is read: 4.5 times
Average amount of time per week spent doing artwork: 12 hours, 15 minutes

Average length of involvement in art: 16.5 years
Average annual art supply purchases: $427
70% are female
66% are married
 Average age: 49 years
 Average education: 14.3 years
 Average household income: $32,760

With its rapid circulation growth, **The Artist's Magazine** will continue to expand the market for your products. You can take advantage of this active and responsive audience at the lowest cost per reader in the art materials industry.

The Artist's MAGAZINE

9933 Alliance Road • Cincinnati, Ohio 45242
513/984-0717 • 800/543-2610

...survey of 1,899 subscribers, conducted during February, 1985.
...were randomly selected on an Nth name basis. Usable returns were 58% of the total mailing.

Cover styling

The first task when designing a new magazine is to decide on a logo. This is similar to designing a company logo, with one major difference: the title of a new magazine will probably be chosen with design considerations in mind. Long titles, or long words within a title, create typographical problems: they must be set in a condensed face, or else the word trails all the way across the magazine cover. On the news-stand, other publications may obscure all but the top left hand corner of the cover, making long words illegible, and concealing the magazine's identity. The same restrictions rule out a logo that is very deep (extending a long way down the cover).

The typeface used for the logo is also of vital importance. The typeface must be adaptable enough to work in conjunction with a range of different cover styles. The title should appear as recognizable when reversed out as it is when printed in black on a light background. The logo should be legible as an outline, as well as in normal type. And the title must be easy to see from a distance, so that it immediately catches the buyer's eye.

The position of the logo is dictated by the newstand practice of overlapping magazines so that they take up less space. The suggestion that the magazine name should be moved from the top left is usually met with fierce opposition or an outright "no". The same is true of size and shape. Magazine distributors are geared up to deal with publications around 8 × 11 in (200 × 280mm) in size; any publication that deviates considerably from these dimensions causes problems.

Choice of paper for a cover is particularly important. Monthly magazines need a heavier, better paper than weeklies, because they are displayed for longer. In practice, though, it is wise to choose a resilient paper whatever the frequency, because scuffed magazines do not sell. Varnishing or laminating after printing helps to protect a cover, but these processes add to the print cost, and may introduce production delays into the schedule.

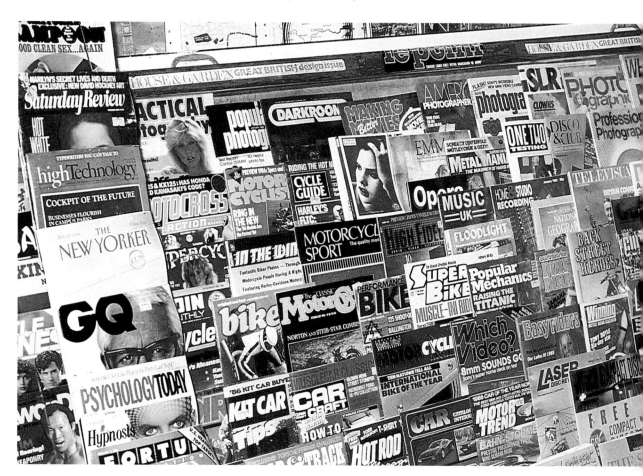

With the exception of the logo, the only other graphic elements that are usually specified in the initial design process are the size, typeface and position of the date, the price, and possibly the issue number. In the USA the position of the bar code is specified by statute, so the designer has no control over this aspect of the cover.

Cover design must anticipate the future needs of the publication. Try out your initial attempts at cover styling by copying them onto acetate using a photocopier or PMT machine, so that you can place the logo and other text over a variety of photographs, some in boxes, some bleeding off on all sides. See how the cover works when decorated with contents lists or "tasters": short ten- or twelve-word paragraphs which preview features inside the magazine. Does your design look good when there are 2 or 4 pictures together on the cover? Remember that when you finish the design you probably have no control over the material that appears on the front of the magazine.

The magazine cover you design has to be good – it faces some stiff competition. Weak designs simply disappear among the forest of other titles on the news-stands.

Designing the editorial pages

Open a magazine that you read regularly at a random editorial page. If the design is good, you should be able to recognize the magazine immediately even if you did not look at the title. The way that type, pictures and headings are used should give the publication a clear identity.

For uniform style and sheer economy of production, the bulk of body type in a magazine is set in just one typeface and one size, and captions in one other. The choice of fully justified or left-aligned body text is also taken at an early stage in the design process. This decision is subjective, but some people believe that justified text is slightly easier to read. If you choose unjustified text, be wary of narrow column widths: unless you specify a minimum acceptable line length that is quite close to the full column width, the text may look very ragged.

The actual layout of editorial pages is defined by a grid that is drawn up at the design stage. The grid specifies the width of the margins, the position of running heads, of the page number and perhaps of the name and issue date of the magazine. In most magazines the grid provides for several different column widths – usually 2 and 3 columns, but often there is provision for 4 columns as well. A two column grid is very restrictive, in that it provides for just two different picture widths; it also effectively excludes very short news articles, since these would run to only a few lines of copy when set to a wide measure. So when designing the grid for a magazine, bear in mind practical considerations like these, and again, try out several different layouts with sample setting.

Headline setting Budgetary and stylistic considerations limit the number of display typefaces that are used in a magazine. Decorative typefaces are often difficult to read, and boost the typesetting bill. A sensible approach is to use just one display face regularly for headlines, and revert to unusual faces only when a special feature really calls for a unique typographic approach. Running heads and bylines that appear in every issue are the exception; these are set only once, and can be held on film for future issues, so they can be set in virtually any typeface without incurring great extra expense.

Rules, boxes and tints These three devices are all valuable for dividing up the page. Photographs often benefit from a narrow enclosing box, particularly if there is an area of sky at the top which would otherwise blend into the margin above. Before you specify a rule as a regular column-dividing feature, though, think how it will look up against a boxed photograph: do the adjacent rules form a confusion of parallel lines? Tints can help isolate any text which provides background information not strictly necessary for an understanding of the main story. However, production costs will almost certainly limit when and where any coloured text, rules and tints appear, so in your initial design it is futile to specify coloured elements, except on pages that are always printed in colour.

The contents page This is a very important part of the design of a magazine. It must act as an efficient signpost for the regular reader, and yet it must attract the casual browser into making a purchase. Here you can be quite specific in your design specification, and you are also more likely to have colour available on a regular basis, so you can use this to draw attention to leading articles.

WATERCOLOR

Step 1

I use grid lines to transfer the outline of my image to cold-pressed watercolor paper. When the drawing is complete, I'm ready to begin painting. Working with a palette consisting of primary colors and earth tones, I mix warm and cool grays that fall in the middle of the value scale. Using a one-inch flat sable brush, I apply these tones to all the shadowed areas. Already, I see the direction of light and the overall design.

Step 2

Next, I paint in the very dark areas with the same gray mixtures, using less water. My warm gray consists of equal portions of ultramarine blue and burnt umber (or burnt sienna). For a neutral gray, I mix equal portions of cerulean blue and raw sienna with a touch of alizarin crimson. For cooler grays I add more blue.

Step 3

I begin by adding color to the lightest areas with diluted washes. I match the local color (the actual color) of the objects either with straight tube color or mixed color. Where I want warm colors, I use cadmium red, Indian yellow and ultramarine blue. For cooler areas, I rely on alizarin crimson, lemon yellow and Winsor blue.

Step 4

To finish Park's Fruits and Vegetables II (22x30), I make final color and value adjustments. I intensify a color with additional washes or deepen its value by adding a gray tone. I'll often use a pure color wash over the darkest shadows to add interest to the area and to tie it into the rest of the painting.

I also use both warm and cool grays. In *Park's Fruit and Vegetables* (page 51) I used a warm gray for the brick building. This wash was mixed from equal portions of ultramarine blue and burnt umber, diluted considerably with water. Another warm gray can be mixed from equal portions of ultramarine and burnt sienna. For a neutral gray, I add a touch of alizarin crimson to equal portions of cerulean blue and raw sienna. For cooler shadows I just add more blue to the gray mixture.

This stage of painting takes only about twenty minutes for a 22x30-inch sheet, and immediately the overall design becomes apparent. The rest of the painting, then, is built on this foundation.

The final stage of the underpainting is to use the same gray mixtures but with less water, making a denser, darker paint. With this deep rich mixture, I paint in the darkest areas. In addition to the one-inch sable, I use a #12 round brush. It holds a fine point for fine touches and details. After this step, the white paper glistens in contrast to these darks. The design has strength and I have yet to add color.

ON TO COLOR

When I first started painting I used twenty-four colors. Now I know better and only use twelve. It's easier to manipulate and control a limited palette, and I've found that I like the mixing process. I use at least two colors for each primary—one warm and one cool—plus the umbers and siennas, which are fairly neutral.

I start adding color in pale tints to the lightest areas. Sometimes I use diluted color straight from the tube, like lemon yellow for fruit. Other times, I mix primaries to create oranges, greens and violets to the intensity that I want. I'll often use different color mixtures within the same area. For instance, the lighter brick color in *Park's Fruit and Vegetables* was mixed from burnt sienna, cadmium red and cerulean blue; the darker bricks were made from a mixture of burnt umber and cadmium red.

If I need a cool red for a shadow, I'll use mixtures with alizarin crimson. For a warmer red I'll use cadmium. When I want a warm yellow I'll use Indian yellow instead of the cooler lemon yellow. For a cool blue I rely on Winsor blue, and for warmer tones I use cerulean, ultramarine or permanent blue. I won't hesitate to use color straight from the tube if it is appropriate—the Seven-Up sign is painted in cadmium red. The whites, if I leave any, are created by the untouched paper.

In the deep shadow areas, I often use a wash of pure color as a thin glaze over the dark-gray underpainting. I've found that a dilute wash of pure cerulean blue looks well by itself over a dark area. These pure color washes liven up the deep shadows and tie them into the rest of the painting.

After I place color where I want it, I make final adjustments. If an area is not dark enough, for example, then I'll deepen the value with either an additional color wash or a gray tone. For instance, the green awning in *Park's Fruit and Vegetables* (mixed from cerulean blue, Indian yellow and raw sienna) was not dark enough in the folds. I added ultramarine blue to this same mixture and re-applied it to the folds until I got the value dark enough. If an area turns out too dark, I try to remove the color as quickly as possible by blotting gently with a paper towel.

At this stage I also pay attention to the edges of my forms. If I want an area to recede, I'll soften the edge with a wet brush. On the other hand, if I want an area to come forward, I'll either use a crisp edge, strong color or interesting texture. On the jacket of the right-hand figure in *Park's Fruit and Vegetables*, for instance, I used a razor blade to scrape out white spots of texture. Other times I'll create texture with a dry brush.

All in all, it takes me about twenty hours, spread out over two weeks or so, to complete a painting using the techniques I've just described. With this method, however, I always know where I'm going, and I know how to get there—even if it is just down to the corner market. ■

Simply Real

By limiting my palette to warm and cool primaries, plus earth tones, I can mix any color I want. I try not to overmix my colors on the palette to keep the color washes more lively. Over the gray underpainting for Ethnic Deli (40x60), I primarily used earth tones (mixed with blue in the deep shadow areas) to build up the forms. I used raw sienna for the painted metal sign, drybrushing burnt sienna along the edges.

About the Artist

"I paint New York City market scenes because I know them well," says Thomas P. Valenti. "Besides, I like to think that I'm preserving something from the past."

Born and raised in Bronx, New York, Valenti studied at the Newark School of Fine and Industrial Arts and graduated as a fine art major. Valenti is a member of the Salmagundi Club, the New Jersey Watercolor Society, American Artists Professional League and the Garden State Watercolor Society, among others. He has received numerous awards and commissions, and is in many corporate and private collections. Valenti currently teaches watercolor painting at the Yard School of Art (Montclair, New Jersey) and lives in Washington Township, New Jersey.

50 THE ARTIST'S MAGAZINE

OCTOBER 1985 51

Initial styling of a magazine must be free and loose enough to give designers multiple options when laying out the pages. In this example, you can see how one designer makes the fullest possible use of the various house styles for copy, headlines and captions in order to make a feature look attractive and accessible to the reader. Instead of setting all the text in one monolithic block, the designer has broken the copy up into several smaller sections. The reader is thus presented with many different ways of approaching the piece. The casual browser can read captions alone, then return to the main text later; the serious reader can work through the article from beginning to end; and the art-lover who is interested as much in the artist as the technique can quickly find the biography without reading every word. Cross-heads provide convenient points for readers to pause, then resume reading without hunting for the point where they left off.

The Tonal Technique for Watercolor

How to use a shadow underpainting to create realistic scenes.

BY THOMAS P. VALENTI

I am always drawn to Manhattan's outdoor markets for my subject matter. The contrasts of the old buildings, colorful fruits and vegetables, and people of all shapes and sizes intrigue me. Since I live near the city, I don't have to travel far to find interesting places to paint. And after twelve years of working in watercolor, I've developed an almost foolproof method for capturing slices of this environment: By starting with a gray underpainting and *then* adding color, I'm able to tackle the most complex scenes.

Whatever painting technique I use, however, one aspect remains the same: I always collect solid reference material first. I've found that a 35mm camera and color slide film are the best tools for gathering this information. On-the-spot sketching may work fine in a rural setting, but it poses a problem on a crowded city street. Besides, I don't like people looking over my shoulder when I work. And with a camera I can travel light and go unnoticed. I use a zoom lens, 36-85mm, so I can easily record tight shots and wide angles. Black-and-white Polaroid pictures are also an excellent source for value studies; they instantly analyze a scene in terms of its design.

Usually, I'll meander about a marketplace until something catches my attention. I'll take some shots, then walk over and get a better view. Many times, while stopped at a street light, I've seen a dazzling array of lights falling upon a display of fruits, crates and shoppers. Some of my best work, in fact, is done from photos taken right from my car.

Once the color slides are developed, I select the shots I like and have them made into 5x7-inch prints. To transfer the image accurately to my paper, I use the grid system. I draw three vertical and three horizontal lines on the photo, dividing it into boxes. Then, I draw corresponding light grid lines on a sheet of 140-pound, cold-pressed watercolor paper with a 2H pencil.

The next step of my process actually takes the longest. I draw lightly with an HB pencil, carefully transferring the forms in each box in the photo to my paper. I don't indicate shades or values at this point. I use mostly contour lines to get the correct placement of forms. Often, I'll erase or redo an area until the composition looks just right. Then, I switch to a No. 2 pencil and darken the lines to see them better. Most of these lines get covered with paint, but those that remain visible are easily removed with a white drafting eraser (such as Magic Rub).

MIXING IN THE MIDDLE

My first step in the actual painting process is to block in the shadow areas with gray washes. I mix several grays that fall in the middle of the value scale. That is, from one to ten (light to dark), these grays would be numbers four, five and six. By starting with these middle values and painting shadows I can set the direction and pattern of light. This also allows me to maintain a certain balance by being in the center of things; I can work toward the lights or the darks and better control the painting.

I mix my own grays from primary colors and earth tones, obtaining greater depth and range than I could with any gray from a tube. I keep the paints fairly fluid, and apply them quickly with a flat one-inch pure sable brush.

A Strong Foundation

I've developed a method of handling involved urban scenes like Winter Market, 22x30. First, I establish the middle values of the painting with various grays, and then I add the darks. This sets the structure of the light and dark pattern before adding color washes.

48 THE ARTIST'S MAGAZINE

OCTOBER 1985 49

Magazine production

The weekly or monthly business of putting a magazine together is theoretically routine. However, any designer who works on a magazine soon learns that this is far from the reality. The logistics of laying out the editorial pages are quite complex, and the longer the magazine, the more complexity is introduced.

In planning the magazine, you and the editor are working within certain fixed guidelines, the most fundamental of which are the number of editorial pages, and how many are in colour. Generally these are fixed quantities from month to month, but special issues may boost editorial or colour content. The first step is therefore to produce a page-by-page plan of the magazine, and assign space for each feature. Remember that the copy for the issue may not be complete at this stage, so any planning is provisional.

Distributing text and pictures is easiest if you draw up a flat-plan. This is a large sheet of paper with a small rectangle representing each spread. Indicate the distribution of colour by outlining the colour spreads with a marker. Colour fall depends on imposition (see page 84), but the availability of colour for editorial use must be decided in cooperation with advertising department, who may, for example, want to sell two consecutive double-page spreads to a single advertiser. Use of colour on editorial pages is also restricted by the magazine's contract with the printer and colour origination house. Generally, this specifies a fixed number of colour photographs and other colour elements per issue. Any excess incurs extra costs.

Scheduling for magazine production is often staggered – there are several deadlines for layouts or finished mechanical artwork, not just one. Colour pages have a longer lead-time than the bulk of the

Magazine layouts generally start as thumbnail sketches and very rough concepts. These simple visuals led to the layout shown opposite, and eventually to the printed magazine spreads illustrated on pages 158-9.

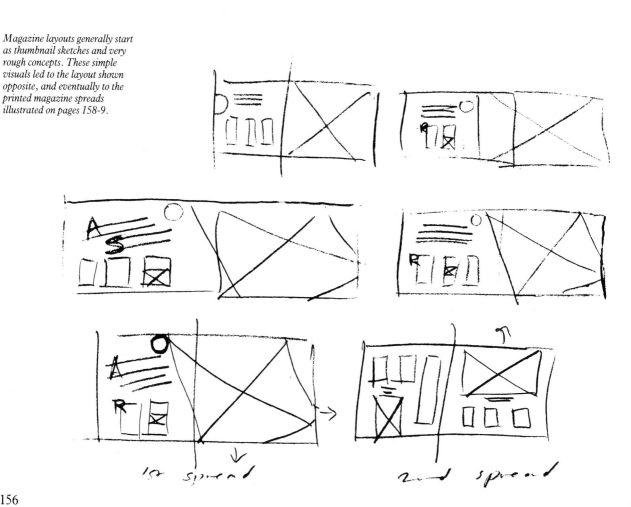

1st spread   2nd spread

magazine, and on monthlies the cover is usually printed well in advance. Some sections of the magazine are on very short lead-times, so that there is the opportunity to put in news that breaks shortly before the publication date. These topical pages are laid out by copy-fitting from the typescript, and are pasted up into pages immediately the copy is set; the editorial staff thus do not have the opportunity to check the copy for accuracy and fit at galley proof stage. The rest of the magazine is laid out much as a company newsletter: the editor makes sure that copy roughly fits the space assigned to it, and fine-tuning takes place only when the galley proofs have arrived back from the typesetters.

Within this broad outline there is much variation; the pace on a weekly magazine is naturally much faster than on a monthly. High-circulation magazines have more scope for variety and imaginative design: they have more editorial colour available; design staff have more time, so they can be creative, rather than simply fitting copy and pictures into the space available; and there is a bigger budget for commissioning special photography and illustration. Conversely, special interest and trade magazines are often run with a very small staff and a low budget: the only pictures are those supplied free by manufacturers hoping to promote their products; copy may be little more than re-written press releases. Many magazines are part of large publishing groups, and there may be a pool of staff on which to draw for specialist services.

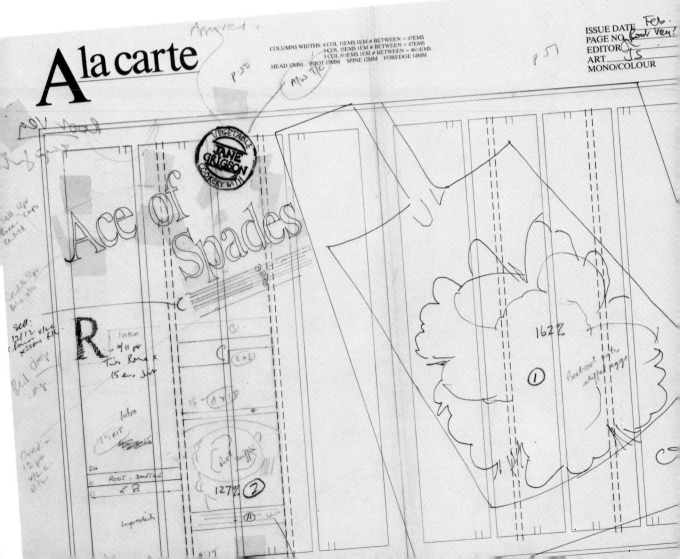

Magazine production: case history

A la carte is a glossy food, drink and entertainment magazine aimed at A B consumers, and is published monthly by IPC Magazines. This story, about root vegetables, illustrates how the design and editorial staff turn a typed manuscript into printed pages.

The author of the feature was Jane Grigson, Britain's leading food writer, and an authority on vegetables and their preparation. The feature was one of a series on vegetables, and by convention the articles start with a strong, witty photograph that is specially commissioned – as is virtually all the photography in the magazine.

The design staff were in the fortunate position of having few restrictions on their creativity. Colour printing is available on every page, and the house style is relatively flexible. The feature ran to two spreads in all, and none of the editorial pages faced advertising matter.

The idea for the picture came from the photographer, Tim Hazael. Some time before, he had brought in to the magazine a photograph of a fried egg and bacon on a shovel, and although there was no way to use the picture immediately, the creative staff recalled the image while searching for new ideas to illustrate Jane Grigson's feature. Several possibilities were proposed. One was to show the finished dishes being dug out of the ground; another proposal was to photograph several shovels, each with a completed dish on it. These ideas were discarded as too muddled and fussy, and the team opted for the simpler concept shown here.

The photographer was not supplied with a layout – he was simply told that the picture had to be an upright. Despite the pristine appearance, the shovel was not specially made for the photograph: it was a regular stainless steel gardening tool carefully polished up.

The finished 8 × 10 inch transparency was so successful that the design staff used it larger than was originally planned. Preliminary sketches led to a finished layout on which the photograph was positioned diagonally across the page to provide a more energetic feel (see previous page). The transparency was dark overall, so a butting rule was not necessary to lift the picture off the page.

Once the position of main photograph had been decided, the rest of the spread fell naturally into place. The red dropped cap (1) is a house style, but the approved/tested stamp (2) was a new idea. It has since been adopted as regular feature of the vegetable series.

The magazine goes straight to page-proof – the editorial staff do not see galley proofs, so copy was fitted to the layout by casting off from the typescript. Cutting and filling of text, and any corrections to position were therefore made on the page-proof (3) which was then returned to the printer so that text and colour films could be combined.

The colour proof took the form of a Cromalin (4) of the whole printed page – rather than just the colour images. Changes at this stage are expensive, so the Cromalin is used only as a final check on colour.

The magazine is printed web offset on 100gsm glossy paper. The heavy-weight paper and the high quality printing give the magazine the prestigious feel which the buyers expect – *A la carte* is the leading British "foodie" magazine. The printed pages (5) look lively and exciting, in line with the vigorous, young feel of the magazine as a whole.

Photographer Tim Hazael used a large-format camera not only for the high definition of the images it produces, but also because, by tilting the front panel, he was able to keep the shovel sharp from front to back.

Book publishing

To appreciate the graphic opportunities in book publishing, it is necessary to know a little about the industry as a whole, and about how an idea in the author's or publisher's head is transformed into printed and bound volumes.

Non-illustrated books such as novels offer the designer very limited opportunities. Generally a designer's attention is required only for the cover, though often a typographer styles the overall page layout of a hardback book. Sometimes the first page of a chapter is set apart from the rest of the text by a characteristic rule or symbol, and this too requires some design input. However, on non-illustrated books the designer's role is essentially a very minor one.

Illustrated book production offers far more scope for your creative skills. Here writer, photographer, designer, typographer and illustrator all join hands in producing the printed book. Here also is the opportunity for the inexperienced graphic designer to receive a first commission. The pages that follow trace these two areas of book design.

Understanding the publishing industry

The traditional view of book publishing is of an author submitting a manuscript to a publisher, who in turn produces the book, and pays the author a fee based on book sales. While this was indeed typical of book publishing for many years, the publishing industry

now also functions in a number of other ways. Books today are not always initiated by the author: the publisher is just as likely to have an idea for a book, and then seek a suitable author to write it. Publishing is also more heavily influenced by the accountants than in the past: book production is a relatively risky business, and before making a commitment to publish, a publisher takes care to ensure that a book will make a profit, or at least break even on first printing. This is done by selling the rights to publish the book in as many markets as possible, before actually instigating production and printing, and sometimes even before commissioning an author to write a book.

A market for a book is not defined just by geographical or national boundaries, but also by different forms of publishing. For example, a book which initially appears in hardback may later appear as a paperback from a different publisher. Later still, a special book-club edition appears, and perhaps the book is serialized in a magazine. Some books – especially multi-volume 'continuity sets' – are sold by direct mail; two or three of these books may subsequently be combined into one thick volume for sale as a 'trade book' – that's to say, a book sold in a book store. Each of these forms constitutes a different market for a book, and the process could potentially be repeated in a number of different countries, with text translated into foreign languages. The shrewd publisher will seek to sell the rights to publish the book in as many forms as possible. In fact, illustrated books printed in colour are often uneconomic to produce unless the rights to publish are sold in several different markets.

Book production is not always carried out by the publishers themselves. Book packaging companies are in the business of selling rights and producing books, but do not publish a single title. Instead they negotiate a price with the publisher, and in return agree to supply a fixed number of books. Small packaging companies are able to function more cost-effectively than large publishing conglomerates, so the publisher gets finished books at a lower price than they could be produced in-house. The arrangement benefits the packager too, in that the publisher carries the financial risk of the book failing to sell; and the packager can sell rights to the book in other territories.

How does this affect you, as the designer of a book? The relevance lies in the scope for creative design, and in the size of your budget. A major illustrated book series that has been pre-sold in several different markets is likely to have a lavish budget, with colour printing available on every page, and a budget for commissioned photography in addition to bought-in stock pictures.

As the cost of printing books increases, publishers look for new ways of spreading expenses. The two books on the far left were created not through the traditional publishing structures, but by recycling material which first appeared in the periodical "You and Your Camera". Individual features from the magazine were grouped by subject matter, and published as books both in English, and as foreign language editions.

Much of the world's trade in books takes place at the Frankfurt Book Fair (right), yet few printed volumes actually change hands. Instead "rights" are bought and sold – the right to publish a title in a particular territory.

Book jackets

The cliché "you can't tell a book by its cover" is as true as it ever was, yet millions of people still buy a book purely because the jacket catches their eye. For this reason, publishers attach enormous importance to the design of book jackets. A jacket must reflect not only the content of the book, but also where and how it is to be sold, and who is expected to buy and read it. Books bought at railway stations or airports have very direct and immediate covers: these books are usually purchased on impulse. On the other hand, a book sold primarily by mail order is examined by the reader over a longer period of time, and the jacket can therefore have a more subtle appeal.

A jacket design is constrained by certain fixed factors, and to an extent by convention: the title must be clearly legible on the front; the author's or editor's name must be visible here too; the publisher's name or colophon always appears on the spine and often elsewhere on the jacket; on the spine too the title is repeated, together with the author's full name or just the surname. The back of the book usually carries a list of contents or, for fiction, a brief taste of the setting or style of the book. The back also carries the International Standard Book Number (ISBN) and the corresponding machine-readable bar-code.

On dust jackets, the design also includes front and back flaps. By convention, the front flap generally incorporates a "blurb" – selling copy which invites a potential reader to buy the book. This may continue on the back flap, but there may instead be a biography of the author or a list of books by the same publisher.

Within these guidelines, the jacket you design generally needs to be descriptive of the contents of the book, and to catch the book buyer's eye. The design solution you choose depends first on whether the book is a fiction title, or non-fiction. Fiction publishers frequently favour illustrations on the covers of their books, rather than photographs, since a drawing or painting provides more scope for the book-buyer's imagination. Typography is as important to the success of a jacket as the picture. The typography on the jacket of "The Illustrated Brontës of Haworth" below is a carefully observed homage to the graphic styles that were current at the time when the sisters were writing.

If the author of the book is well-known, either as a writer or as a celebrity in some other field, then some of the conventions of publishing undergo a subtle change. This is best illustrated by example. In the design approach to the two fiction titles shown below, the author's name dominates the jacket completely. On the book by Catherine Cookson, the name runs with a flourish across the top half of the jacket, dwarfing the title and illustration below. This approach is easy to understand – regular readers of a well-know author look for the name on the bookstand,

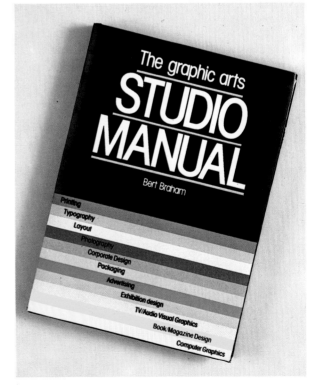

Book jacket designs are often evolved through lengthy discussion with the publisher, as can be seen from early roughs of the jacket for the book you are reading. On the left are six of the twelve designs that were rejected. The final approved version of the jacket for the UK edition is shown below. The jacket for the USA edition was designed quite independently by the American publisher.

and will buy any new title. By contrast, when the writer is a new name, and has yet to develop a following, the book has to sell much more on the title and cover illustration, so the author's name is reproduced very much smaller.

After the initial design concept for a jacket has been approved by the publisher, you will need to prepare the artwork. This is generally done well ahead of the printing of the book, because the jacket is used for promotional purposes. The fit of a jacket is very important, and although you will be supplied with nominal sizes for the jacket, you need to make allowance for the paper used up where the jacket folds around the spine and the edges of the cover boards. You should therefore always start the artwork by measuring a bulking dummy. This is a dummy of the book, prepared with samples of the paper, cover boards, and binding that will be used in the final printed edition. Wrap paper around the bulking dummy, and mark on it the points where the jacket is creased to fit the book. Consider at this stage the effect of errors in trimming the jacket. For example, if the flaps are different colours to the covers, make sure that the cover colour wraps well round the edges of the boards, so that any misalignment does not create an unsightly line down the extreme edge of the cover.

Illustrated book production

1 There is plenty of work available in illustrated book production, but who do you contact initially to obtain commissions of this type? How do the fees compare with mainstream advertising and other design work, and what type of work is available in book publishing?

To answer the first question, it is necessary only to look at the list of credits on the copyright page of any illustrated book to see the team of people that are required in the production of a single title: art director 10 or art editor, designers and picture researchers are all involved in making up the book, and there are other staff on the editorial side who may have some say in the design process.

Your first contact should be the in-house art director or art editor (right). This individual usually supervises the production of several titles simultaneously, with each title at a different stage of production. Most art editors are interested in seeing new designers and illustrators, not just because they 20 like to view fresh approaches to traditional themes, but because much book design work is seasonal; a sudden build-up of work may provide you with an unexpected job from a company to whom you took your portfolio months before.

You will find that working for a publishing company pays less than mainline advertising work. In the advertising industry, a client's money pays for the design work regardless of whether or not the product sells; a publisher, however, receives nothing if a book 30 fails to sell, and must therefore cut costs to a minimum. This can however work in favour of the young designer who is prepared to work hard and gain experience for a lower financial reward.

The art director is responsible for controlling the overall appearance of the entire output of a publishing house.

40

Pre-printed grid sheets make the task of positioning copy and pictures very much quicker. Printed in pale blue, the grid lines 50 *are not picked up when a negative is made from the finished* 52 *mechanical artwork.*

1 What sort of work is required in illustrated book production? The first requirement is for a book dummy or presentation. However, the real work starts once a title is approved, and the publisher is committed to the project. The first step is to work out a page-by-page synopsis. This is a task carried out jointly by the project editor, the art editor and the author. The sheer volume of research and writing involved in a book takes a considerable time, so very 10often the synopsis is produced before the manuscript is complete; design of one part of the book then proceeds while the author completes the remainder of the text. The synopsis to a certain extent dictates the shape of the finished work: some illustrated books are produced on a spread-by-spread basis, so that each double page spread is virtually self-contained, and text is edited to fit precisely into a layout designed by the art department. Just as often, though, text runs on

from one spread to the next. In this book you can see both approaches at work.

For design purposes, the book synopsis is turned into a flat-plan (below). On this you can mark the colour-fall for the title, and thereby see where colour printing is available. Colour-fall is dictated by imposition (see page 84) which in turn is decided by negotiation with the printer. Within the limits of the imposition, though, there is still some flexibility in colour fall. For example, if the specification of a book is nominally two-back-four (two colours on one side of each sheet, four colours on the other) you may be able to juggle the colour around so that one signature prints entirely in colour, in return for the sacrifice of full-colour printing in another section. This is a particularly valuable facility if there are appendices or glossaries at the back of the book where colour illustrations are not required.

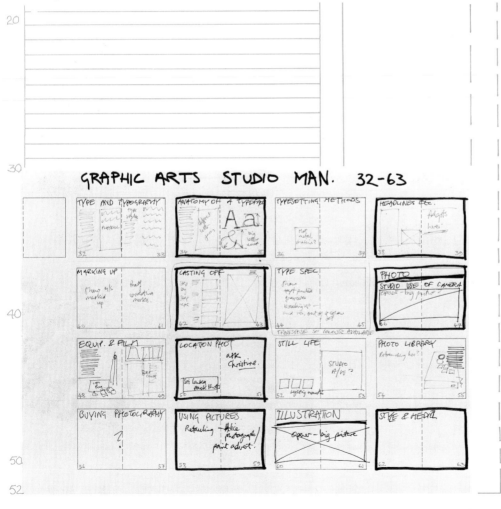

The flatplan for a book may be simply a list of headings with an indication of the colour fall – or, as here, it may carry specific information about the visual content of each spread.

Before design work can proceed any further, the art director needs to make decisions about typesetting. Here the design process is similar to that for a magazine: faces and sizes are selected for body copy, headlines and captions, and a basic grid is drawn up to aid the process of layout. The manuscript can then be sent out for setting.

The set text returns as galley proofs, and copies of these are distributed to the editor, the designer and the author. One set is pasted into position on the printed grid sheets, and the sizes and positions of pictures and illustrations are finalized. Editorial galleys are checked for errors, and may be cut in length to fit into the correct space onto the layout, or to eliminate widows – single words on the last line of a paragraph. This may also require the writing of a few lines of extra copy to make the text fit the layout. Captions for illustrated books may be sent out for setting at the same time as body text. Often, though, they are written to fit into specific spaces on the layout, and therefore go for setting at a later date.

Once these initial stages are complete, much of the remaining design work is concerned with checking and correction. The marked-up galley proofs are sent back to the typesetter for correction, and when the corrected galleys return, they are again checked to make sure that they fit into the space available; completed illustrations are checked, and any annotation or call-outs added; commissioned and stock photographs are either traced to size or converted into sized bromide prints, and these are pasted into position on the layouts. The completed package of layouts and corrected galleys are sent out to be made up into finished mechanical artwork, and all illustrations are despatched for colour origination.

Proofs of colour-and-black and white illustrations are checked as explained on page 86, and the completed artwork is compared with the layouts and corrected galleys. Finally, the corrected artwork and colour proofs are returned, and the book is made up into film. This means that the printer shoots the boards on a process camera, and makes up one sheet of film for each of the four process colours. For final checking, the printer normally supplies an 'Ozalid' or diazo print shortly before the book goes to press.

Finally, printing of the book is almost always supervised by a member of the design team, who travels to the printing works to pass each printed sheet as it rolls off the press.

Presentations

To sell the rights of an illustrated book, a publisher or packager often creates a dummy to show what the final book is going to look like. Almost all dummies and presentations include a jacket design (below) wrapped around a bulking dummy of the book. This dummy may also contain simulations of several spreads of the book usually including the title page. However, the simulated spreads are often made up on separate presentation boards (opposite).

These presentations need to resemble the finished volume as closely as possible, so if you are commissioned to produce one, you should refer to pages 26-7 for an explanation of how the printed work can be simulated.

Design on screen

Most of your graphic works necessarily end up as static images printed on paper. However, design does not need to be bound to the printed page or the side of a package. On a screen, your ideas can flicker into life, constantly shifting and changing to put a message across.

This description perhaps evokes the world of high-budget TV commercials, and it does indeed encompass that field of activity. However, design for the screen need not be complex or expensive: a carefully designed and projected slide-show can be a valuable visual aid that is within the budget of even the smallest of companies. Add a recorded sound-track, and you have created a portable sales presentation that can be supplied to members of a large sales-force easily and economically.

Visual aids

The simplest use of an image on screen is to accompany a text delivered verbally by a live speaker. In this context, the images can be projected not only by a 35mm slide projector, but also by an overhead projector of the type shown on the opposite page. The speaker may also use a flip-chart or writing board to illustrate points of importance.

Such a presentation is inexpensive and modest in its aims, but it can sometimes be more effective than an elaborate slide-tape or video feature. The speaker's own personality plays a larger role, and members of the audience are often more attentive than they would be when viewing a totally recorded message. Budgetary restrictions may in any case prevent the presentation from taking a more elaborate form.

For such a talk, choose your visual aids with care. 35mm slides lend themselves to presentations in which conventional photographs must be interspersed with title slides carrying a written message. Overhead projection transparencies can if necessary carry regular colour photographs, but the process of enlarging them onto the necessary large sheets of acetate is

costly. Overhead projection is better suited to situations in which the speaker wishes to add supplementary information to an existing chart on the screen, either by drawing on the transparency, or by superimposing further transparencies on the first. Flip charts and writing boards are especially useful in venues which are impossible to darken – though for a small audience, a high-gain screen makes projection possible under even quite bright conditions.

Preparing transparencies

Overhead projection (OHP) transparencies and 35mm transparencies (slides) are prepared in quite different ways, though the same artwork can potentially be used for both. OHP transparencies are generally made up actual size (S/S), either by working directly on an acetate sheet using self-adhesive coloured acetate strips, or by preparing line artwork on paper, then photocopying this onto acetate to make the transparency. You can load the paper tray of a regular office photocopier with acetate sheets to make the conversion, or for stronger blacks, use a PMT machine. For coloured images, make the copy on an electrostatic colour copier. If you wish to project photographs using an overhead projector, you can have ordinary 35mm, roll-film or sheet-film transparencies enlarged onto acetate by a colour lab. The service usually costs about 20 percent more than a high-quality colour print on a paper base.

Many projected 35mm transparencies are of course photographs of people, products and scenes, but this format is also ideal for throwing graphic messages and information onto a screen in foot-high letters. Speakers can reinforce their words by projecting key phrases or campaign aims onto a screen behind them.

Statistics such as growth planned and achieved are more easily absorbed from projected charts than from spoken figures.

Making 35mm lecture slides is not difficult, but it is time-consuming, and some of the processes are best

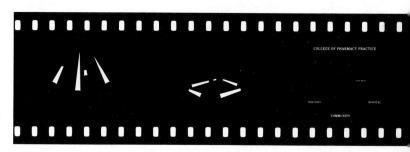

These disjointed images are actually individual components of a coloured 35mm slide (see text above). Once rephotographed using coloured filters and a special camera, they create the full-colour image shown on the next page.

left to specialized laboratories. The simplest way to create graphics for projection is to produce the artwork in full colour at some convenient format such as 8 × 12 in or A4, then copy this using colour reversal film in a 35mm camera. For best results, use slow film and a tripod-mounted camera fitted with a macro lens.

You can make even better title and text slides using a two-stage process. First, create the line artwork in black and white, and copy it as before onto 35mm film, loading the camera with a lith film such as Kodalith. This is a graphic arts film that renders the subject as areas of clear film base, and solid black. If your artwork consists of black letters on a white background, the lith copy will be a negative – white letters on a black background. You can now recopy this onto regular colour reversal film, using coloured filters to produce brilliantly coloured letters against a black background. Many specialised labs will carry out this work from artwork which you supply; if you make registered overlays, as when specifying colour on finished mechanical artwork, the lab can even create multi-coloured slides from monochrome artwork.

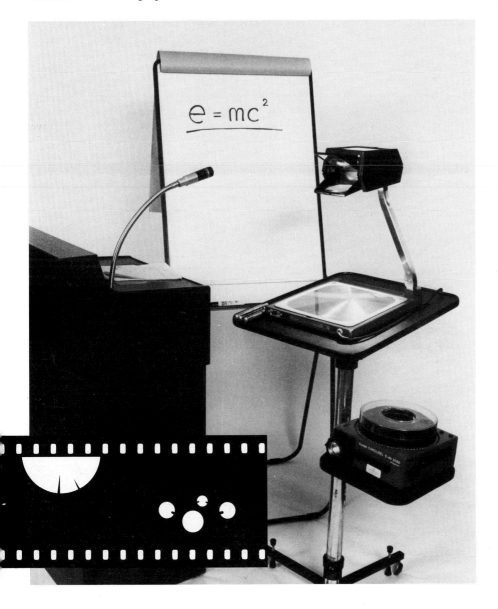

Visual aids need to be matched to the speaker's style, and the location in which the presentation is being made. In brightly-lit rooms, for example, the flip-chart (background) is a far more sensible choice than either of the projectors.

Presentation tips

To be successful, a visual aid presentation must obey a few simple rules. Not all of these are concerned with graphic design: the most important, in fact, are to do with the script that the speaker uses. You may not be expected to write the text yourself, but since you are designing the slides that accompany the speaker's words, the script has a major bearing on what you do.

Length How long can your presentation keep the attention of the audience? This depends both on the script and on the visual material projected to illustrate and emphasize the speaker's words. The appropriate duration for a presentation also depends on how much the audience already understand the subject. If the topic is completely new, the presentation needs to be longer than if you are explaining a new approach to a familiar subject.

Relevance The script should address the subject directly, without rambling off into irrelevance or repetition. The last few phrases (and slides) should sum up the whole of the presentation.

Legibility Design your slides for ease of reading. A concise phrase or a schematic diagram always looks better on screen than a rambling paragraph or a column of figures. Keep slogans short – preferably no more than three or four lines of text should appear on screen at once while the presenter is speaking.

Appropriate graphics Different types of information demand varied presentations. Choose carefully from the four main types of format for graphic representation of statistics, as explained at right.

Liveliness Unless your client is very conservative, don't just use words and figures on the screen. A bar chart explaining the menace of stray dogs really comes to life when the bars are made up of snarling hounds.

Timing Change slides often to provide pace and rhythm, but keep each slide in view long enough for the audience to take in their message.

Format Don't mix landscape and portrait slides.

Tell a story Use the slides themselves to get the client's message across: don't rely too much on the speaker's words.

Check the venue If the presentation area is not familiar, check for ceiling height and acoustics, and make sure that the windows can be blacked-out.

Charting statistics

These are the four visual forms that are most often used to represent statistics on screen, and make them more quickly and easily assimilable.

Bar charts (1) Best used when the audience needs to make comparisons between several commodities, or between the performance of individual units such as countries or subsidiaries of a parent company. Bar charts often contain a time element – such as separate bars for each of several years – but this is not the best medium for illustrating change or growth relative to time.

Pie charts (2) When you need to show how some total quantity is divided up into several different shares, use a pie chart. A typical application is to show how much of the market one company has secured, against the market share of the competitors. Not a suitable medium for illustrating changes against time.

Line graphs and fever charts (3) These plot how some value is affected by regular changes in another value. The commonest example is growth against time: population, say, is plotted at the end of each year, and the dots are joined up to make a line. These charts are an ideal way to illustrate trends and changes.

Lists and tables These are the least easy to read and understand, but they are the only way to present very diverse information, and exact – rather than approximate – data. For legibility, keep the number of rows and columns as small as possible.

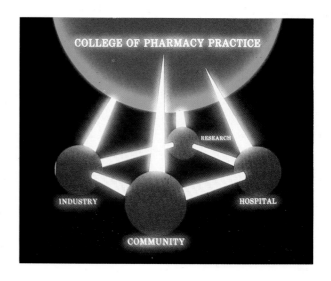

Full colour slides such as this are created from black and white artwork as explained on the previous page.

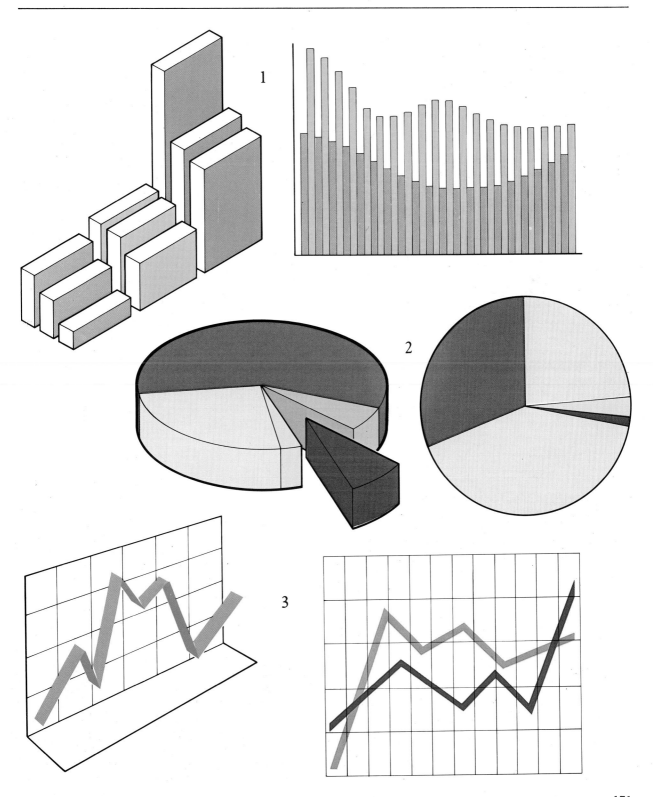

The audio-visual

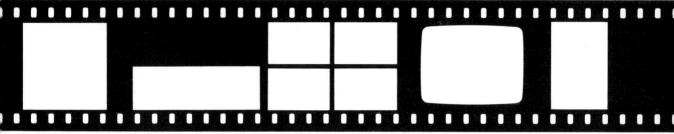

An audio-visual, or "AV" presentation differs from a simple slide show in that the changing images on screen are accompanied by a recorded sound track rather than a spoken commentary. The AV is therefore suited to presentations that must run unaccompanied by a live speaker, that must be repeated numerous times, or in several different venues.

The use of AV is most apparent at exhibitions. A well-produced programme makes visitors stop, look and listen, and addresses a large audience even when staff on the stand are busy dealing with individual inquiries. The projected slide-show repeats the same basic information over and over again, and of course the recorded presenter never sounds tired or bored.

Unlike a video or a movie, an audio-visual show can easily be updated by substituting a slide of a new product. The sound-track can be re-recorded in a different language, and one tape can potentially carry several different languages, so that the presentation can be changed instantly to suit foreign-speaking groups.

The basic principle of an AV is simple: as with a slide-show, you start with a script, and decide what should appear on screen to illustrate each spoken phrase. Once you have prepared all the slides, you record the speaker, using a special tape-recorder. This puts inaudible control tones on a spare track of the tape at the points where the picture on screen is to change. Once the magazine of transparencies has been loaded into the projector and the tape rewound, the presentation can be repeated automatically. The pulses on the tape control the projector so that the commentary is synchronized with the pictures.

Such a presentation is ideal for use as a sales aid: each sales representative is supplied with an integrated unit comprising a back-projection screen, a projector and a cassette tape recorder. However, AV presentations can be much more sophisticated than this.

Extra projectors With two projectors and a suitable control unit, there is no blank screen between pictures; one image fades into the next. Adding further projectors increases the versatility of the medium: a six-projector show can create a wide-screen effect, with three projectors making up a single image between them. The hard dividing line between images is eliminated using special soft edge masks.

Matrix screens Alternatively, the screen can be divided up into separate compartments, each served by a pair of projectors. Every compartment can display a different picture, the same picture, or a single picture can cover the whole screen, with each "cell" showing just a portion of the whole.

Movement Using pin-registered slide mounts and special copying techniques, you can create an illusion of movement by fading from one slide to the next. For example, by fading gradually from a flower in bud to the same flower in bloom, you could simulate the flower gradually opening.

These advanced techniques demand complex equipment and programming, and it is wise to seek advice from designers and photographers experienced in AV work before tackling a complex assignment.

Sandwiched inside a slide mount, a hard-edge mask (left) permits projection on just part of the screen.

Purpose-built AV presentation rooms (below) may incorporate three or more projection media. This room features OHP, video and slide projectors.

An infrared handset (above) allows speakers to control all projection functions without trailing leads.

With a soft-edged mask (left), the AV producer can merge images from several projectors seamlessly together.

This tower of components throws images across the presentation room shown above left. At the base of the stack are U-Matic and VHS video recorders, with audio tape and slide synchronizers above, then twin slide projectors, and a projection TV system at the top.

Making a commercial

If your mate's in a state, steer him away from his car.

The most expensive, time consuming and labour intensive of all advertising agency work – but potentially the most rewarding – is the TV commercial. Just half a minute of viewing time may take weeks of work and involve anything up to 60 people from conception to final edited film ready for screening.

This large team enters the picture only at a fairly advanced stage, though: a commercial starts life just like any other piece of graphic work, in the hands of the art director and copywriter. Together they study the client's brief supplied to them by the account team. This includes the message that the client wishes to put across to the television audience, the times, dates, and TV regions for which the commercial is scheduled (this defines the audience) and the budget.

As the script for a 30-second commercial averages only about 60 words, the members of the creative team concentrate first on getting the script right, then on the visual impact of the film. They build up a combination of ideas until they reach a point where they can discuss the various outlines with account team. This can be done by story telling, using words to set the scene, define the characters and camera movements, and to show how the commercial will achieve the client's aims. At this point the account team put forward suggestions for improving the story, or perhaps propose an alternative.

Before the client is introduced to the concept for the

commercial, the creative team must prepare some detailed visual material. This is done in various ways, but the storyboard approach is perhaps the most commonly used. A storyboard is a selection of still images – drawings of the filmed action at the most important points in the narrative. The standard of finish varies, just as it does with any other visual.

If the client has already demonstrated a good ability to understand sketchy concepts, then the storyboards do not need to be highly finished. Visually naive clients require more detailed presentations, as shown above, or perhaps even rough-and-ready cut-out animation using movie film. This sort of presentation is known as an animatic, and is made using a special rostrum animation camera.

Another approach is to show key frames. These are highly-finished fairly large coloured layouts, which the copywriter uses as visual aids to act out the commercial to the client. With just a few of these key frames, it is quite possible to convey the visual appearance of the film, and explain the camera angles and movements. The soundtrack is either typed underneath the storyboard, or spoken by the copywriter who is explaining the commercial.

A narrative tape provides a more sophisticated way of conveying sound to the client. This is a combination of voice and music or sound effects. The tape is played while the creative team shows key frames.

On the set of a commercial, a professional technician takes care of every detail. Here the director lines up the shot, while the clapper/loader chalks the shot number onto the clapperboard (top). The noise of the clapperboard slamming shut marks the beginning of the sequence, and enables the film editor to synchronize sound and vision (centre). After the shot, the director checks all details with the continuity girl, while a camera assistant inspects the film gate for dirt which would spoil the shot (bottom).

Pre-production

Once the client has agreed the outline that the commercial will take, the main preparation for the production begins. The agency approaches a film production company specializing in commercials, and asks for a quote, based on the storyboard. The agency choose a production company who are already well known for the style of commercial required, or because the company has presented an impressive showreel. This is like the portfolio of a graphic designer: a compilation of the best commercials recently produced by the company, reflecting its style and experience.

When a final selection has been made, a script goes to the production company, and the budget is finalized. The agency then holds a series of pre-production meetings, involving the client and the production company, to plan the fine details of the commercial. At this stage, the production company chooses their own art director to create a series of drawings showing camera angles. These may be on tracing paper, to give a better sense of perspective and movement.

Shooting a 30 second commercial takes about two or three days, with 30 to 40 film industry specialists taking care of every aspect of lighting, props and staging. To enable the director to preview each shot before processing film, a video camera is coupled to the 35mm movie camera used to shoot the commercial. As filming progresses, lighting, camera angle and exposure are checked by viewing rapidly processed film or "rushes".

As soon as filming is complete an editor assembles the shots in order to make a rough cut. The objective at this stage is to make sure that the whole narrative fits into the time available, and that there are no major gaps. Using the rough cut and a series of prompts as a guide, an actor in a sound studio records the client's message that will later be mixed with the sound track recorded on the set. The spoken commentary is called a voice-over.

The last steps in post-production are to do a final cut; to add sound effects, the voice-over, and music to the original sound recorded at the time of filming; and to do 'opticals' – any added text that is to appear on the screen, superimposed on the main action.

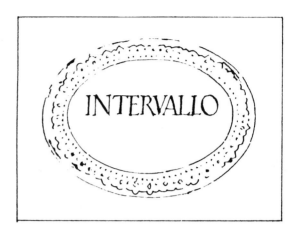

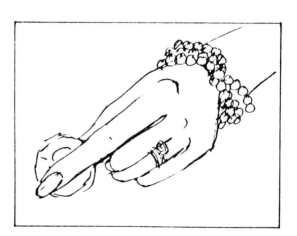

Client **FERRERO ROCHER**

Publication 30 second TV   Space

Issue   Size

"CHRISTMAS"   Job No.

AUDIO

VIDEO
FVO:

COMMERCIAL OPENS ON
INTERVALLO WRITTEN ON WHITE
SCREEN.
DISSOLVE TO ESTABLISHING SHOT
OF RICH LOOKING MAN AND WOMAN
SITTING ON SOFA, DOG AT FIREPLACE.

MAN IS WRAPPING PRESENTS,
WRITING GIFT TAGS, WOMAN LOOKS
AT CLOCK.

Christmas is coming ....

and you can make sure

CU OF ATTRACTIVE ANTIQUE
CLOCK SHOWING IT IS NEARLY
MIDNIGHT.
CUT BACK TO MAN WHO IS ABOUT
TO WRAP A BOX OF ROCHER
WOMAN REACHES
TEMPTE

Computer graphics

The impact of the computer on graphic design is only just beginning to be felt: commonplace for years as the 'front end' of phototypesetting machines, the ubiquitous micro is now appearing in increasing numbers on designers' desks. Hand in hand with the spread of computer power and the dramatic fall in its cost has come a revolution in ease of use. Early pioneers of computer graphics were programmers and technicians, who wrote complex routines to manipulate shapes and colours on screen. While these people still play a major role in the industry, many computer graphics terminals can be operated by designers who have no knowledge of computers or programming. Today, it is the creative designer – not the introverted technician – who produces brilliant and innovative computer graphics.

The background
The earliest computer output appeared as print-out: letters and numbers typed on strips of paper. Computer graphics only really began with the advent of the TV screen or visual display unit (VDU) as a display device. Computer programmers were quick to realize that complex numerical information was clearer and easier to understand if it was displayed in the form of a graph or chart. So they wrote simple routines which converted data into graphic form: pie charts, bar charts or line graphs (fever charts).

These elementary computer graphics programs are now widely available in an easy-to-use form for microcomputers. However, they are of limited interest to the graphic designer, since generally the programs are capable only of extracting information from spreadsheets (financial projection programs) and databases (electronic card indexes), and displaying the data in graphic form.

Creative graphics programs have their roots in a variety of other areas. One of these is the computer game. The first animated games were produced by computer programmers as a diversion from more sensible applications in the 1960s. Though these games pushed existing computer technology to the limits, they were crude compared to present-day arcade games: the simple shapes moved slowly across the screen, and there was no colour or sound.

Industrial applications of the silicon chip have also influenced computer-aided graphic design. Manufacturers recognized that a computer could control processes such as milling and grinding, and that a drawing created on a computer terminal could be translated directly into a finished three-dimensional object. The Boeing aircraft company were early

```
CIRCLE(188,64),32,2,,,3
PAINT(188,64),2
CIRCLE(136,48),27,12,,,3
PAINT(136,48),12
```
F5

The simplest of home computers can produce pictures – of a kind. Without special software, the user must write a laborious series of commands, building images from geometric shapes. "Paint and doodle" programs provide much more versatility, but on a home micro, resolution (sharpness) is still limited, and there may be only a small choice in colours.

pioneers of computer graphics, using the medium for cockpit design, and to create perspective views of airports for flight simulators.

All these early graphics programs were limited by the relatively primitive character of the computers on which they operated. The microprocessors at the heart of the computers were slow, so drawings tied up the machine for long periods; information had to be stored using bulky punched cards or paper tape instead of compact magnetic discs; resolution was limited, and solid objects appeared transparent, as if they were wire skeletons.

Gradually, though, better data storage methods evolved, and programmers wrote more sophisticated software (the programs that make the computer carry out a specific task). Most important, though, the cost of the computers themselves fell dramatically while their raw power increased at a similar rate. The computing ability that in the 1960s was available only to privileged designers in huge corporations is now commonplace in desk-top personal computers.

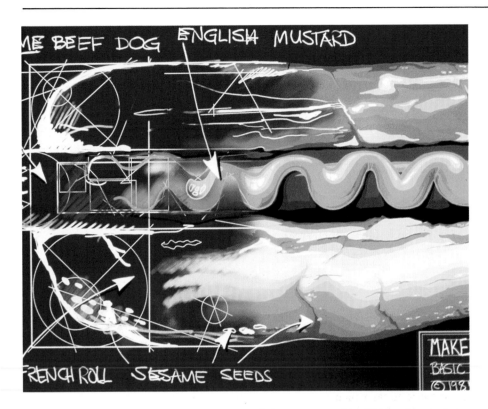

Sophisticated purpose-built graphics computers are capable of creating images which give no hint of their origin, and can imitate a whole range of graphic styles. These machines are described on pages 182-3.

Traditionally the computer has been associated with wire-frame images, and stick men. As this picture illustrates, the stereotype is no longer valid – objects can now be drawn with ample texture, form and depth. Though the structure of the picture is still visible in a still frame, the regular pattern effectively vanishes when the image is made to move. This, of course, makes the computer a powerful tool for TV titles.

Graphics on the micro

Your first hands-on contact with a computer graphics program will probably be through the use of a home computer or office personal computer. Although both the hardware and software of such machines set upper limits on quality of graphics that can be produced, these simple graphics applications in some respects resemble the more complex systems that are in commercial use.

The graphics program is stored on a magnetic disc – either a removable floppy disc, or a fixed hard disc. When you start the program, you are generally presented with a blank screen, surrounded on two or more sides by a series of symbols or "icons". In the centre of the blank screen is a position marker called a "cursor" – usually a tiny cross. This is your drawing implement, and you can control its position on the screen using several devices. The most common is a mouse: a block the size of a cigarette pack with a rubber ball on the underside, and a cable connecting it to the computer. Slide the mouse across the desk to the right, and the cursor moves across the screen to the right. Hold down a button on top of the mouse while you do this, and the cursor leaves a line tracing its path

across the screen. You can also control the cursor using a joystick – which resembles the joystick found in aircraft cockpits – or a track-ball, which is like a mouse turned on its back.

You alter the line drawn on the screen by moving the cursor to one of the symbols at the edge, and clicking the button. The cursor will imitate most of the mark-making tools that can be found in the graphic studio – and some which cannot. Most drawing programs supply you with the electronic equivalents of an airbrush, paintbrushes, pencils and pens of various widths, an eraser, and a means of creating perfect circles, ellipses, squares, arcs and rectangles. By choosing from a "palette" you can paint in many different tones or colours – even with striped paint! And by choosing a symbol for text, you can type words directly onto the screen.

Painting programs also let you change your mind. You can enlarge sections of your drawing, cut them out, duplicate them, move them around, and paste them down into new positions. When your work is complete, you print it out using a dot-matrix printer, which builds up the patterns using tiny black dots on

Most small computers need a degree of adaptation before they can create sophisticated graphics. Usually the bare minimum requirements are an add-in graphics board and a high resolution monitor. This system, from IO research, supplements the PC shown with a range of peripherals, so that the system can not only create images from scratch, but also "grab" them from a video camera or tape, and then manipulate them on screen.

paper; or just save the drawing on disc for later revision or printing.

Once you have tried a few drawing programs, you will notice that, broadly speaking, there are two kinds. The easiest for the beginner to master are so-called "paint" or "doodle" programs. These can be compared with paintings or collages on paper: once you have made a mark, it is there for good, though you can always paint over, cut out unwanted bits of paper, or paste new sections on top. The more sophisticated programs are like sheets of acetate: each mark you make appears on a different transparent sheet, and you can alter every sheet independently, bringing some sheets to the front, and hiding others in the background. The forms you draw can be either transparent, so that the shapes behind are visible, or opaque – as if you had filled in the outline with paint. These programs are less easy to use for quick sketches, but they are inherently more versatile, provide you with more creative scope, and offer more opportunities for revision. They also bear a closer resemblance to the professional computer graphics systems described on the pages that follow.

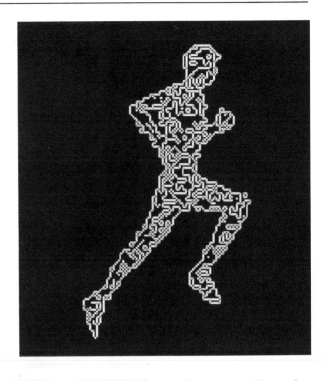

These two images illustrate the potential of a micro-based graphics system. Unlike the graphics generated on a home computer, these pictures are good enough to integrate into more conventional graphic work produced on a drawing board.

The graphics workstation

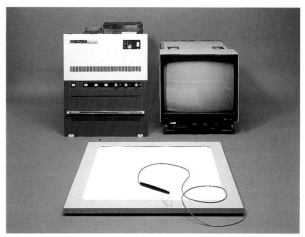

In use, the Quantel Paintbox has a "feel" that is immediately familar to any designer or artist: pressing the stylus down harder makes a thicker or darker line – just like a pencil.

General-purpose personal computers are of limited use for graphic applications, and at present few can produce artwork that compares with that created manually using conventional studio tools. For professional results, a dedicated graphics system is essential. One of the most widely used is the Quantel Paintbox illustrated here, though other manufacturers supply similar systems with comparable functions.

Superficially the Paintbox differs from a personal computer in many ways: it has a much higher resolution screen than that found on a personal computer; instead of a mouse there is a stylus, for more sensitive application of line and colour; there is no operating console as such – just a simple electronic stylus and palette; and the system offers the designer more ways of producing finished artwork or "hard copy". Many of the most important differences cannot be seen visually; the system is more sophisticated both in hardware and software terms. These are a few of the many functions.

Colour and resolution The Quantel Paintbox has a vast palette of colours: potentially you can choose from some 16 million different hues. You can choose colours from a palette, and mix them together, or point to an existing colour area to produce a perfect colour match. The final picture has a resolution (fineness of detail) as much as 16 times the visual power of a regular TV screen in its high resolution

form (an alternative, more powerful version called the Quantel Graphic Paintbox).

Drawing and painting In addition to the graphic techniques available on a home computer, the Paintbox offers a wash effect resembling watercolour, and shading, to add a 3-D look to your graphics. Images can be rotated in a single plane or in space or 'borrowed' from other media, such as a regular TV screen, then retouched just as if they were colour photographs.

Cut and paste Images can be cut up and collaged together, with either a hard or a soft edge. You can also choose images from a library stored on disc, and paste these into your picture, moving them and enlarging or reducing them to fit. Elements of the picture need not be permanently fixed until the end of the session: you can simply tack them down temporarily if you think you may change your mind.

Text mode You can put text on the screen in a wide variety of fonts, which you choose by name from the keyboard, or by browsing through a library. Having picked a face, you simply type in the required text, and position each letter or word individually, rather like transfer lettering. You can also specify a drop shadow on each letter, or simulate blind embossing. Text can appear in any colour, making this a versatile and rapid means of creating film or TV titles without the need for laborious artwork.

At their best, computer graphic images have a unique quality all of their own – they resemble paintings and photographs in equal measure. This image was created entirely on the Quantel system – no part of it has been borrowed from real life.

Even when a portion of a Paintbox image is enlarged, the individual picture elements are not immediately obvious.

Enlargement of detail Areas of a drawing requiring very fine detail can be enlarged on screen to double size, carefully drawn in or altered, then reduced to fit.
Stencils Any shape you choose can be used as a stencil: you can even use stencils as masks in combination with the airbrush option.
The finished product You can transfer images stored on disc to paper in a number of ways, but the most common method is conventional photography. Using a specially modified 4 × 5 or 8 × 10 inch sheet-film camera, you simply photograph the output from the image store that appears on the colour TV screen. Alternatively, the red, green and blue portions of the image are displayed sequentially on a special high-resolution monochrome screen, and photographed through three filters of corresponding colours to build up the full-colour picture with very fine detail. If the camera is loaded with 35mm film, this technique is capable of producing complex slides for audio-visual use quickly and effectively. The Graphic Paintbox outputs directly to a colour scanner.

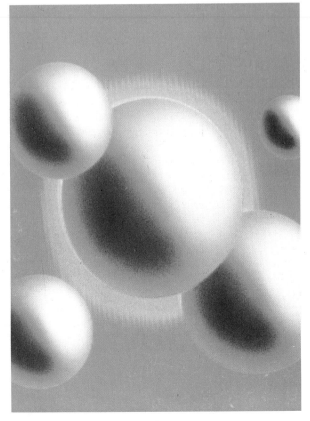

Graphic reference and presentation

Many designers are bad at drawing, and rely on specialized colleagues to interpret roughs into finished layouts. However, clients will sometimes require you to produce fairly finished layouts with some illustrative content: perhaps a montage of company employees engaged in various jobs, and using anything from a truck to a computer. Whatever the subject, drawing is easier if you have reference material around. An instant camera is a great aid in this respect, and for drawing figures there are several resource books containing photographs of people of all races and ages in every conceivable posture. However, both these forms of reference are costly, and there is abundant free visual material in newspapers and magazines.

Building up a library of such reference pictures means being selective: time spent searching through useless pages is time wasted. So when leafing through any periodical, tear out and file only selected images, not the whole magazine. Mark folders with the subject matter they contain: "men working", "children", "motor vehicles" and so on, so that you can locate images quickly.

Copyright and the law

If you collect visual material for reference purposes, you must be very careful how you use it. The copyright laws provide protection for the photographer or artist who originated the picture, and this protection continues for 50 years after the artist's death, and sometimes longer. Unless you are working from very old illustrations, you should never make a direct copy of an existing piece of work. Your own drawing must differ substantially from the artwork reference – it is not good enough to simply reverse the picture left to right, and make minor changes.

TRAVEL

FAMOUS LANDMARKS

Presentation

Whether you have just left college, or you are trying to break into graphic design from some other direction, you will inevitably be required to show a portfolio of work at some point. Potential employers cannot assess your track record in the industry if you have little experience, so the appearance of your portfolio is all they have to go on.

The specimens of work that you include in your portfolio must therefore be an accurate reflection of what you are capable of today – not what you have done over the last five years. An experienced art director will in any case probably overlook work that was completed some time ago, and will pay more attention to what you have created in recent months.

If you have little recent work available, how can you add weight to your portfolio, and gain the attention of an art buyer or studio chief? One way is to take an existing advertisement or brochure, and try putting together your own graphic interpretation of the same material; or choose a product, and put forward a new creative approach to its sale. If you spend time adding self-motivated ideas such as these to your portfolio, you will demonstrate that you have enthusiasm and the ability to work on your own. You will also sharpen your creative skills, and be able to analyse and discuss with the agency staff your reasons for taking a particular creative approach. Many art directors will be interested in your interpretation of a piece of graphics, especially if it originated in their own agency. They will not necessarily agree with your reasoning, but will perhaps be more inclined to listen to you, and to explain how the final form of the agency's original campaign evolved.

The appearance of your portfolio is of crucial importance. Spend time mounting work on boards, marrying up various items with a similar theme. Protect everything with acetate or lamination to prevent scuffing: nobody likes to look at worn boards that appear to have been dragged round every agency in town. Try to secure pages into the portfolio so that they do not drop out onto the floor; if you can afford one, a portfolio with ringbound plastic sleeves is ideal in this respect. If you are showing colour transparencies, mount these in black window boards, or plastic sleeves, so that they can be examined in groups of 20 or 24 at a time.

Climbing the design ladder

Formal design education is obviously an advantage when it comes to getting work. However, it would be a mistake to assume that an art school training is absolutely essential. A host of people at the top of the profession have no such advantage, but progressed by virtue of sheer guts and hard work, learning from their own mistakes and those of others.

If you aim to specialize in a particular area of graphics, don't make the mistake of turning down general work when it is offered. If you can get experience in a small studio producing fast, full-colour, highly-finished visuals, you will find this a valuable source of income when your own chosen avenue of work fails to provide the required number of commissions. Advertising agencies have a constant requirement for this kind of work, and when their own staff cannot keep up, the agency will employ competent freelances. The illustrator who masters the technique of using magic markers, putting them down in a fast, professional manner, often finds that this is a good way of making a regular living, and subsidizing the less profitable – but more rewarding – types of illustrative work.

As in any business, you need talent to succeed in graphics, but talent alone is not always enough: for the inexperienced, perseverance and personality are almost as important. Few designers walk into a job or pick up work at the first agency they visit, so don't get despondent if it takes time to break into the business. Keep knocking on doors, and one will be sure to open eventually.

Glossary

Account director Senior person dealing with a client, in charge of handling high-level contact with the client's management.

Account manager As account director.

Account team Combination of account director and account executive, dealing directly with the client's management.

Against the grain Folding a sheet at right angles to the grain of the paper.

Airbrush A small gun that sprays ink by means of compressed air. Used to create graduated tonal effects in artwork.

Align To arrange letters or words on the same horizontal or vertical line.

Animatic Simple cut-out animation used to demonstrate an idea for a television advertisement to a client.

Antique finish A term describing a paper that has a naturally rough surface (usually a book or cover paper).

Antique laid A rough-surface laid paper.

Art Paper Coated one or both sides with casein mixed with starch and china clay.

Art buyer Staff member who commissions specialist photography, illustration, and artwork outside the agency.

Art director Member of the creative team responsible for visualizing the original creative concepts.

Art studio Team of graphic personnel who complete a more finished style of work for client presentation and finished artwork.

Artwork Finished graphic work ready for reproduction by the printer.

Ascender The part of a lower case letter that rises above the x-height.

Author's proofs Proofs with setting errors corrected by the typesetter's reader. The author reads the proofs and makes any necessary changes.

Back lining A paper or fabric strip fixed to the back of the book before casing in.

Backbone The bound end of a book.

Backing up Printing the second side of a sheet of paper, the first side having been printed earlier.

Banner A main headline across the full width of the page.

Basis weight The weight of a ream of paper of standard size. The size varies according to the paper – for book papers, the standard size is 25 × 38 in.

Batter Metal type that is damaged and worn, thus giving a defective impression.

Below the line A term used to describe a portion of the client's budget that is not spent directly on media advertising in newspapers or on TV.

Benday prints Mechanical tints used in blockmaking to add texture and shading to line drawing. Largely superseded by adhesive or rub-down tints such as Zip-a-Tone

or Letratone.

Bit The smallest unit of computer data – 32, 16, or 8 bits are usually needed to create a single byte.

Bite In photoengraving, the various stages of etching, accomplished by the action of acid, the depth increasing after each bite.

Blanket In offset lithography, a sheet of rubber clamped around the cylinder, which transfers the image from the plate to the paper.

Bleed The part of the image that extends beyond the trim lines of the page, so that there is no margin around the picture.

Blind stamp A design on the cover of a book stamped without gold leaf or ink.

Block A halftone or line illustration that is engraved or etched on a metal plate, used in letterpress printing.

Blowup An enlargement.

Blueline A final proof from film – the last opportunity to make changes to text or pictures before a work is printed.

Blurb Description of a book or its author, printed on the jacket.

Body type Type used for the main text.

Bold face Type that has a black, heavy appearance, but based on the same design as a medium face in the same fount.

Bond paper A broad term used for paper suitable for letterheads, forms, and general business purposes.

Book paper A class of paper used for books, catalogues, periodicals, booklets, and general advertising literature.

Brand name A distinctive name given to a group of products.

Brief A written or verbal indication of the client's requirements, on which the agency bases all creative planning.

Bristol board Fine cardboard usually with a smooth finish, used for artwork, painting and drawing.

Brochure Any short printed work with stitched pages.

Budget The amount of client's money set aside to undertake a specific piece of advertising work.

Bulk The thickness of a book excluding its covers. Also refers to the thickness of a sheet of paper in relation to its weight.

Byte A single character of computer data.

CPU Central processing unit. The chip at the heart of a computer that carries out the primary tasks of calculation.

Caliper The thickness of a single sheet of paper measured under specified conditions, and usually expressed in thousandths of an inch.

Cap-height The height of a capital letter.

Caps and smalls Capital letters and small caps, with capitals used for the initial letters of the word: CAPS AND SMALLS.

Caption Descriptive text printed alongside an illustration.

Carbro A photograph in full colour, frequently used for process colour reproduction.

Cartridge paper A rough surface printing paper widely used for drawing, envelopes, book jackets, offset printing and wrapping.

Cast-off Calculation of the space into which a piece of typewritten copy will fit when set in type.

Centred Type set so that the lines are of unequal length, and positioned equidistant between the margins.

Chain marks The lines on laid paper parallel with the grain, usually about an inch (25 mm) apart.

Character A single unit of type, including letters, numbers, spaces and punctuation marks.

Character count The number of characters in a piece of copy.

Cromalin A colour proofing method which does not utilize printing ink.

Chrome *See* transparency.

Chromo paper Paper that is more heavily coated than art paper: the surface can be dull or glazed.

Close up An instruction to remove space between characters or lines.

Coated paper Paper with a surface coating giving it a smooth glossy finish.

Collation In binding, checking the sequence of gathered sheets or signatures.

Collotype A photomechanical, non-screen process suitable for finely detailed reproduction.

Colophon A publisher's trade mark.

Colour guide Set of small register marks placed on each negative used when making blocks or plates for colour printing. Also the set of progressive proofs supplied by the colour origination house as a guide to the printer.

Colour separation The creation from a colour image of four separate pieces of black-and-white film, each one representing that part of the picture that will print in each of the four process colours.

Colour sequence The normal order in which the four process colours are laid onto the paper – yellow, red (magenta), blue (cyan), and black.

Column rule A rule used to separate columns – on a newspaper page, for example.

Combination line and halftone A block used to reproduce photographs with superimposed letters or diagrams.

Combination plate As above.

Commercial Any advertising on TV or radio, as opposed to print media.

Commercial artist A person undertaking finished artwork.

Competitive advertising One firm's attempt to expand its market share at the expense of its rivals.

Compose To set in type.

Condensed type A narrow or slender typeface.

Contact print A photograph made from either a negative or positive in contact with sensitized paper. The copy is thus exactly the same size as the original.

Contact report A written report of a meeting between client and agency, with a summary of action to be taken.

Contrast The difference in tone between the darkest and lightest areas of a picture.

Copy Written work presented by copywriters for use in a client's printed material. Also used to describe finished artwork – such as a press ad – supplied to a publication in a ready-to-use form.

Copy chief Head of the creative team or in direct control of agency copy strategy.

Copyfitting See casting-off.

Copywriter A person who thinks up slogans and words used in selling a client's products.

Corporate image Term used to describe the controlled use of graphics over an assortment of a company's printed material.

Cover The paper, board, cloth or leather to which the pages of a book are secured by glue or thread.

Cover paper A term applied to a great variety of papers used for the outside covers of catalogues, brochures and booklets to enhance the appearance, and provide protection from handling.

Creative team Normally composed of copy chief and art director who combine to think up the creative strategy – ideas for the client's campaign.

Crop To indicate which section of an illustration is to be used for reproduction, and which parts are to be eliminated.

Crosshead A headline at the beginning of a subsection of text, set right in with the body copy, rather than at the top of a column of text.

Crown A standard size of printing paper – 15 × 20 in.

Cutscore In die-cutting, a sharp-edged knife usually several thousandths of an inch lower than the cutting rules in a die, made to cut part-way into paper or board to aid folding.

Cylinder press A press on which the type form is flat, but the printing is done against a revolving cylinder which carries the paper.

Dandy roll In papermaking, a wire cylinder that forms the watermark and wove or laid effects on the paper surface.

Used in the manufacture of better grades of business and book paper.

Deep-etch In offset lithography, a plate for long runs where the inked areas are slightly recessed below the plate surface.

Demand The market requirement by the purchasers of a product or service.

Demy A standard size of printing paper: $17\frac{1}{2} \times 22\frac{1}{2}$ in.

Descender The part of a lower case letter that extends below the main body, such as the tail of a y, g, p or q.

Diazo A method of reproduction used largely for proofing or copying pages onto film or paper.

Didot point Continental European measurement for type. One Didot point equals 0.0148 in.

Die-stamping Stamping of a relief impression into the cover of a book, usually with foil or ink to colour the impression.

Differential spacing The spacing of each character of type according to its individual width.

Digitizing tablet Computer input device on which the operator draws using an electronic pencil.

Disk drive Means of storing computer data on magnetically-coated discs.

Display type A larger face used for headings.

Dot The individual element of a halftone.

Drop folio Page numbers printed at the foot of the page.

Dry mounting Mounting using heat-sensitive adhesives.

Dummy A very realistic simulation of a piece of printed work.

Duotone Any picture printed using two impressions. One of these is usually black, but the second colour may be in any colour – sometimes grey, to give enhanced tonal range to black and white photographs.

Edges The three cut sides of a book.

Egyptian A group of display types with heavy slab serifs and little contrast in the thickness of the slopes.

Em Unit of measurement equal to the height of the type in use; a 12 point em is therefore 12 points wide. So called because the letter M is cast on a square piece of metal type.

Embossed finish Paper with a raised or depressed surface resembling cloth, leather or some other pattern.

En Unit of measurement half the width of an Em.

End-papers The leaves at the front and back of a book covering the inner sides and securing the book to its case or binding.

Expanded Type with a flattened, oblong appearance.

Face That part of the type or plate that

makes the impression on the paper. Also used as an abbreviation for typeface.

Family A group of typefaces with common design characteristics, but different weight or emphasis, such as medium, italic, bold, or condensed.

Fashion boards Boards lined on one side with a good cartridge paper, and a thin paper on the other. Used when preparing artwork.

Felt side Usually the preferable side of the paper for printing. The top side of the sheet in paper manufacturing.

Filling in A problem arising in letterpress printing whereby the area between the halftone dots fills with ink.

Filling up As above.

Filmsetting Form of phototypesetting.

Fine line work As the name suggests, artwork composed of especially fine lines. More costly than ordinary line illustration.

Finished artwork See below.

Finished mechanical artwork Any artwork in its final form, ready for the printer.

Flexography A method of letterpress printing using flexible rubber plates.

Flimsy Tough, semi-transparent bond paper used for layouts.

Floppy disc Removeable plastic disc coated with magnetic compound, used to store computer data.

Flush cover A cover trimmed to the same size as the inside text pages.

Flush left or right Type set so that only one margin forms a straight line – lines are of uneven length, so that the second margin looks ragged in appearance.

Flush paragraphs Paragraphs set so that the first line is not indented.

Folio A page number.

Font or fount Complete set of all characters of a single typeface and size.

Foolscap Standard size of printing paper $13\frac{1}{2} \times 17$ in.

Format The size, style, shape, printing requirements of any magazine catalogue or other printed piece.

Four-colour set See process colours.

Full point A period or full stop.

Galley In letterpress printing, a shallow tray containing a long column of type. More often used as an abbreviation for galley proof.

Galley proof A proof from a galley, or a single column of typesetting output from a photocomposition machine.

Gatefold Any page of a publication that folds out, creating a double width page.

Grain The direction in which the fibres lie in a sheet of paper.

Graining Roughing the surface of lithographic plates to retain water in the non-printing sections.

Grant enlarger or camera A visualizing aid which forms an enlarged or reduced image of anything placed on an illuminated board. Handles control the exact degree of enlargement, allowing the designer to make tracings at any scale.

Graphics tablet See digitizing tablet.

Grid A sheet printed with the format of a multi-page publication to aid design and paste-up. Shows type widths, picture areas and margins.

Gripper edge The leading edge of the paper as it passes through the press; always the longer side of the sheet.

Gripper margin Unprintable blank edge of the sheet on which the grippers bear, usually ½ in (12 mm) or less.

Grippers Metal fingers which hold the paper in position during printing.

Gutter The inside margin between the printed area and the spine.

Hair lines The thin strokes of a typeface.

Half title Title of a book printed on the leaf preceding the title page.

Halftone A representation of the full range of tones from black to white, using only black dots of varying size.

Hand set Type set manually by picking each individual character up, and assembling in the correct order.

Hard copy A printed version of computer output, as opposed to a screeen display.

Hard disc Metal disc coated with magnetic compound, used to store computer data or software.

Hard sell Very punchy high presure form of advertising.

Highlight The lightest part of a picture.

House style The style of spelling, punctuation and spacing systematically adopted by a publisher and used throughout a printed work.

Imperial A size of printing and drawing paper, 22 × 30 in.

Imposition The arrangement of the pages on the plate, so that they are positioned correctly in relation to each other when the printed work is folded, bound and trimmed.

Impression The pressure of the type or plate upon the paper as the two come into contact.

Initial A large capital at the beginning of a piece of text, occupying several lines.

Input Information fed into a computer by the operator in any form.

Insert A special printed piece or sample prepared for insertion in a publication

Italic Type with sloping letter.

Jingle Catchy tune used to accompany a TV or radio commercial.

Justify To add space between words so that all lines of type are of equal length.

K *See* kilobyte.

Keyline A line on artwork: either non-printing, to show the position of an illustration; or printing, to frame the illustration in black or colour.

Kilobyte One thousand bytes of computer data. Usually used as a measure of storage capacity, or program length. Abbreviated to K.

Lacquer A clear coating applied to the surface of a printed job to protect against marking and improve appearance.

Laid paper Paper that shows the wire marks of the mould or dandy roll used in manufacture.

Layout An outline or sketch indicating the position of all text and illustration.

Leader A group of dots, usually three, used to lead the eye across the page to a word or figure in another column.

Leading In letterpress printing, the thickness of the strips of lead spacing between lines. More commonly used, though, to mean the line spacing.

Letterspacing The insertion of space between the letters of a word.

Light pencil Pointing device similar to a tiny flashlight or torch; used to draw on a computer screen.

Linen finish Embossing process that makes paper resemble woven linen.

Literal A typesetting error – as opposed to a mistake that appears on the manuscript supplied for setting.

Lith Light sensitive paper or film that is capable of representing only black and white, without intermediate grey tones.

Lithography *See* offset lithography.

Lockup In letterpress, to position the printing elements (blocks, type and rules) reading for printing.

Logo Symbol designed and registered for sole use by an organization – part of the corporate identity of a company.

Lower case Small letters, rather than capitals.

Machine coated Paper coated one or both sides on the papermaking machine.

Makeup Assembly of type and illustrations into complete pages.

Mark up The specification of every detail that the typesetter requires to set copy.

Market Term used to describe the buyers of a client's products, or the area of their application.

Market research manager An executive of the agency responsible for analyzing information, and helping shape market strategy.

Measure Width or depth of type matter, usually in picas.

Mechanicals See finished mechanical artwork.

Media A term used to describe all types of communication available to an agency as means of putting across a client's message.

Media buyer Executive responsible for purchasing advertising space of every type – newspaper, TV, etc.

Media planner Person in charge of putting together a schedule of newspaper advertising and/or TV time slots, with the aim of reaching the people most likely to buy a client's products.

Moiré Undesirable pattern in colour printing, caused by misalignment of the four halftone screens.

Mottle The spotty or uneven appearance of printed matter caused by unsuitable paper or ink.

Mouse Desk-top pointing device used to create computer input.

OHP Overhead projection.

Offset lithography Printing process that relies on the mutual repulsion of ink and water, rather than on a relief image. Commonly called offset.

Old face Typeface characterized by diagonal stress and sloped, bracketed serifs.

Opacity The ability of a paper to minimize show-through.

Opticals Material such as titles superimposed on a film during post-production.

Origination The process of creating from a photograph or illustration one or more pieces of film from which printing plates can be made.

Out of register Incorrect registration.

Output The result of a computing operation, displayed on a screen, or printed out.

Overlay Translucent or transparent sheet over finished mechanical artwork showing the position of extra colours, or carrying reproduction instructions.

Overmatter Set type in excess of the space allocated for it.

Overprinting Printing on an area that has already been printed one or more times.

Overset *See* overmatter.

Ozalid Trade name for a diazo page proof on paper.

PMT Abbreviation of photo-mechanical transfer. A rapid access photographic process used to make line prints. Hence PMT machine or camera – an optical device used to create PMT prints.

Pagination The number of pages of a book.

Paste-up A term for putting together all material on a board to form finished artwork.

Pebbling A process of graining paper after printing to give a rippled effect.

Perfecting press A press that prints both sides of the paper at a single pass.

Photosetting *See below.*

Phototypesetting Any method of typesetting that creates letters by the action of light on sensitive paper, rather than by using ink on metal letters. Also called photocomposition.

Pica A unit of measure equal to 12 points.

Picking The removal of the surface of the paper during printing. It occurs when the pulling force (tack) of the ink is greater than the surface strength of the paper.

Pixel Smallest point on a computer screen that can be individually changed or manipulated by the operator.

Point Standard unit of type size in the UK and US. There are about 72 points to the inch.

Point-of-purchase Any advertising material designed to be placed near the product where it is on sale in stores or supermarkets.

Point-of-sale *See above.*

Post-production The finishing-off of a film after shooting – editing, adding titles and mixing sound.

Press proof A finished proof taken on the press in one or more colours.

Press relations Staff responsible, for obtaining favourable comments for the client's products or services in the editorial sections of the media (as opposed to paid advertising).

Press release An informative story supplied to the media together with photographs, specially written and directly related to a client's products.

Primary colours In printing, the process colours. In light and painting, the three colours red, green and blue.

Process colours The four colours – yellow, cyan, magenta and black – that are used in colour printing to create all other hues of the spectrum.

Process plates Two or more halftone plates used to produce a variety of colours and shades, usually in the four process colours.

Production controller In an advertising agency, the person in charge of making up origination blocks to despatch to newspapers or magazines. In a publishing company, the member of the design staff responsible for communicating directly with the printer or colour origination house.

Progressive proofs Series of proofs showing how the image appears as the four process colours are printed in turn.

Quad Blank spacing material used to fill out lines in typesetting.

Ragged right or left *See* flush left or right.

Ream Five hundred sheets of paper.

Recto The right hand page of a book.

Register The correct superimposition of two or more printed colours on the paper.

Registration *See above.*

Rivers Irregular white streaks produced in text setting when spaces in consecutive lines coincide.

Scamp A quickly-prepared rough illustration of a creative idea.

Scanner An electronic device used for making colour separations.

Scatter proofs Proofs positioned at random on the sheet, rather than in their correct positions on each page.

Score To impress or indent paper with a mark with a string or rule, thus making folding easier.

Scraperboard *See below.*

Scratchboard Board with an inked surface which is scratched away to simulate a line engraving.

Screen Cross-ruled opaque lines used in a process camera to break continuous-tone illustrations up into halftones.

Self-cover A cover made by using the outside pages of a publication.

Serif Small cross strokes at the end of the main strokes of a letter.

Set close A term describing type set with the minimum of space between words.

Set-off Ink from the printed side of the sheet rubbing off on the unprinted side of the adjacent sheet.

Show-through The ability to see the printed image from the reverse side of the sheet because the paper is too thin and transparent.

Slide A mounted 35mm colour transparency.

Slug A piece of spacing 6 points or more thick, used in letterpress printing.

Software Series of coded instructions that makes a computer perform a specific task.

Spiral binding A book bound with wires in spiral form.

Stereotype In letterpress, a printing plate cast in a single piece from a mould of the matter to be printed.

Stet Instruction to a typesetter to ignore a marked correction.

Stock Any material produced to carry a printed image, such as paper or board.

Storyboard A series of drawings indicating key scenes in the action of a TV commercial.

Strapline A secondary heading to a newspaper or magazine story, amplifying the main heading.

Stripping In offset lithography and photoengraving, the arranging and fixing of negatives or positives in the correct position, on the film from which the plate will be made.

Substance *See* basis weight.

Subtitle A phrase following the main title, often amplifying it.

Super-calendered Paper highly polished by heat and pressure.

Text paper A high grade of antique, laid or wove book paper, frequently watermarked and used for deluxe booklets, announcements and advertising literature.

Thermographic printing A process which creates raised letters without the need for pressure. The printed sheet is dusted with a resinous powder which swells up on heating.

Tint Any light colour, usually used for backgrounds.

Title page The right-hand page at the front of the book, bearing the title, the names of the author and publisher, and usually the date and place of publication.

Transfer lettering Form of headline typesetting in which individual letters are transferred to the artwork by rubbing the back of a clear plastic sheet which carries an entire fount.

Transparency A full colour photographic positive.

Transpose To exchange the positions of type matter or illustrations.

Underscore To set a rule under a word or group of words to add emphasis.

Upper case Capital letters.

VDU Visual display unit – the screen of a computer.

Verso The left-hand page of a book.

Visual First impression of the way a promotional or advertising campaign would work. Often used interchangeably with rough or scamp.

Watermark A name or design embossed into a sheet of paper during manufacture.

Web A continuous length of paper that is fed through the press from a roll, rather than in sheets.

With the grain A term applied to the folding of paper parallel to the grain.

Work and tumble Printing of the second side of a sheet by turning over from gripper to back, using the same side guide.

Work and turn Printing of the second side of a sheet by turning it over from left to right, using the same edge of paper as gripper.

Wove paper Paper made on a roll of finely-texture wire, which leaves no marks on the paper surface.

x-height The height of a lower case letter without ascenders or descenders, such as x, n, z or c.

Zip-a-Tone Tints composed of lines, dots or patterns, printed on self-adhesive plastic, and applied to finished mechanical artwork to create tonal effects.

Index

Acknowledgements

With the exception of images individually credited below, all design by Bert Braham: all photographs by Michael Busselle Studio and Bert Braham.

Abbreviations: T, top; B, bottom; R, right; L, left; C, centre.

6-7 Bill Bradshaw; **9** Rick Blakely; **10T** Roy Williams; **10B** Richard Platt; **11** Rick Blakely; **12** courtesy of Neville Russell; **28-29** Rick Blakely; **31** Rick Blakely; **36** courtesy of Hunter Print Group; **42L & 42R** Richard Platt; **52** courtesy of Johnson & Jorgenson: **53B** courtesy of BWP studio; **54-55** courtesy of Photobank International; **58-59** Photocomposition and retouching by T & S; pictures by courtesy of T & S; advertising agency, FCB; art direction by Joanna Dickerson; photography by Bryce Atwell; **61** courtesy of Schafline Group/Schaedler Quinzel Lenhert Green Inc.; Schafline and High Definition are registered trademarks; **63TL & 63R** Julia Stiles; **63BL** Rosalind Caldecott; **67** courtesy of Delux Advertising and Design; **68T** courtesy of V.S. Engineering; **68B** courtesy of Hallmark Cards; **69T** Illustration courtesy of ZOOBOOKS; copyright 1984, John Bonnett Wexo; Richard Orr, Illustrator; **70** Rick Blakely; **71** courtesy of Hunter Print Group; **72L** Rick Blakely; **72R** Richard Platt; **73T** Rick Blakely; **73B** courtesy of Celia Russell; **76T** courtesy of Hunter Print Group; **77** courtesy of Schafline Group/Schaedler Quinzel Lenhert Green Inc.; **78** courtesy of Daniel West & Associates Ltd.; **80** Rick Blakely; **81** courtesy of Hunter Print Group; **82** stickers courtesy of Townsend Engineering; **83** courtesy of Hanover Studios; **84T, 85, 91** Rick Blakely; **92-93** courtesy of Judge Marketing Services; **94-95** courtesy of Garotta Garden Products; **101** courtesy of British Airways; **102-103** courtesy of 1986 Artist's Markets © 1986; **105T** courtesy of Townsend Engineering; **105B** (tub) courtesy of Johnson & Jorgenson, (truck) courtesy of Centrum Ltd.; **106-107** courtesy of Portland Outdoor Advertising; **108** Richard Platt; **109** courtesy of Portland Outdoor Advertising; **112** courtesy of Pedigree Pet Products; **114** courtesy of Johnson and Jorgenson; **116-119** courtesy of Imperial Chemical Industries; **120** Richard and Sally Greenhill; **121, 122, 123TL & TR** courtesy of Daniel West & Associates Ltd; **124** courtesy of Derek Steffens; **125, 126** courtesy of Cape Boards; **127** courtesy of Joel; **128-129** courtesy of Coca-Cola; **129T, C, BL** Martin Salisbury; **129BR** Richard Platt; **130-131** courtesy of Express Travel Ltd.; **136** Rick Blakely; **138** courtesy of Eastman Kodak Company; **138** courtesy of Garotta Garden Products; **141** Martin Salisbury; **142** courtesy of Garotta Garden Products; **144-145** courtesy of Allied International Designers/Standard Chartered Bank; **146-147** courtesy of Honeywell; **148-149T** courtesy of Centrum; **148-149B** courtesy of Pirelli; **150-151** courtesy of The Artist's Magazine; **152** Richard Platt; **154-155** courtesy of The Artist's Magazine; **156-159** photography by Tim Hazael/courtesy of A la Carte © IPC Magazines; **160-161** book cover photograph by Eric Crichton/courtesy of Eaglemoss Publications; **161** courtesy of The Bookseller ©; **162C & 162R** courtesy of W.H. Allen Publishers; **168-169, 170** courtesy of GHA Group; **171** Rick Blakely; **172-173** courtesy of GHA Group; **174** courtesy of Bill Bradshaw; **175** courtesy of BFCS; **176-177** (photo) courtesy of BFCS, other material courtesy of Landsdowne Euro/Ferrero Rocher; **178** courtesy of Toshiba; **179T** courtesy of Quantel; **179B, 180-181** design by Wyn Davies/courtesy of IO Research; **182-183** courtesy of Quantel.